W9-AWP-447

A
TALENT
FOR
LUCK

Helen M. Strauss

A TALENT FOR LUCK

AN AUTOBIOGRAPHY

RANDOM HOUSE
New York

Copyright © 1979 by Helen Marion Strauss
All rights reserved under International and Pan-American
Copyright Conventions. Published in the United States by
Random House, Inc., New York, and simultaneously in Canada
by Random House of Canada Limited, Toronto.

Library of Congress Cataloging in Publication Data
Strauss, Helen M
A talent for luck.
1. Strauss, Helen M. 2. Literary agents–United States–Biography. I. Title.
PN149.9.S75A37   070.5'2'0924 [B]   78-21804
ISBN 0-394-50428-3
Manufactured in the United States of America
First Edition
2 4 6 8 7 5 3

For my mother and father

"The luck of talent is not enough;
one must also have a talent for luck."

—HECTOR BERLIOZ

PREFACE

Through the years several publishers suggested I write my memoirs, but I never really thought they were serious. The idea of writing this book germinated during the first time I thought I'd retire. It seemed like an ideal way to spend the rest of my life. Not so. I was not ready to spend "those golden years," nor to become a senior citizen, living in a warm climate and traveling in groups. I had too much energy and, blessed with good health and a very active mind, I took another job and another challenge, so the book idea lay dormant. I did, however, have some intimation that some day, perhaps, in desperation, "quiet desperation" to be sure, I would have to work on something which would keep me occupied. Now, having completed this book, I am embarked on another career—writing.

PART
ONE

I SUSPECT I shall not fill in the blanks of a by-the-numbers personal portrait nor surface the whole iceberg, nor will I indulge fancy to fashion the Most Unforgettable Character You've Ever Met or I Ever Hope to Be. If that was my angle or my art, I would be more encouraged by friends like Angela Lansbury, who cornered me at a party when I told her that I was writing this epic and said that she was the one to play me in the film version. A movie I'll never be.

At various times, I have been called "Mrs. Grand," "Auntie Mame" and "Craig's Wife," and in the isolated moments that those nicknames were bestowed they were accurate enough in pinpointing some individual facet of my personality. The "Craig's Wife" label, for example, relates to an almost obsessive penchant for neatness. But all of the labels spotlight a small surface quirk, a momentary attitude, only.

What I accomplished was to succeed in a man's world, and most of the time I enjoyed being there. Yet I do not imagine that this volume will find a niche in the cells of the Women's Liberation movement. Only once that I can recall was I discriminated against because of my sex, and had I wanted the job in question, I am convinced that terms could have been reached which were the equal or better of those offered the competing male.

While I think some people may anticipate in my story episodes of discrimination at the whim of the men in my business and some pioneering feminist zeal behind my success in the field, I have never been a joiner of movements or any sort of flag-bearing soloist. With a degree of allowable professional and individual pride, I admit to a certain pioneering spirit, but I have never been solicited to join the Women's Liberation movement or to share credit for personal accomplishments with their number. I do not feel slighted, and I am relieved that I have been ignored. In the last lap of life, one either becomes more valuable as a human being by virtue of experience, or completely worthless. In laying out the course of my life, I have set my own standards, seeking to define myself in self-critical and highly personal terms and with dignity, without subscribing to the can't or the can'ts of the times.

Perhaps the shareholders in the Women's Lib movement know what they are doing, but as an innocent and disinterested by-stander, I wonder whether the entire movement could not have been handled with better public relations, projecting a more attractive image, a sense of grace and a greater attention to solid issues than to the freakish stunts which simultaneously catch the public eye and ruffle its sensibilities. Most women, looking at the pictures in newspapers, magazines and on television, see little common bond in the unladylike and unattractive demonstrations of the leadership.

I know few Women's Libbers. I met Bella Abzug years ago when I was the literary agent for her husband, Martin Abzug. She is intelligent and knows what she wants, but I wonder why she settled for becoming the movement's clown and is so self-righteous in her zeal that she defies one to join her in common cause.

From where I sit, the rank and file of the movement seem to be women who have done everything to make themselves undesirable. Many, I suppose, are lesbians, and that is certainly their business. Many have vehemently protested that they are not sex objects, the one point on which there is general agreement.

I will not be exploited in my professional or personal life, but I do not find that conviction incompatible with a belief that women should remain women. Colette said, "When a woman remains a woman, she is a complete human being." Men don't respect or admire women who come on like gangbusters. I never believed in seeming helpless, and I am not, but I do believe in listening and asking questions when I don't know the answers, regardless of the sex of the person holding those answers.

I've always enjoyed being a woman. If a man I know and respect tries to make love to me, I an not offended. I'm pleased, but that doesn't mean that I'll hop into bed with him to prove to myself I am desirable.

A few years ago a man with whom I once worked at Paramount Pictures greeted me at a New York restaurant where I was having a business lunch and proceeded to recall for the gentlemen around the table a fiery phase of my youth when I threatened to gain a reputation as a modern Manhattan version of Lily Langtry. He kept calling me "melody by Strauss," as he had those many years earlier. For a moment I was embarrassed, but only for a moment.

Actually, for a brief period, in youthful folly and disillusionment, I could have become a trollop and wasted my life, but I was soon bored and set about work that was to consume and satisfy ninety percent of my life—most of the time, seven days a week. If at the same time I could be a sex object and do my job to the best of my ability, hurray! But I never mixed sex and business.

Still, I often think that I would have enjoyed living in the era of Madame du Barry or Lily Langtry. If I had been born a hundred years earlier, I would love to have been a courtesan—not a whore. Instead I've worked hard for whatever I have.

Frankly, I was never really ambitious. If I had been, I believe that with my energy and self-confidence I could have been the head of some large company, even though I happen to be a woman. I was liberated long before there was a movement which made headlines for many women who would have spent their lives in total obscurity if a few had not suddenly realized that men were their peers. I always believed I was at least equal to any man.

Men were never my enemies, and through the years I was helped in business by several. I don't understand women who—whether consciously or unconsciously—emasculate men. I've admired many, and if they were capable in their jobs and when they knew more than I, and many did, I respected them and in many instances learned from them.

Despite the fact that some—if not most—of my friends are men, I've battled with many. But some of the most nettlesome situations and some of the most irreconcilable problems were generated by women, their attitudes, resentments and fears regarding women in business, the irrational threat a woman executive or associate poses for wives and career women who are insecure in their own life roles.

I was a successful literary agent for twenty-three years, representing some of the most talented, temperamental, temporal, tormented and tormenting authors and personalities of those decades. During the Depression years I served an apprenticeship in the New York home offices of several motion picture companies and was involved with what was then the waning production activity on the East Coast. Throughout the twenty-three following years as a literary agent, it would be an incidental but crucial part of my job to negotiate from the other side of the desk with the midgets and moguls of that industry on behalf of my clients.

I was called to Hollywood in 1967 to function as a vice-president for two different major film companies. Neither assignment lasted more than two years, and following an impulsive and premature retirement—so brief it passed for a vacation—I was again in a job which involved opening up a new territory, with the freedom to set up my own command post for motion pictures with the *Reader's Digest*. This diversification into the entertainment business by the *Digest* drew upon a vast literary heritage in the course of establishing new avenues of outside production in the changing structure of today's film and television production, but unfortunately it did not succeed, and I learned quickly and painfully that it was better to work with people who are in show business than with those who know nothing about it.

Writing this is a difficult experience for me, for I remain a very private person, with a combination of Victorian and contemporary ideas which has added confusion to what I thought was my well-ordered mind. To make things even more difficult, I have a blind spot. For example, I not only cannot remember what people wear, I can't even remember what I wear most of the time. My mother, to whom such matters were of great importance, found my lack of concern for such details of décor and costuming maddening. I would go to parties and come home to face a debriefing session. "How were they furnished?" she would ask. "I didn't notice" was my usual response. But she would persist. Ultimately, I reached a point where I would dash into the house, chanting, "It was traditional (or modern). The furniture was gorgeous. But don't ask me to describe it, because I don't remember what it looked like!"

With the exception of a couple of very short periods when I disciplined myself to honor the good intentions of someone dear who had presented me with a leather-bound volume, I have never kept diaries.

Unlike Garson Kanin, who on the drive home apparently makes transcriptions of every evening's idle chatter and keeps them cross-filed for instant reference to eulogize or fink upon his famous friends before their bodies are interred, and unlike the fan-magazine writers who simply make it up, I cannot reconstruct the dialogues of a lifetime career, and won't fake them.

Nor have I maintained files of correspondence, neither those personal letters Gertrude Stein called "the flowers of friendship" nor those business memos which have charted the details and direction of careers. I am chided for letting pass over my desk and into oblivion letters of special wit, sentiment and sensibility from such diverse and distinctive author friends as Edna Ferber, Edith Sitwell and Fred Allen. But I neither savor nor stash the past, never have. I have dealt in tomorrows.

In an effort to retrieve and reconstruct some anecdotes otherwise lost, I wrote to a number of former clients, asking them to recall amusing moments or memorable impressions from the years during which we were associated. Several will be included in the chapters which follow. A number, like this one from Gore Vidal, are typical of the wit of the writers and abandon *this* unwilling writer to her own wits.

Dear Helen,
    I don't remember anything! So that gives you absolute freedom to invent the past for both of us. All luck on the book.
Love,
Gore

I do know where I have been and what I did and how I did it. There will not be a great many villains in this text. I have known my share of heels, and found them easily forgotten. To recall them now would do them honor inconsistent with my estimation of their importance.

I have reached that beautiful time of my life when what people think of me is of little importance. People are people and no one is all good or all bad. All of us can repeat phrases like that one in our youth, but it takes a lifetime to accept and understand their meaning.

Living is great fun and I have a built-in survival kit. It's self-protection, but I've always had the faculty of forgetting unpleasant things. I expect little of anyone but myself, with whom I have been very strict. I appreciate the kindness and consideration of others, but I never counted on being the recipient of either one. I am grateful to the people who have been fond of me and treated me well. The others, and there were many, hurt themselves, not me, and I can have compassion for them. I've met many people. I've never been impressed by great wealth, but I have been very impressed by great accomplishment.

I know my shortcomings, and they are many. I am stubborn, impatient, periodically penurious and periodically overgenerous. I say exactly what I think. I am opinionated and my opinions are not always right.

I have always enjoyed working and I loved my jobs. When I didn't, I changed them. I have made a lot of money and spent a good deal, but I have always maintained a sizable cache of what I call "Go to Hell Money," the best subsidy I know for continued independence. As a child I was given a combination Christmas and birthday gift of cash by my father. He would say to put it in the bank, and, in fact, I had no alternative. So I have always been ready for the rainy day.

I've had more than my share of the material things, but I earned the money which paid for all these trappings. Work is great therapy, especially if you enjoy what you do. It keeps one from imaginary illnesses, self-pity and boredom. It also helps pay the bills. Actually, during most of my working days I could never quite differentiate between work and pleasure. Work was pleasure and pleasure ofttimes was work.

I have been blessed by Pope John, insulted by Joseph Kennedy, praised by Justice William O. Douglas, James A. Michener, Dame Edith Sitwell, Gore Vidal, Robert Penn Warren, Edna Ferber, Archibald MacLeish and numerous others. I have been helped by many people, among them, Muriel Fuller, Herbert Mayes, Frank MacGregor, Arthur Thornhill, Sr., Joe McCarthy, Harry Sions,

Frances Lastfogel, Charles Baker, Barbara Leveaux and John Mahoney.

I have been kissed by movie actors, actresses, producers and directors, a habit which disguises not a bit the fact that ninety-nine percent of them are suffering from such extreme cases of megalomania that they are inarticulate and unthinking.

I have been yelled at by Samuel Goldwyn and David O. Selznick and complimented by Harry Cohn—all former greats of the film business.

I am proud to have represented clients who won Pulitzer Prizes—Leon Edel, Archibald MacLeish, Bill Mauldin, James A. Michener, Edwin O'Connor, Robert Penn Warren. I have also served history by encouraging some valuable additions to contemporary biography and have been involved with a few flamboyant personalities who could not write and had no opinions until popular magazines and book clubs were willing to pay them extravagantly for advice and confessions for which they had to be primed.

I represented black writers before it was "in": Frank Yerby, friend, scholar and great storyteller; Ralph Ellison, a marvelously talented gentleman; and Jimmy Baldwin, whose essays are masterpieces, whose plays and novels are not. Jimmy can be engaging, charming and irritating. On some occasions I could have slapped him as I would a naughty child.

I never wanted to be a mother. Perhaps whatever maternal instinct I had was fulfilled in the care and feeding of writers. I like animals, but I don't have any. They invade my privacy and as I am a fanatic about cleanliness, a dog in my establishment would truly lead "a dog's life."

I have always liked men, and the kind of men I liked have felt the same about me. I was lucky. My attitude toward sex from the time I was in my teens would have shocked many people then—particularly my parents, but they never knew and the last thing I wanted to do was hurt them. I tried to live by the golden rule. It was not always possible, but I gave it a good try.

From the time I had my first job I knew that mixing sex with business could only end in disaster. There is no substitute for a job well done, and I always believed that whatever success I might have would have to be achieved the hard way. Looking back, there were quite a few married men in influential positions whose wives didn't understand them, or so the patter has gone since Eve passed the apple to Adam.

I've had more than my share of exercise running around desks. Being human, I found myself tempted on occasion. Some of the men with whom I've been associated through the years were attractive; a few were fascinating, exciting and bright.

But I learned very early in my career, when I worked for producer Walter Wanger, whose personal life was almost as well known as his motion picture credits, that too many ambitious girls said "yes" too quickly when "no" would have been more expedient. Emotional entanglements in business are hindrances most of the time. It is more practical to fall in love with a man you don't have to face in the office the next day. And it is fatal for a girl to fall into bed with a man who won't want to face her in the office in the days to come.

I am not against marriage, but even when I was young, its disadvantages seemed greater to me than its advantages. I can be a geisha girl for about a month. I can cater to a man, make divine breakfasts, let him read the daily newspaper first, look at the bathroom in disarray without uttering a word, be quiet if he's moody, bring slippers and a drink, and give my all and enjoy it. But after a while it becomes routine and a bore.

Still, I loved and was loved by two wonderful men, neither of whom I married. They were fortunate and so was I. As I said, I'm not the marrying kind. When I was in love with the first one, both of us were too immature. Then when I met Bill, it was not too little, simply too late.

I was married once, a long time ago, to an Alsatian who was raised in Basel, Switzerland, and who later disguised himself as a Parisian. The marriage was a fiasco, though all of my friends thought he was charming. Of course, they didn't live with him.

I lived most of my life in New York City, but I lived in Paris before World War II and in London during the swinging sixties. The most miserable sojourn of my life was the year in Paris during my ill-fated marriage. The London tenure was an experience worth all the trouble. After a four-year international romance with a charming Englishman, Bill, whom I met on the *Queen Mary* "across a crowded room," I moved to London. Days and weeks with him in New York, Paris and London were gay, exciting, romantic, full of promise beyond reason, but the timing was wrong.

There is no doubt that my miserable marriage at a foolishly early age and the almost ten years of waiting to get my estranged husband to agree to a divorce, without alimony, prejudiced me against and made me wary of that holy state. I wouldn't be telling the whole truth if I said I've always been happy and never lonely, but I do not regret never remarrying. I was capable of making a good living. The jobs I held were interesting, and through the jobs I met some fascinating people who became friends. I was lucky to have a way of life that suited me. Not that I believe one chooses a way of life. Life happens and one does what he or she thinks is best, and it helps considerably to be in the right place at the right time.

I've never minded paying my own bills, for houses, clothes, cars and servants. I was glad to have been in a position to be able to earn the money to have all these things. I've tried not to take myself too seriously. Certainly, my career was launched inauspiciously enough. I started as an incompetent secretary who never had any rapport with a typewriter, moving through a couple of jobs with large motion picture companies, scouting for story material. While that experience greatly enhanced my background for a future as a literary agent, it soon proved a frustration.

Similarly, when the agency business was no longer a challenge, I was lured back to the motion picture business, taking those two high-level executive jobs with major companies, largely as a lark. Had it been anything more, had it been twenty years earlier, that experience might easily have broken my heart. As it was, both were fun and games—but mostly games—and the money was interesting.

Perhaps that was only just compensation for childhood years which had allowed far too little time for game playing. But one of the great advantages of having been born early in this century is that I've had the best of then and now.

"I was born (as I have been informed and believe)" in the early part of the twentieth century, on Boxing Day, a day which has nothing to do with the rules set down by the Marquis of Queensberry or the Boxer Rebellion. I should have arrived on Christmas, and spent the better part of my childhood saying that Christmas was my birthday. It seemed to me that being born the same day as Christ would have made me very special. But eventually I found out that it was hardly a commercial idea, since I would have had many more presents if I had been born on any other day. That was the beginning of my knack for spotting the business angles.

There was nothing auspicious about my birth. My parents, Edward and Josephine Strauss, were intelligent, middle class, but with sporadic delusions of grandeur. My mother was a native New Yorker, born on Manhattan Island, as was I, their only child.

I never knew my paternal grandparents. They died when my father was a small boy. That is why he came here from Heilbronn, near Stuttgart, Germany, in 1901, to live with rich relatives on 63rd Street, between Park and Lexington Avenue. He left them quickly because while the silver and china were plentiful and first-rate, the food was not.

My father had the Midas touch. On the other hand, he had an Achilles pocket. He was a shnook for hard-luck stories and he trusted people, so he was easily divested of what he made. He was smart, but never shrewd. For a long time, until a bitter lesson which taught me that you don't trust people that much, I feared that I had inherited that weakness from him. But I recovered.

It was a nutty family, in ways that I find difficult to describe now. Too, it is impossible to describe silly family rituals that were so very funny or so very vexing to the participants. I'll retreat to the line that the comics use when they attempt to retell a story at a party and fail, "Well, you would have to have been there."

To this day I find myself using some of the wild expressions that bear my father's special imprint. Things like "Quiet! I have a sick friend in Denver!"

I was an anti-Establishment infant. The first word I uttered was a four-letter gem—shit! My mother employed a greenhorn as a maid of all work. A greenhorn in those days was any young European woman who sailed steerage class on an ocean liner to come to America, guided by visions of a New York where the streets were paved with gold. They believed implicitly in Emma Lazarus' famous lines on the Statue of Liberty, "Give me your tired, your poor . . ."

Little did they know that the employment in store for them was usually just a different kind of bondage. They got a room and board, and if the lady of the house was kind, the room wasn't a closet and the food not always leftovers. The pay per month rarely exceeded six dollars.

The girl who worked for my mother was Hungarian and knew no English. None of these girls spoke anything but her mother tongue. Mary used one Hungarian word frequently, "*egan*," which means "yes." It has remained my Hungarian vocabulary and would later get me started on an inconsequential romance with a Hungarian writer.

The first English word Mary learned on her time off was "shit." And according to family lore, I staged a spectacular scene sitting in my highchair when I knocked my arm against the chair and shouted "Shit!"

As an only child, I suffered not from neglect but too much love and protection, amplified, I am sure, by protracted childhood illness which demanded greater attention and would keep me home and absented from many of the adventures in independence I would have experienced in school. As I am strong-willed, I recognized the signs of my parents' possessiveness long before I had the slightest knowledge of Freudian psychiatry.

My father was not as formidable as he appeared in some later family photographs, taken after he had retired and become very clothes-conscious and dapper. My mother, too, gave the impression of being formidable, but truly was not.

Actually, my mother was jealous of any relationship I had with my father. She was the more possessive, but I always understood that, because she had suffered through so many troubles with me as a child, standing sentry through years of illness and operations.

I was blond-haired but olive-complexioned, and I am told that everyone thought it was very attractive. But when I was rushed to the hospital with appendicitis, the doctors discovered that my liver was going to hell! I don't remember the details, nor do I want to. It is long past and I survived, but from the time I was not quite five until I was about ten, I underwent a series of eight operations to put it right. After the last one, I really became religious, because I almost died and had reason to pray that I would live through it and be able to walk again. It was not enough to drive me to any organized religion; quite the opposite.

If anyone should have borne the title "Mrs. Grand," it was my mother. I always thought she was gorgeous. She was a lady of impeccable taste, and her greatest pleasure in life as she grew older was collecting expensive jewelry, clothes and furs. She was constantly flattered to be told she looked like the young Ethel Barrymore. In fact, she was much better-looking than Miss Barrymore, and to my father she was always radiantly lovely.

She never questioned that the best was none too good. As a result, I have always loved good things, though I have never bought anything I could not afford. Mother taught me that quality was more important than quantity, and in the long run a saving. As the same time, it never occurred to her that one had to have the money to begin with.

Saving money was a very special kind of game for her, a game with rules subject solely to her own peculiar standards of practicality. She would hire a Cadillac and chauffeur to drive from 88th Street and Riverside Drive in Manhattan, where we lived for a number of years, to East Hampton, Long Island, a distance of roughly two hundred round-trip miles. The goal of these expeditions was the duck farms where Long Island ducks could be bought directly at a substantial saving.

It never dawned on my mother, on these long and adventuresome journeys to beat the middlemen, that she was incurring the very costs of transport which accounted for the differential. To have acknowledged that would only have robbed the days of their joyous connivance and the satisfaction of imagined savings.

My mother lusted to frequent "the best places," which were, in fact, the appropriate settings for her. She determined that I, too, would shine in those surroundings. I remember vividly the first time she dressed me up for a luncheon appearance at the Waldorf-Astoria. The Waldorf was at 34th Street and Fifth Avenue, now the site of the Empire State Building. The *pièce de résistance* of the outfit was my short white kid gloves, and Mother pinned another pair inside one of my numerous petticoats in case I should be so indiscreet as to soil the first pair.

To get downtown, we rode on the Fifth Avenue bus. The fare was then ten cents, while the streetcars cost only five. But on the bus, one was guaranteed a seat, since no standing was permitted.

I came by my love of writing and writers quite naturally. Because of my illnesses, I had little formal education, and my mother taught me. It was a stroke of good luck that she had worked for the New York Public Library and had been graduated from New York's Normal College, which later became Hunter. I was an avid reader, encouraged and guided, and that background helped considerably when I eventually became a literary agent.

At intervals I did attend a number of schools. In the aftermath of my illnesses, my metabolism accelerated. I was such a hyperactive child that it was necessary for my mother to write notes to my teachers, explaining that I could not sit down for extended periods. Alert to my lessons, nonetheless, I was allowed to pace about the classroom, literally learning on the run.

Because of this condition, when it came time to submit to the inevitable music lessons that were an essential part of the grooming of young ladies of my generation, I optioned for the violin, a lightweight instrument which would have ensured maximum mobility. But my own strong will was tempered upon the anvil of the ever-dominant will of my parents and further galvanized through the eight dreary years of the piano lessons which they dictated.

I tried to finish Hunter High School in New York, because I thought it was important for me to go to college, but I was again ill and was out most of my second year. By the time I was able to go back, pride got in my way—I couldn't face schoolmates who by then were a year ahead of me. Later I was able to take extension courses at Columbia University.

Unlocking the world of knowledge and adventure stored in literature was only one part of my mother's important legacy to me. She was stage-struck. She didn't know it, but I did. The Broadway theater of my childhood yielded such stars as the Barrymores, Jane Cowl, Ina Claire, Lenore Ulric, Richard Bennett, Marilyn Miller, Fanny Brice and the headliners of the Ziegfeld Follies. I spent most Saturdays at the theater, much to the displeasure of my father, who never knew just how many times a year my mother and I sneaked to matinees. In those years, most people worked on Saturdays. If Dad had some leisure time, he was either at a baseball game or out fishing on Long Island.

Between my illnesses and relapses, my mother fell sick, and my father, who had an old friend who owned a farm in the Catskill Mountains, sent Mother and me there until she recuperated. I must have been eight or nine at the time. It was that part of the Catskills chosen by Washington Irving as the setting for Rip Van Winkle. Whenever there were thunderstorms, my mother told me that the dwarfs were playing ninepins. In those days there were still vast farms and acres of beautiful and unspoiled country stretching endlessly beyond the horizon.

Here it was that I fell in love with nature and nurtured a secret wish that some day I would have a home in the country where I could putter around in the garden. The wish was fulfilled, but it took years of hard work before I had the money to acquire that house which faced Long Island Sound in Old Field. It was a great satisfaction to build it, furnish it, and at last to surround it with that long-wished-for garden.

It was a sad day when I sold it to move to California. I will always be sentimental about that house, its surroundings and the friends and neighbors who were so kind to me there.

If my mother was possessive, she was not overprotective once my crises had passed. Having seen me through those years of sickness and hospitalization, she might have been expected to hover over my every cough, or even encourage me to act the dependent invalid. She did not. As I grew older and was really in very good shape, there were inevitably those days when I would wake up with a slight sore throat or a cough and say that I didn't think I could go to school or work that day. She would always shake her head and say, "Oh no, you don't. Don't baby yourself!" So, I'd get up and go, and that was that.

My mother was the shrewd one. Like many mothers, she got her way and made her desires known by attributing them to another, if not higher, authority. Her general tactic involved a preface of

"Wait until your father gets home." At most of the important family summits, "your father's" decisions were laid down through his spokeswoman and volunteer interlocutor. Only once that I can remember did he disown the attribution, and I was too young to appreciate how very close we were in that moment.

Mother always used to say, as she checked my whereabouts or noted the hours of my return, "It's not that I'm worried about your morals, but I'm afraid you're going to be in some kind of accident." Actually, she was worried about my morals.

I adored my maternal grandfather, Leon Kahn, probably in part because he was the black sheep of his family and, for those days, anti-Establishment. He was tall, with red hair, aquiline nose and blue eyes, and held himself very erect. With his black fedora hat, a winged collar, a rakish waxed mustache and an omnipresent walking stick with gold handle, he was the most distinguished and romantic figure of my childhood. He had fought in the Franco-Prussian War on the French side and was later a member of the Foreign Legion.

He was stingy, forthright and proud and had great eyes for the girls. He was born in Alsace and had been sent to Paris, where he got into some trouble—which still remains a well-guarded family secret. I have never been able to find out what really happened, even when I went to visit and pump some cousins in Strasbourg years ago.

Although he was born in Alsace, he was a true Frenchman, his eyes ever darting in reconnaissance for the exposed ankles of New York's fairest ladies and I like to blame the trouble I've had with my feet on this fetish for girls' well-turned ankles and tiny feet. During my childhood my grandfather used to buy my shoes, and somehow, I was always fitted with short ones. He dearly wanted me to have small feet. He'd take me to Cammeyer's, which was a fine shoestore on Fifth Avenue. I looked forward to these excursions and was proud to walk along the street with him.

As I remember it now, he never did much of anything else. He retired when my mother married. He was then about fifty and he lived to be eighty-six. But he continued to maintain real estate interests in New York. I had two not too bright uncles who advised him on these investments. Unfortunately, he took their advice and ended up with real estate in Harlem which wasn't as valuable as the real estate he should have kept. Though he could have been very rich, when he died he did leave a fairly substantial amount to my mother. Ironically, she decided her two brothers needed the money more than she did, and that was true enough. So she divided the inheritance between them.

I never had any affection for my maternal grandmother, who was born Mathilda Hammerschlag. She, too, was proud, handsome, but arrogant as well, a woman whose only interest in life was herself. Although she spent time and energy trying to buy my love, I never had any feeling for her other than hostility, and not without reason.

When I was a child I saw her slap a maid-of-all-work who had worked for her for many years. I loved Jenny, and my grandmother was embarrassed when she discovered that I had witnessed her cruelty. When Jenny died, I felt that I had lost a friend. When my grandmother died, my parents had to force me to go to the funeral.

My maternal grandfather cherished my grandmother, as my father adored my mother. Both couples celebrated golden wedding anniversaries, and both men had extramarital affairs. With wives like those two ladies, who shared the opinion that beds were made for sleeping, I salute my father and grandfather for enjoying one of the best things in life. Yet since both gentlemen were Europeans, the home was sacred, and their tact, diplomacy and discretion never brought about any scandal that I knew of, nor any loud screams for divorce.

My father had many Teutonic characteristics, and like many German Jews, frequently passed as a Christian, which gave him some inexplicable feeling of superiority. My mother had this same failing, and it had its effects on me. I was brought up without any formal religion other than a general belief in God.

My Uncle Albert, my father's brother, who had been in the German army and fought in World War I, added to my religious confusion when I visited him in Munich in the late twenties. His branch of the family had converted to Catholicism. Whether or not my father was aware of this I'll never know, because when I expressed my surprise and bewilderment to him, he changed the subject and there were no further discussions. I never saw Uncle Albert again. All of my father's family left in Germany were wiped out in World War II.

As a child, when a friend of mine went to Sacred Heart Convent, I wanted to attend too. Though my father strenuously objected, I was permitted to go to church with her and her family. The mysticism and pageantry of Catholicism had a fascination for my mother, and when I was very ill she prayed in church and lit candles for me.

When I was about sixteen I had another friend who was Jewish whose family belonged to a synagogue, and I suggested we join it. Again the answer was negative. I was curious about religion and I wanted to be something and have a sense of belonging. When my parents and I talked about it, the final result of the discussions was I could be whatever I chose, but my parents would not join me in any organized religion.

I have always been religious in my own way; I believe in God and pray frequently, but never in a house of worship. I pray for guidance, which gives me a feeling of peace and serenity and the reassurance that "someone up there loves me."

About a year before my mother died, when I arrived home one evening from the office the first thing I heard her say was, "I've decided we should join Temple Emanu-El." We lived on East 66th Street, and the synagogue is on 65th Street and Fifth Avenue. By this time in my life it mattered little, but joining a synagogue did seem a little ludicrous, since I felt it was late for me to learn how to be a good Jew.

When my mother became seriously ill, although still unaware she had cancer, she told me it was good that we had joined the congregation of Emanu-El, which is very Reformed, because without any difficulty I could arrange for her funeral services and my father's at the Temple and it would be well organized and dignified.

My father outlived Mother about a year, although he was hospitalized long before she was. I never told him of Mother's turn to religion. He was very ill, his mind had gone, and he would not have understood.

Both are in a nonsectarian cemetery in Westchester County, New York. Years before my parents' deaths, Mother decided one day to prepare what she called "our final resting place," which I now call my Westchester home. She telephoned me at the office and we drove from New York City to Hartsdale in Westchester County to Ferncliff, where she selected a nice mausoleum for three. I had the temerity to ask why three places, and Mother's prophetic answer was: "You'll never marry again."

In 1963 I went to Israel to visit James A. Michener while he was writing *The Source.* I had hoped to find some identification with my past. I wanted to feel like a Jew. Perhaps I was not there long enough, and the discussions I had with people I met through Jim were political rather than religious. All I know is that I felt completely alien. I could not have had a better guide or a more informed one, historically, than Jim, and I wanted to belong, but sadly, I didn't.

I was with my maternal grandfather at the hospital the night he died. He was almost eighty-six and had survived my grandmother by five years. Since Grandfather believed in nothing but the truth, I hoped he would say something about God in his last moments.

I was in his room. Mother and the nurse left me alone with him. He had been ill only a few days. Like many stricken elderly people, he had developed pneumonia, but his mind was as alert as ever. He looked at me, pointed to the closed door and said, "They don't know what they're talking about. I'll never recover. The machinery has worn out. It can't be repaired."

The first time I was allowed to go out on New Year's Eve, my date had been arranged by my grandfather. He had a friend with a grandson who was a young lawyer I found dull, though not unattractive. I had suspicions that my grandfather was doing a bit of Old World matchmaking and I was at that age when I had begun to bristle at my family's rigid management of my life.

The young man whose name I can't even recall took me to one of those typical gala New Year's parties at the Roosevelt Hotel, where Guy Lombardo and His Royal Canadians dispensed "the sweetest music this side of heaven." The love light in my escort's eyes cautioned me that if I didn't nip this ready-to-wear courtship in the bud, I would at the very least be obligated to be courteous to him for a few weeks, while Grandfather and the family would be encouraged to escalate their hopes for my future.

When my mother and father debriefed their darling daughter the following morning, how I enjoyed myself. I became the Baroness Münchhausen. The evening was a bore, to be sure, but I determined that my account of it would be most interesting.

With a straight face I told my parents that my grandfather's choice of prospective husband had tried to rape me in the taxi en route home. My mother relayed the tale of terror to my grandfather, who threatened murder. Eventually I got a little scared and confessed that I lied. By then, any prospects for that match were off.

My father was basically a very gentle and retiring man. I can't remember his ever getting terribly angry. From him I inherited a number of Teutonic characteristics, especially regarding punctuality. Dinner had to be served promptly at seven o'clock, a routine which was maintained until the illness that ultimately took his life—a standing order to be obeyed so long as we shared the same roof, even after I had become a very busy literary agent.

If I rushed into the house at five minutes to seven and dashed into the bathroom to wash my hands, he would tap impatiently on his water glass until I had taken my place at the table. If I slipped into my seat a minute after seven, he would mutter coldly, "Who's running this house, you or I?" But when boyfriends came to the house, he would always retreat from the living room and hide out in his bedroom. He didn't want to meet them.

He read a great deal and loved music, travel, baseball games and fishing. My mother not only loved to read, she also adored the theater and motion pictures. Throughout my career with the William Morris Agency, she was as omnipresent as any performer's stage mother, going everywhere with me.

When I was entering my teens, my mother let me know that I was good-natured and bright but would never be a *femme fatale*. My mouth was too big and my nose was not the fine straight nose that should have been her legacy to me. She even told me I had absolutely no taste, no flair for clothes. Fortunately, I did have a will and a mind of my own, and we did love each other, so that our life together involved those compromises which allowed both of us the greatest satisfactions and the least frustrations.

And of course, though my mother's methods could be rough, her judgments were often very sound, particularly when I was young. My very first torrid romance erupted when I was barely seventeen. He was a fine person, but we were kids and foolish and marriage would have been disastrous for him, for me and for the love we had for each other. My mother broke it up, and I'm glad she did and I knew it was right even then. If she had not, I would not carry the fond memories I do for that tender and tempestuous moment, which did not sour only because it did not progress.

I felt even then that sex, love and marriage do not necessarily go hand in hand, as many more people know today, including many of my friends who have schlepped down the aisle to get into bed and battled in court to get out.

It was during that teenage romance that I surrendered (let's be honest, I volunteered) my virginity. My young lover, impassioned by that guilt which used to pass for chivalry, swirled his cape across the broken bloom of my maidenhood and vowed that he would escort me to the holy and honorable state of matrimony.

"Why bother?" I laughed. "Oh no, that's not the way it's supposed to be. I wanted to find out what it was all about, too. What does that have to do with marriage?" His noble offer rejected, he pouted and called me a slut.

I have seen him in recent years. He is very rich and successful. I hope that he is happy as well, but we would not have been had that mutual experiment been binding.

My father did not retreat into his room during my next romantic affair. Far from it! His Old World attitudes boiled up and over and he laid down the law like one of those illustrations from a Victorian melodrama poster, the one in which the angry father stands in a doorway opened unto the night blizzard, pointing with a "Go, and never darken my door again!" gesture.

The inspiration for this dramatic stand was the discovery that his daughter had fallen madly in love with . . . an actor! He had a fit. Fathers of his generation still believed that daughters who fell into the clutches of actors would be raped before the cab had turned the first corner.

The actor in question was Borrah Minnevitch, the harmonica virtuoso, who had co-starred with Elsie Janis in *Puzzles* and with Marilyn Miller in *Sunny* and the Ziegfeld Follies. I don't remember how we met, but I knew when he telephoned me that this was going to be an episode I would long remember.

When I first went to Borrah's apartment in a brownstone on 51st Street between Fifth and Sixth avenues, he greeted me with an outrageous question, which seems curiously old-fashioned now: "Are you a virgin?"

I responded with a lie that I was to find handy in getting out of many future tight spots: "Yes, I am." We left the apartment in a mad rush.

I still have a book he gave me, a collection of Shelley's poems, inscribed with "The inspirations of Shelley must surely have been mild—had he known you!!!—ah well!"

It ended finally when my father threatened to throw me out of the house, but after my short-lived marriage we were to meet again. I'll always remember his beautiful hands, his hair, his voice and the way he smelled. He died some time ago in Paris. I think he married twice.

I became an adult in the twenties. It was the decade which ushered in speakeasies, flappers, the gangster boom, a big revival of the Ku Klux Klan, the Florida land boom, Lindbergh's flight to Paris, Byrd's flight over the South Pole, and the ill-fated League of Nations.

Women and girls with rouged knees dared to smoke and drink in public. The young college coeds necked, though sex was not openly discussed and promiscuity was frowned upon, but the younger generation was becoming emancipated, or at least they, like many now, thought they knew it all. But politically, they were not very aware. World War I was quickly forgotten. The stock market hit new highs, like everything else on the margin of reason, on a crash course toward that decade's final October.

Out on the town one night, at a party, I met Walter Donaldson, the composer of "My Blue Heaven," "Love Me or Leave Me," "My Mammy," "My Buddy," "Makin' Whoopee!" and "How Ya Gonna Keep 'Em Down on the Farm?" He told me that I was just like a melody out of the sky and offered me a chance at immortality. The song he composed for me, "Just Like a Melody Out of the Sky," was introduced with fanfare by the Paul Whiteman Orchestra. It bombed, and I caught hell from my parents for going out with the Tin Pan Alley tunesmith, despite a vain attempt on my part to warble a few choruses of "Little White Lies."

The big success launched by Whiteman during that period was a trio which had been introduced as the Three Rhythm Boys during a "New Faces" week at Keith's Palace sometime earlier. As the Rhythm Boys with Whiteman, Bing Crosby, Harry Barris and Al Rinker had made a hit of "Mississippi Mud." Harry, Bing and I used to go to a speakeasy on 45th Street when they got off work.

One night we went instead to the Chateau Madrid. Bing, enjoying the first flush of success and anxious for the next break, had a miserable evening. I'll always remember the gloom that descended upon him as the night wore away. He had hoped to be recognized and asked to sing, but no one called him up. They missed their chance.

Though Crosby loved to tour the speakeasies, he was in those days not infrequently shy of cash, a condition from which he was soon to have a permanent recovery. When his cash ran out before the tours did, I would lend him money. Each payday I appeared to collect the previous week's debt. Both of us were quite careful to keep the ledger up to date. It was a pleasant, but brief, friendship, nothing serious. Shortly thereafter he married Dixie Lee.

I was still in my teens. My father was in business with a friend, a man in whom he placed that blind trust that was his curse. He trusted him so implicitly, they had never bothered to incorporate. By the time the gloss of friendship on my father's partner had worn sufficiently to reveal the crook at base, my father found himself liable under the laws of New York State for all of his vanished friend's debts.

Mortified, my father contrived a romantic scheme to leave us very well off. He decided to commit suicide. He planned it all, not realizing that his insurance policy would be voided by suicide. He did it in a most peculiar way. We were all driven from the house on various ruses. Then, when he was alone with his notes and policies, taking care to leave some windows open, he turned all of the gas jets on.

I prefer to think that in addition to some strong subconscious will to survive, my father's actions evidenced the same sweetly myopic concern as his well-intentioned motives, in that last effort to see that windows were open so that there would be no explosions and damage to our property. How typical, in the futility of his grand plan, that he would not immediately correlate efforts of meticulous concern on our behalf with their effect upon his own.

That's when I decided to go to work.

I had no set goal. I wanted to be able to pay my own way and be independent. I had no consuming ambition to be rich and famous, though I was determined to live my life with dignity. I was never poor, neither was my family rich. We were comfortable. There were periods of affluence. When Riverside Drive began to deteriorate we had moved to the East Side.

My first assault on a prospective employer proved to be a bitter disappointment initially and eventually a rebuff that spurred me beyond the tight ripples of home to the farther shores of possibility. I asked my father to give me a job, to take me into his business. He knew my negotiable skills better than others I would soon meet, and we haggled over price. He said I wasn't worth fifteen dollars a week. I knew I was. I wouldn't settle for less.

One day my mother, the compulsive shopper, was on her rounds, walking down Fifth Avenue, when she ran into an old friend of the family. The essential pleasantries out of the way—or in their course—he asked about me.

His name was Claud Saunders. He was a former theatrical advance agent and manager of theatrical companies, and had established an early association with the motion picture business, having managed presentations of David Wark Griffith's *Birth of a Nation* and *Intolerance*, among other early epics. He had joined Famous Players–Lasky Corporation to organize and direct the first motion picture exploitation department.

On the word of that highly placed executive, I was quickly given an interview with the office manager and hired. It was a very good thing that I was not called upon to prove my claim of skills as a typist and stenographer. If I had, I would never have been hired and would not now be sending off the pages of this book in longhand for someone else to type.

To this day anything mechanical stumps me, typewriters in particular. I had only learned the fundamentals of stenography, but my memory was always very good. The fact that I used common sense and was interested in everything going on gave me the reputation of being bright, even if I wasn't about to win any typewriting sweepstakes.

My first assignment in Jesse L. Lasky's Manhattan hierarchy was as an assistant secretary to his personal eastern representative. Don't ask me what that meant. I never did find out, and after six months I decided that assignment had no future and went to the office manager, demanding a job in which I might show my talent.

He sent me to a man who did not strike me as being terribly bright. It was one thing to think that I knew more than the boss, but when I began to learn that I in fact did, I knew we were in for trouble. I never listened to him. We had a big fight. He pouted that I was insubordinate—and I was again looking for the first available opening.

Under similar circumstances, years later, but early in my career as a literary agent, I was given some prudent advice by George Joel, head of a small book-publishing firm, Dial Press. He was probably the wisest man I ever knew and also one of the best-informed, and he told me, when I was beginning to make a reputation for myself, "Always remember, Helen, it isn't that you're so brilliant. It's that the rest of the world is so stupid."

I was making a huge salary for those times—$20 a week, I believe—when an average salary was closer to twelve or fourteen. My mother decided to take me for a coat. She chose a very good store in Manhattan that sold coats and furs. The coat I selected bore a $195 price tag.

"I'm sorry," I said. "I just can't afford this."

But my mother insisted. "You'll pay me back out of your salary," she commanded. "But you must always look well and have good clothes, wherever you go." And I have always bought the best.

It was typical of my mother's extravagant practicality. Three years before, prior to the collapse of my father's business partnership, when he was making good money, Mother bought a Rolls-Royce—a second-hand Rolls, to be sure, but quite unheard of in those days. A year later, when my father lost his money, we sold the Rolls. A year later, when he was successfully establishing himself in a new business, she was one of the first to buy the elegant new Lincoln.

She also advised me never to associate with the girls in the office. She did not approve. "They gossip, no point," she cautioned. "It is to the advantage of anyone who wants to progress to remain aloof, not to be just one of the girls."

Well, I never was.

My next stop along the dreary hallways of the Famous Players offices at Broadway and 44th was in the publicity department, and this time I was even more determined to learn everything I could and make my presence felt. I was constantly wandering through the building, trying to find out what everyone did there, how movies got made, how stories in print emerged as shadow dreams, which courses were the swiftest.

The man I worked with was a charmer, and every time anyone would call up for me, he'd answer, saying, "Oh, she's off on her Cook's tour."

Famous Players–Lasky had emerged from the combine of Adolph Zukor's Famous Players Film Company and Jesse L. Lasky's Feature Play Company more than a decade earlier. At the same time, the two producers had sought to ensure the stability of their distribution outlet by absorbing Paramount Pictures Corporation, a distribution and sales organization. As new theater outlets were built or acquired through various subsidiaries, the company was briefly known as Paramount Famous–Lasky Corporation, and with its greatest surge of theater-chain acquisition, had become Paramount Publix. It was the first motion picture stock to be traded on the New York Stock Exchange.

James R. Cowan, who had been with the Balaban and Katz circuit of theaters when Paramount took them over, was brought to Paramount's Astoria, Long Island, studios to be general manager of the studio.

My next job for Paramount took me out to the Island as Cowan's personal secretary. I was just recovering from an operation, however, and my mother called Cowan to say that I could not work for him unless he sent his car and chauffeur. Cowan met the demands, and each morning I would be picked up and chauffeured to work at the Astoria studios and transported home in time for my father's seven-o'clock dinner deadline each night.

Many of the important associations of my subsequent career began in that office, as did a great share of the practical experience. But the continuity of my life would soon be interrupted. I was already being courted by Mathieu.

My first encounter with Walter Wanger was in the hall in the New York office of Famous Players–Lasky. At that time Walter was head of eastern production. He was in a class by himself.

In those days of motion picture production most of the so-called moguls were illiterate first-generation Americans, lacking in social graces even though they were not without great business acumen and a street-level instinct for the public's taste. Walter was different. Brought up with Warburgs, he had been graduated from Dartmouth, inaugurated the Theatre Guild with Anne Morgan, J. P. Morgan's sister, and was a prodigious reader. From his early youth most of his friends were those German Jews whose parents had come here at least one or two generations before, having acquired great wealth, art collections, and all the trappings of refinement, including, in some cases, taste. They were also snobs.

Walter was a product of that background and he had the social assurance which flourished in that environment. He was also attractive, had a wry sense of humor and a quick mind. With his connections, he started at the top.

There wasn't anyone like him in the film business, not even Irving Thalberg. He lent an elegant façade and a respectability to the motion picture business on the East Coast such as it had not yet gained or aspired to until that time.

When I came home the day he talked to me, I told my mother very excitedly about the incident. I was thrilled. He was rich, influential and attractive and he had singled me out. My mother told me something which was not only wise but probably the best kind of advice for a young girl. She looked at me and said, "Do you think Mr. Wanger is better than you are? If you do, you're wrong. The most important thing in life is to be a good human being. No one should be judged by wealth, position, race or color." That statement, all through my life, has been a guidepost.

When I went to work for Walter, I learned other things. He liked women and women liked him, but on the whole he had little respect for them, and woman's place, whether glamour girl, star or whatever, was in bed. Having seen a number of these ladies come and go rapidly in his life, and being practical, I concluded that it would be better to have him as a good friend, which he was, than to be one of the girls.

Through Walter, I would meet Noel Coward, Flo Ziegfeld and other legendary talents of the era. And he was charming to my mother, so, naturally, she adored him.

Later, when I was working for Walter's production company, he asked me to go to his suite at the Waldorf Towers and act as his hostess for a very influential, fabulously wealthy gentleman until he arrived. When Walter came home, he asked me whether I was going to have dinner with his friend. I said, "No." Walter predicted a dismal future for me. This man could do everything for me—money, furs, jewels, and if I wanted a career, he could be helpful there too. Why didn't I want to spend an evening with him? "He is old and he is married," I replied tartly.

A short time before he died, Walter and I met for lunch at the St. Regis Hotel in New York. Picking at bits of veal and memory, he had looked up and said, quite simply, "I was wrong about you. You did what you wanted—your way."

Temporarily blinded by polka dots and moonbeams, I brought my future husband, Mathieu, to the Astoria studio. Wanger looked him over, detected the star-diffusion in my eyes and said, "Okay, go ahead and marry him. He looks pretty substantial." Wanger was also suitably impressed by Mathieu's automobile, an ornate status symbol in those days of pre-Cadillac elegance, a special-body Packard. So I told him we'd set the date—and I kissed my momentum at Paramount adieu.

Everyone thought Mathieu was wonderful. He had an accent like Maurice Chevalier, was slim, over six feet tall, had blue eyes, danced divinely and made a more than substantial income. Why he married—I'll never know. During the period of our engagement he was so romantic. All he wanted out of life was me, a house in the country—and children. After we were married, there was no evidence that he wanted me, the house in the country—or children.

The day I was married was a beautiful spring day in April. We had a lovely wedding at the Plaza Hotel in New York. Just before the ceremony, as my mother and I looked out across Central Park, she reminded me that it was a very good omen to be married on a sunny day. Since then omens mean nothing to me.

We spent the first year of our marriage in Paris. By the time Mathieu and I returned to New York, the marriage was rapidly going to hell. I decided—actually, it would soon be decided for me—that I would not do the same. We were living on East 57th Street, so it was quite convenient for me to go over to the Long Island studio to visit my old friends. We had a chauffeur, but as if to signal my regained sense of independence, I learned to drive.

One of my first solos behind the wheel proved both disastrous and catalytic. Mathieu was off on a business trip through the Midwest. The chauffeur was off for the day, a Sunday afternoon as I remember. I arranged to pick up my parents and started out along 57th toward Park Avenue.

My driving must have been afflicted by an excess of nerves and caution, for I suddenly heard a carload of kids behind me, honking persistently. The rude and strange blare and an instinct to accommodate prompted me to spin the wheel in an insane right turn over the sidewalk and straight into the Ritz Towers, demolishing an ancient wrought-iron canopy. Surprisingly, the car survived with relatively little damage.

In the aftermath, I did have the presence of mind to slip the policeman who arrived on the scene a ten-dollar bill. When I finally went to court I got off with a suspended sentence. But I did not notice the *Daily News* photographer who happened to see and photograph the accident. The following morning the *News* carried pictures of the crumpled canopy and a picture of the frightened driver, clutching my fur collar about my chin, a wild lock of hair cascading from beneath my cloche hat.

On the night following the wild ride I reached Mathieu by telephone in Chicago. "I've had an accident," I told him.

There was a long pause at the other end of the line. Then, "Was there much damage . . . to the car? How much?"

It was only a short time afterward that we officially separated, though it was ten years before I would be granted a divorce. In the wake of that perfect storybook wedding and the disillusionment which followed, Mathieu, who was surely as miserable in the marriage as I, salved a bruised ego by refusing to void a contract neither of us wished to fulfill a day longer.

I really hadn't wanted to get married in the first place. I suppose my view of marriage is not too unlike that which is being voiced increasingly by many young people today. While I would not have presumed to force my own feelings upon other and unwilling ears, nor formulate a socio-political religion based on a personal preference in a single aspect of my life, marriage never appealed to me as goal or fulfillment. It seemed an obsolete ritual. Domesticity as a full-time occupation bored me. There had to be more.

Nor were my parents any more anxious for me to get married. That I ever got married was a miracle, except that there were greater social and family pressures then to intimidate and drive a young woman to the altar than exist today. Certainly my parents were possessive and, in many ways, impossible, but I enjoyed being with them and loved them dearly. So, unlike other girls I knew, I didn't consider marriage as an escape from them.

The pressure for a wedding probably began with my grandmother, who had begun to threaten me with the ultimate stigma, that of becoming an "old maid." She delighted in reminding me that she had married when she was seventeen, that my mother had waited until she was eighteen, neither age especially young for matrimony in their times. If I was to be saved, to ensure my immortality, to be kept from being "washed up" at twenty, Mathieu was surely the most suitable of the suitors who had checked in: "a great catch," as the saying went.

He satisfied the family. He pleased everyone. He had been born only five miles from where my grandfather was born in Alsace. He had very good manners, was polite to the family and was fourteen years older than I. Everybody went mad for him. My friends envied me and were quick to run after him when I eventually left him. For a time it didn't seem to matter that he bored me. We tried to make it work, but it didn't and I cannot blame him.

Since then, every man I met throughout my life, no matter how attractive he was, how intelligent, I asked myself, "Can I spend the rest of my life with him: can I sacrifice any part of the satisfaction I find in my professional life?" The answer was always no. Men liked me and I liked them. I could be intrigued and flattered, enjoyed the flirting and the attention, but I had no desire for "entangling alliances."

I wanted much more.

I continued to drive out to the Astoria, Long Island, studios. I was not looking for a job, but I showed up with such frequency that Walter Wanger stopped me one day. "Since you're going to be spending so much time here," he said, "why don't you make it official, get back on the payroll and back to work." I was ready.

Through Wanger, I was hired as a junior writer and returned to the Paramount studio. Paramount had been hiring top Broadway stage and vaudeville stars and developing them in one- and two-reel comedy shorts. A number of these performers were simultaneously capturing the American public on radio and some would later establish themselves as top film draws. Rudy Vallee, Eddie Cantor, Jack Benny and Burns and Allen were among the headliners turning out these quickies, assisted by fine supporting players from the Broadway stage. I was assigned to write adaptations for several and received the only screen credits of my career. Fred Allen was writing his own scripts down the hall, and George Burns was turning out the stories for a percentage of the Burns and Allen one-reelers with a screenplay credit of "George N. Burns." I worked on several of the Burns and Allen and Fred Allen comedies, but essentially these pictures drew upon the well-tempered vaudeville routines of the recruited performers.

I have never been much of a social creature. I have tried, but I really don't like to be with groups. Even when I was younger I had few girl friends. Women's clubs and similarly oriented organizations hold no appeal for me. I know that they accomplish many good things and I admire the ladies who have the time to turn their energies and talent toward helping others. While I have initiated scholarships, organized a few benefit programs and lent various degrees of support to a number of causes, my jobs have always demanded so much of my time that even occasional meetings would have been impossible to attend. Basically, I simply am not a joiner. Most of my life I have preferred to do what I wanted to do, to be with people after a busy week of dealing with people in business only if I wanted to. I don't mind being alone. In fact, I prefer it.

But when Mathieu and I separated, I briefly reveled in having a midtown Manhattan apartment. I fancied myself very sophisticated. I threw myself into a social whirl that seemed appealing for the first time simply by virtue of having been several thousand miles away during my exile in Paris. So I gave parties. Giving parties, one always gets to know a lot of people, especially if the price is right—free booze and food. It was supposed to be fun. It really wasn't. I was also receiving invitations to parties and places. I met a motley assemblage of people—songwriters, song pluggers, some theatrical laborers and some theatrical talkers, some racketeers.

I have never been awed by actors, and the ego required to survive as an actor does not make the actor or actress a particularly intelligent or interesting companion. There are always exceptions, to be sure. I've often said that while writers are frequently as neurotic as actors, they are considerably more interesting. But to that season's newest party girl, actors were the pick of the litter.

When Mathieu returned to New York from one of his business trips, he stopped at the apartment, but not before he had engaged in an in-depth debriefing session with one of the building's elevator operators.

When I saw him, his first words were "Did you have Gary Cooper here last night?"

"Yes."

He looked surprised. "I don't believe you," he insisted.

"Well, you asked—and I assumed you already knew the answer."

"I don't believe you. Next you'll tell me that you've had Chevalier up here."

"That was last week," I responded truthfully.

I first met Gary Cooper on the Paramount lot. I arrived between the finale of his tempestuous affair with Lupe Velez and before the playgirl countess Dorothy Di Frasso shanghaied him for an African safari and a gentlemanly overhaul by Bond Street tailors. While he was in pursuit, I found it expedient to travel with a girl friend to discourage his advances. The famous taciturn manner which he was to develop into a distinctive and artful screen image did not seem to me at that time to be shielding extraordinary wit or intelligence. He would simply sit and stare at me, at a loss for conversation. The man from Montana and I soon parted company.

I soon realized that I was wasting my life. I knew instinctively that I was running around with the wrong crowd. And the morning I awoke to find a Russian actor, whose name I couldn't remember from the night before, snoring on my living-room couch, I knew that I could not allow myself to become one of the girls around town. At the same time I became increasingly interested in my work at the studio.

Perhaps it was too coincidental when my mother telephoned the next day to inform me that she and my father wanted to have a talk with me. When I went to see them that evening Mother very simply stated that she and my dad wanted me to come back and live with them. It was the answer to my problem.

I'll never know what my parents knew or surmised and nothing was ever said, but I found out immediately that it wasn't my father who had felt I should move home. As I was about to leave he suggested putting me in a taxi. When we reached the street he told me it had been Mother's idea, that as far as he was concerned, I was an adult, and since I seemed responsible and he had every confidence in me, it was important for me to build a life of my own.

My reaction to my father's statement was completely wrong. I thought he didn't love me. I felt a little lost. I wasn't very grown up, really. And so I went home.

Shortly after, I was canned, ever so briefly. I suppose "laid off" is the more euphemistic modern phrase, for the Long Island studio was closed down. These were the Depression years, when many, if not most, studios went into receivership, reorganizing and consolidating production on the more modern studio soundstages of Hollywood. Cartoons and biweekly newsreels were coming in strongly and the live comedy shorts were on the wane. Those who made it in Paramount comedy shorts were moving up to Hollywood feature roles. So I was not destined to challenge such distinguished veteran lady screenwriters as Frances Marion, Dorothy Kingsley, Frances Goodrich, Sonya Levien or Isobel Lennart.

Because of the number of different jobs I held with Paramount, both in progression and under separate tenure, it is hard for me to know just how many times I signed in there. I think there were six, possibly only five, initial start dates, but it was home base for the prodigal during the balance of that decade. Each return marked an advancement. By the same token, each departure led to something better, ensuring that advancement. I first met many lifelong friends during those years and would meet casually many people who were to play key roles in my life and career much later. I have operated on the premise that if you're around long enough, you get to know everyone. Then it is a question whether they are going to like you or hate you, and that is always up to you.

A few years ago I attended the Hollywood gala celebrating the hundredth birthday of Adolph Zukor, the tiny and indestructible mogul who built Paramount—in the course of setting the production and distribution patterns for much of the motion picture business as we have known it. I remember for the first time in years my first and only encounter with Zukor during my tenure at Paramount. It taught me the idiocy of being too eager to volunteer.

Mr. Zukor was in town and wanted to put in some work in the office on Thanksgiving Day. No one wanted to work on the holiday. One by one they were approached and one by one they declined and retreated. Stupidly, I agreed to come in. So it was that Adolph Zukor and I spent that long-ago holiday alone in the Paramount office. However, I arrived to discover that Mr. Zukor had nothing for me to do. He proved to be a very quiet and pleasant man, and we stood at the window and watched the Macy's parade while I silently cursed myself for having made a waste of the day.

Another man I revered was Herman Wobber, my boss when I returned to work at Paramount's Manhattan home offices. An independently wealthy San Franciscan who was one of the original franchise holders of Famous Players–Lasky and had helped build the Curran and Geary theaters in San Francisco, he had one of those fancy, incomprehensible jobs organizing sales drives.

Wobber also made an immediate conquest of my mother, calling her to ask her permission to take me to dinner. My mother, of course, immediately asked where. He said that he was taking me to the Colony restaurant. That was the first time I ever went to the Colony.

My stenographic skills had not improved at all. I couldn't take his dictation because he spoke so fast. Years later he wrote me acknowledging that my letters were never anything he had dictated, but he added that they were substantially true to his intentions and in much better English than I had been given. I was very fond of him and visited him many times in San Francisco in later years.

At one point, Wobber was called to the Fox Film Corporation to work as division sales manager under Sidney Kent. Kent was one of the most strikingly successful pioneers in the young movie industry. An engineer who had literally opened up new territories in Colorado, he began in the picture business with the old Vitagraph Company. He had helped untangle the General Film Company from judgments totaling $25 million under the Sherman Law, before coming to Adolph Zukor as a district manager and, later, general manager of distribution. He rose through Paramount to the company's board of directors, general managership and vice-presidency. When Harley L. Clarke, the Chicago public utilities magnate, acquired control of Fox Film Corporation, he lured Kent over as president of the company, and Kent would be instrumental in the subsequent merger of Fox and Twentieth Century Pictures in 1935.

Without delay, Kent took Wobber with him, and Wobber paged me. When you are brought from one studio to another, there is an added and different stature which descends upon you. At Paramount it had been "Oh yeah, Helen, she started here when she was just a kid out of school."

I moved from Paramount's offices at Broadway and 44th to the Fox building at 56th and Tenth Avenue, an unfortunate location. Aside from its selection in the first place, the founding father was responsible for its décor, which all who have encountered and been oppressed by it can only describe as "early William Fox": part penal institution, with social-service-agency-office compartments and windows; part Byzantine powder room, with overhangings and outcroppings of gold leaf and fruit-salad masonry overwhelming you in the most unlikely places.

Paramount's New York offices had simply been very ordinary, with merely functional facilities, but the Long Island studio had a touch of that Hollywood flair that stars and visiting press people of the day must have expected. While I had been a junior writer there, I had been celled in an office with satin walls—surrounded by phony antique furniture, all of it crafted for less heavy-duty use by the properties department.

While I was at Fox, Wobber introduced me to Spyros and Charles Skouras, who were running the Fox theaters in their rise through the company. In the years to come I would have many dealings with Spyros, who would become president of the emerging combine. More immediately, Charlie would inspire me to new records in the familiar around-the-desk-sprint sweepstakes. As he pursued he recounted the famous names who had thrown the fight and taken a dive.

"If they will, why won't you?" he protested.

"Why should I?" I panted.

The answer seemed to throw him, for he never found a convincing response as I dashed for the door.

Occasionally, I would receive an offer of a job in Hollywood. But I was not particularly interested in going there. I was comfortable in Manhattan, and besides, my mother would have tried her best to discourage me, though it would have been done in the most oblique way. Then came an offer which I didn't think I could resist, an assignment to the London office for Fox. I rushed home, excited, greeting my mother with what seemed to me the very generous and accommodating details of the projected transfer.

"They are willing to pay your expenses for the first six months, until you're satisfied that I'm settled," I told her. She turned to me coolly, then announced, "I hope that you thanked them. But what makes you think I'd leave your father for that length of time?" And that was that. And I didn't go.

Meanwhile Walter Wanger, with the backing of Jay Paley, whose nephew became the chairman of the board of Columbia Broadcasting Company, had launched his own production company. Paramount was committed to release his independent productions, and Walter asked me to be his New York representative—beginning two years during which I attended every New York theater opening night, dashing off a full report on the film potential the following morning, in addition to maintaining contact with New York-based publishers, agents and authors and visiting Wanger talents from the Continent and the Coast. I was running my own office operation for the first time, savoring the autonomy as much as the responsibility. It did spoil me, caused the next job to frustrate me sooner and determined not only the course I followed in the coming years but the manner in which I traveled it.

Walter, whom Ben Hecht called "the most elegant and learned of the movie potentates," remained as volatile as ever, always close to controversy but equally close to the essential humor of situations. During the making of *The President Vanishes*, he tried to phone Louella Parsons with an urgent tidbit of gossip. Placing the call himself, he became offended when the operator demanded more information than just his name. Walter, who kept writers churning out by-line articles on the art of film and peppered the fan columns with daily quotes of pith and promotion, snapped, "I guess you don't read the newspapers. Now get Louella on the line."

Another time he directed me to his window to view the new silver Rolls he had purchased to convey his rising status. He turned to me finally, winked and said, "Of course, it can always be converted into a taxi in a pinch."

We remained friends until his death, and he was always my number-one volunteer press agent.

As Hitler's shadow spread across the European continent and voices of isolation, forecasts of imminent war and the angry chants of the American Bund echoing their Nazi inspiration were heard across an America just beginning to emerge from the Depression, I returned to Paramount.

I finally grew up there and worked my way up to the post of associate story editor, first under Richard Halliday, who married Mary Martin and later settled in Brazil, then under Richard Mealand. I visited literary agents, book publishers, magazine editors and talked unaware writers into writing stories that had potential for filming. The job seemed important and glamorous. It wasn't, though it was always of interest—and I continued to learn.

But it was frustrating, and each month I realized more and more that the future there was a dead-end street. The pay wasn't so hot either. I had this wild notion of becoming a literary agent. It took four years to get off my can to make the leap. When I did, it was again the right time, and luckily, the right leap.

Each of the big film companies was buying approximately fifty pieces of material annually—novels, plays, magazine scrials and short stories, in addition to material written directly for the screen. They bought more than they needed, more than they could produce, not knowing what they would or could do with it. They bought everything. They gobbled up the best-seller lists and the bulk of magazine fiction. They bought the rights to life stories they weren't likely to be able to show. The raw material piled up on shelves and gathered dust in storerooms, where much of it remains today. No one in the present management of Hollywood studios knows precisely what is owned in those lock-me-tights, what past or subsequently great authors are represented, what fortunes are buried in that raw ore.

There was great competition then. If you got the new John Steinbeck book two days before Metro, that made you a genius. You knew that if the synopsis of a new book or the galleys went out to California from your New York readers twenty-four hours ahead, that meant you had a lead of twenty-four more hours to consider it, to reach a decision. The competition was so great, the agents could usually decide the prices.

Sometimes deals were lost because an agent gambled on too high a price. If he held out, he could get stuck. The story editors were always advised as to how much they were authorized to spend. If the studio said $50,000 was the top and an agent tried to escalate an author's price for film rights to $100,000, he'd soon find that no one among the majors wanted it, and he'd be lucky to place it at all at a much reduced price. Once a player defaulted at that game, the goods were tainted. If the majors lost one this week, there was always a fresh harvest of material next week. A few overconfident agents regularly lost rounds for their clients.

It was a game and, of course, it was kind of fun. William Fadiman, who played at the same sport as story editor for Metro while I was at Paramount, used to compare notes with me every day about all we were getting, keeping our confidences a big dark secret. He'd be furious if he learned that I got something before it was submitted to him. We kept timetables. We rated the players and the innings. We kept scores of our own wins and losses.

Studios were turning out as many as seventy-five films each, annually. It seemed that they could afford every gamble. And there were more flagrant examples of wasted money and time. We would receive frantic telegrams from the studio in Hollywood, requesting that we rush by air the newest issue of, say, *The Saturday Evening Post* to Cecil B. DeMille or someone nearly comparable, who could have picked up a copy of the same magazine on his lunch hour in Hollywood.

That also illustrates the sense of caste which still existed in the film companies. Hollywood was a name that struck awe in presumably sophisticated Manhattan offices, just as it did in Keokuk or Biloxi. Sojourners from Hollywood were treated like visiting royalty. You stopped your work and fell on your face if they ordered something. There might be typical New York sneers and gossip about the Hollywood people while they remained on their own turf, but as they approached the Hudson River, mere mortals instinctively moved to part it in their path. Years later, at the William Morris Agency, visiting Hollywood moguls and legendary faces still generated excitement and red-carpet courtesies not necessarily earned.

Power was still rather evenly split between the eastern and western company offices, the New York grasp on money and decisions affecting the creative talents in the West not yet strongly manifest. It became a tug of war as the stakes grew higher and the surviving founding fathers found themselves beholden to boards of directors, banks and stockholders after the wartime boom and the first postwar television frosts.

For those four years in the story department at Paramount, it had been my function to do all of the contact work on story material. I had to find out what well-known writers were doing, what book publishers were contracting for, what plans the magazines had for forthcoming fiction and what plays were eventually going to be produced, and in my continuing search for suitable story matter for motion picture production, to entertain those responsible for these decisions and output.

Through these associations, I met many writers, perhaps the majority of those working at the time. Instinctively I understood them, and there was always a rapport with them which encouraged me to feel that I could help them professionally.

But I was guileless, and had it not been for a friend of mine, Raymond Crossett, who was then an agent, I would have continued to write letters and criticism over the signatures of others. He took me to lunch and told me he knew that most of the letters and comments on story material were mine even though they were all signed by the story editor. It might be a practical idea, he suggested, to use my own name. It turned out to be very sound advice.

The perennial problem in the motion picture business is that a film is a corporate phenomenon, mauled by so many hands from conception to delivery—yet claimed as a personal achievement by so many individuals if successful—that no one could ever know what you did at the studio. The whole studio, its chain of command, took credit for the divine inspiration that brought forth a film whole. A story editor could fight and push to gain attention for a story he/she believed should be made. Producers, executives, directors, stars and department heads then competed for the claim of "creating" the characters, the stories and the inevitable trends and cycles they spawned.

Before I decided to become an agent, I had taken stock of the book-publishing business. In those days few women got very far in that field. Blanche Knopf shared the top position at Alfred A. Knopf, Inc., but it is doubtful if she could have risen to that spot without "marrying the boss."

Oddly enough, most of the literary agents were ladies. Knowing them rather well, I thought that they had satisfactory professional lives. If one had energy, inventiveness, patience and a knowledge of the quality of writing, it could be not only an interesting way to earn a living but the kind of occupation in which success or failure depended in large part upon the individual. I knew also that the most important thing was having a good list of talents to represent, for without that, no matter how hard I worked, I could never hope to become a successful literary agent.

Angus Cameron, the New York editor of Little, Brown, was the first to encourage me, suggesting over lunch one day that I might make a good agent. From time to time I had suggested writers and book ideas to Angus—some of them good, some of them not so good—but they indicated the turn of my thinking.

However, I had yet to acquire enough self-confidence and it was a couple more years before I took the step. One day I confided my desire to another editor, LeBaron Barker of Doubleday, who was always gracious and kind to me during all of my scouting jobs. My timing was again right. It would be nice to take credit for creating those pivotal moments in our lives, but I believe that such efforts never pay off unless and until the time is right.

Lee told me that Harold Matson, a reputable agent, was thinking of expanding. Since I knew Hal well, Lee suggested he'd speak to him on my behalf. Subsequently I had a meeting with Hal and he asked me to join him. The next day I received a call from Albert Schneider, now Albert Taylor, of the William Morris Agency.

He asked if I could do him a favor, and I made a cocktail date with him to discuss the matter. He kept me waiting almost a half-hour, which is something I still cannot tolerate. Albert made it sound as if the Morris Agency were embarking upon some grand international intrigue. In fact, they were considering the establishment of a literary department, and since I knew all the agents in town, they wanted me to recommend a few who I thought might be capable of heading the department. I gladly recommended three or four people.

I don't remember whether I kiddingly recommended myself as well—"How about me?"—or whether he asked me if I wanted the job. After two martinis I'm liable to have said anything.

The next thing I knew, I was in the office of Bill Morris, Jr., and he was chiding me: "Why didn't you tell *me* that you wanted the job?" I explained that I hadn't known they had a job open until then, that I already had a job, and that it was better to have come about as it did.

Bill's father, William Morris, Sr., who founded the agency which still carries his name, had been eulogized as the greatest of agents and managers, was beloved by the acts he represented and had courageously battled Keith and Albee and the monopolies of show business. He was, himself, a tough act for any son to follow, and Bill, Jr., who has now long been retired from the agency, was a contrary and contradictory man, dedicated to fashionably liberal politics and the rights of the oppressed, but when a union tried to start at the agency, he took it as a personal betrayal.

Time ripened and yet another opportunity fell on me. I received a call from Frances Pindyck, who was one of the best agents in the business. She worked for Leland Hayward, had talked to him about me and was calling to tell me that he wanted to see me about a job.

Leland Hayward was one of the outstanding men in show business, then a talent agent, later distinguished as a producer in theater, films and television. His brand of charm and nonchalance made him unique. Other agents, especially those who used to be called "flesh peddlers," used the hard-sell method. When Leland was representing actors and actresses to the film companies, he was the master of underselling. He gave the impression that he might confer a great favor to the producer by consenting to allow his client to appear in the particular project.

The prospect of working for Leland and learning from him fascinated and excited me. Yet I did not want to be an agent for performing talent, was now determined to be a literary agent and knew that Frances Pindyck was already doing a superb job for Leland. Even though Leland was complimentary and assured me that I would be making an important niche for myself with him, the prospect of dealing with actors and actresses was not that appealing.

The opportunity had come—and I worried. I worried more for having the luxury of choice. I spent nights counting sheep. I talked it over with my parents. My father, who had no real conception of what an agent was or did, was horrified at the prospect. It didn't sound quite nice to him. We had a terrible argument about it. It was such a matter of pride to be able to tell his friends that I was associate story editor for Paramount Pictures! Mother, however, encouraged me. I would be dealing with writers, and that was fine. She also was aware of the fact that the William Morris Agency was the largest theatrical agency in the business.

My friend George Joel, in his sardonic way, challenged me to take the Morris post. He baited me, kidding that I was spoiled by working for a big company, where office boys could be sent on errands at whim, long-distance calls made at will. Starting a department from scratch and to my specifications, he thought, offered the greatest challenge and the most fun.

I decided to take the job with the Morris office. No, not quite. The timing was obviously not yet right. I briefly succumbed to forced injections of guilt. I wavered. I teetered. I fell backward.

The head of the home office production staff at the time was a very nice man named Russell Holman, a former newspaperman and novelist. He enjoyed a great deal of authority. Nothing was bought on either coast unless he okayed it. He grew suddenly very paternal, reminding me that I had come to Paramount as a kid right out of school, and tried to talk me out of my plan to become a literary agent.

"Look what we've done for you. Look at the job you have. Don't worry, Helen. You'll get a raise the first of the year," he swore. And so I stayed with my Paramount family, which seemed to have such bright hopes and plans for me. It was October 1943. I forwarded my regrets to Bill Morris and watched the calendar pages ripple toward the end of the year, just like a movie time-lapse. Then it was 1944. I was still in the fold, still wanted to be an agent and still hadn't detected that promised increase in my paycheck.

So I called Bill Morris, telling him that I had changed my mind again. After a moment's pause and a confirmation that the job was still available, he said, "Since you're so whimsical, Helen, would you mind sending me a letter stating your intentions, just so I'll have it in writing. If you should happen to change your mind again, I'll have something to show to Barney Balaban." He was kidding, of course, but Barney Balaban was the president of Paramount. Whether Bill meant it or not, my bridges were already burning. I gave Paramount six weeks' notice.

In anticipation of my start date at the Morris Agency on February 28, 1944, elaborate plans were set in motion for my arrival. But first we had to settle the matter of salary. The Morris men asked me how much I wanted. When I asked for $125 a week, Bill Morris and Nat Lefkowitz, who is now the president of the company, looked at me as if I were crazy.

"That's all I'm worth," I said. "I'm sure that when I am worth more, you'll pay me more." I had a great deal of faith in them—always. As far as I was concerned, it was that kind of company and I was never to be disappointed, except for one early bit of confusion. I had a thing going throughout my years with the agency—if I ever had to ask for money, I would quit. I never had to ask for money again.

I was consulted about the kind of office I wanted, the location and décor in the general scheme of offices in Radio City at 1270 Sixth Avenue. (Sixth Avenue had not yet been rechristened Avenue of the Americas!)

The Morris Agency dates back to 1898, its initial strength rooted in the representation of vaudeville actors as diverse as Sir Harry Lauder, Sophie Tucker, Mae West, Ted Lewis and Australian swimming champion Annette Kellerman. By the forties, the agency was deeply involved in big bands and the swing era. It was a world apart from the literary world I was called upon to lure to the company banner. I'm sure that when I started to represent writers of the stature of Dame Edith Sitwell, Sir Osbert Sitwell and Dylan Thomas, not a few of the staff had never heard of these people of letters.

It was also a man's world. The Morris Agency didn't even believe in female secretaries and would have considered them trespassers in an exclusive club. But I insisted upon bringing my secretary from Paramount with me, and thus began a new era at the agency.

Two obligatory business rituals bridged my old and new careers, a farewell luncheon (without tears, I'm afraid) and a welcome-aboard literary cocktail party. The luncheon Paramount provided included the full ration of speeches and embroidered good wishes, and the presentation of a gold watch, suitably inscribed to commemorate fourteen years of interim employment in the picture business. I promptly buried it at the bottom of my purse.

The agency staged my cocktail party at the Hotel Pierre. I submitted my own guest list. One hundred were invited. One hundred and thirty showed up. Bill Morris had his own barometer to gauge the success of the affair and the prospects for the department it inaugurated. If Bennett Cerf showed up, I was in, and Bennett Cerf showed up, so I was judged a hit. Frankly, everyone jumped at the chance to freeload at the Pierre.

I arrived early at the Morris Agency that first Monday morning only to discover that while the offices opened at nine-thirty, no one ever got there until ten. It was quite a day, filled with lots of conversation about my office, but nothing had been attended to. They didn't even have an office for me yet. They were overcrowded. Finally I was routed to the office of a Mr. Alexander, the head of the band department, who was off on a nervous breakdown. There I sat in an enormous corner room on the twentieth floor of what was then still known as the RKO Building.

I was still sitting there, the promise of a permanent office a running agency joke by then, a promise reduced to frustration, weeks later, when the almost forgotten Mr. Alexander resurfaced. The rest had not noticeably soothed his frayed nerves and he proved to have a very bad temper indeed. The sight of a lady squatter in his tower kingdom threatened to send him into a relapse. He stood there shaking, sputtering in rage and incredulity, "What are you doing in *my* office?"

That vision still awaited me as I sat lost that first day, surrounded by the alien mementos of one-night-stand bus tours and toothy chantoosies and prom-night bookings, the suggestion of fading gardenia corsages evoked by pomade-stained leather upholstery and the fallout of cigars savored long before.

I had it made. I was here. I had arrived and was to begin. Lost behind an expanse of oak desk, I pondered the challenge and the responsibility. There were no guidelines, no precedents. I was inaugurating the literary department. It would be and could be whatever I chose to make it, whatever I was able to make of it. I was in a borrowed office and a different world. I remembered the counsel of my friend George Joel, and then, for a brief moment, I reflected upon the past.

I reached into the bottom of my purse, rummaging for the engraved watch which symbolized where I had been, whatever I had achieved, the known and the sure, what I had to show for more than a decade of work.

I had lost it.

PART TWO

I MIGHT have made more money had I joined Harold Matson, where I would have been a partner, and I probably would have made even more money had I gone with Leland Hayward. He sold out to the Music Corporation of America, that giant agency which booked the bands and packaged the tours. Later, in television, they produced shows. Had I been there, I would probably have become a producer many years ago, made a fortune and retired. What I *chose* was complete autonomy, the opportunity to build from the ground floor with maximum challenge. What I got was satisfaction, pride and an enviably happy life.

A literary agent is a very special occupation, and I didn't *just happen* to become a literary agent. I planned it. Since I was well aware that for the rest of my life the only person who would take care of Helen Strauss was Helen Strauss, I began to work toward a future made to my order.

There are no courses to take. There are several requisites that I believe one must have to be a successful literary agent, which, despite what some people might think, is not an easy occupation. To begin with, one must have an appreciation of good writing and have a feeling for writers, who for the most part are lonely, neurotic and usually insecure about their work. Sitting at a desk for days, months and sometimes years writing a book or play without any way of knowing what will happen to the completed manuscript can be very agonizing, especially if the writer is completely dependent on his writing for his livelihood. An agent must have unlimited patience and sympathy for the writer's problems.

When I started my career as an agent, I was given very sound advice by two men, both fine magazine editors. One was Herbert Mayes, who ran a number of Hearst magazines of the era, notably *Good Housekeeping* and *Cosmopolitan.* The other, Alan Marple, was fiction editor for *Collier's.* Each stressed that the only way to succeed was to try to sell only what you believed in and to tell the truth always. It was not only the best advice I could have gotten, but by following it I gained the respect and confidence of editors and publishers. As time went by I was able to call almost any editor and tell him that I had an idea for a book or an article or had a completed manuscript or an outline for a book, and I would get a quick response. Each of them knew that whatever I was offering had gained my interest and confidence first and was not likely to be a complete waste of his time or mine.

A literary agent nurses a client through to the completion of his manuscript, then works to make the best sale in as many outlets as possible—American hard-cover rights, individual foreign rights, magazine serialization, television, radio, Broadway, theatrical and motion picture rights—and to provide coverage for rights as yet unforeseen, yet to be invented (cable, video cassettes, etc.). He or she seeks to retain for the author the largest possible percentage of profits from whatever use is made of his labors. For this, the agent receives a ten-percent commission on the income. Getting that can very easily seem to occupy ninety percent of the agent's life. A good agent is the pilot of a career.

The ten-percent figure has been credited to a number of twentieth-century agents, including the legendary Myron Selznick. In fact, the ten-percent commission existed in nineteenth-century literary England, and probably before. Even Cyrano got something for his touble.

The "flesh peddlers" of an earlier day had collected such outlandish commissions and deductions as to place their clients in bondage. In the first steps toward the licensing of agents—or artists' managers, as they are legally known—an early ceiling of ten percent made its way into the New York Business and Professional Code. While it stipulated that commissions could not be greater than ten percent, the interpretation ended at the top figure.

In fact, if the agent is doing his job well, the payments and guarantees he secures for his client should often more than make up for the deduction.

Since we are dealing with fragile human beings and the intangibles of talent and temperament, there is a lot more to being an agent. It involves panic calls in the night, luring clients off ledges or out of the pokey, rushing them to hospitals, getting tickets to sold-out Broadway shows for their aged mothers, sobering them up, calming them down, telling them where they can't put their hands or their heads. It means sharing their grief and arching their back-bones. It means knowing the intimate details of every marriage, whether you want to or not. I could have been a marriage counselor. Who am I kidding? I was. I had to be.

It means listening to the storm rumbles of the soul when you haven't the time and knowing when to tell an author to stop talking lest his words flee the paper. It means being the closest person in the world to many of your clients, without ever letting them get too close to you. Or at least not letting them know it. If there are many women agents, it's probably because women have greater strength and patience for the assignment.

I never sold a property I hadn't read. Too many agents today cannot make that claim.

When I joined the Morris Agency, they represented a few writers, but only those who wrote for the screen and radio, among them a few who journeyed from those safer harbors to the Broadway stage. There was an exception, one client who not only wrote for films but also had a career in print. He was Elliot Paul, who had written a series of mystery books with a continuing character, Mickey Finn. Still, his most widely read book was *The Last Time I Saw Paris.*

Simultaneous with the bombing of Hiroshima, Mr. Paul arrived in New York and presented himself in my office, suffering from a dietary deficiency common to writers. He needed some money, fast. I thought it would be a good idea for him to go to Paris immediately after the German evacuation, write a magazine article and then turn that material into a book we would call *The Next Time I Saw Paris.*

Women, I had heard, thought him physically attractive and charming. He was, after all, a celebrity of sorts. Years of living in Paris had festooned an aura of glamour about him. Like many authors, the fantasy of his printed words granted him a reputation as a man of action and adventure.

This international swashbuckler bounded into my office in the afternoon. No, what he did was *bounce* in. He was too fat, and bearded men have never held any appeal for me. I tried to get down to business. So did he. He immediately asked me to go out with him, have a drink and find a place where he could play boogie-woogie for me. Elliot, it developed, was famous not only for his writing, but also for his piano playing.

No doubt I should have been flattered. Dull as it might seem, business was business. I declined, and it was the last time I saw Elliot Paul. I never heard his boogie-woogie, and he promptly left the agency. Strike one. Not a very good beginning.

One of my first coups was acquiring Elizabeth Janeway as a client. Babs—as she is known to her friends—while still at Barnard College, when she was just twenty-one, had won first prize in *Story* magazine's annual competition for college students. The story was "Two Words Are a Story." Later, to encourage a future generation of writers, she was to institute her own annual short-story award at Barnard.

In 1943, when I was still associate story editor at Paramount, she wrote her first novel, *The Walsh Girls*, which would earn a great critical reception, though it did not ultimately register as a best seller. I was anxious to read it prior to its publication to see if it had potential for film production. I knew that she did not have an agent and the publisher had not submitted galleys to us. I tracked her down in a way that would be unheard of in Hollywood but was once reasonably typical in the Big City.

She and her husband, Eliot, lived opposite River House on East 52nd Street in a penthouse apartment that had formerly been Clare Boothe Luce's. Here the Janeways hosted a running series of parties attended by the most prominent literary and political figures of the day. I looked the number up in the Manhattan telephone directory and called her.

When I asked to see *The Walsh Girls*, she very properly suggested that I contact her editor at Doubleday, John K. M. McCaffery. I called Mr. McCaffery and invited him for a drink at the Ritz Bar. We hit if off well and he was soon sharing his frustrations with me. He had a wife and several children and was finding that he really couldn't get along on the salary he was making at Doubleday. He gave me Babs' manuscript, which did not finally inspire a movie sale. Subsequently I got McCaffery out of Doubleday, securing him a job as editor at *American* magazine. He soon established himself as a broadcast personality, hosting the "Author Meets the Critics" radio program. That assignment led to other radio spots as a "guest expert" and host, and he eventually moved before the cameras in the early years of television programming.

After I moved to the Morris Agency, Babs decided that it was time she had an agent, so she came with me. I handled *Daisy Kenyon, The Question of Gregory, Leaving Home, The Third Choice* and the nonfiction works which demonstrated the scope of her interests and intelligence even as they diffused the attention and respect a more prolific flow of her finely written fiction might have commanded. But her vision was always too broad to be limited to the single form. She excelled as a literary critic and reporter, and as an essayist whose attention spanned politics, sociology, anthropology and gourmet cuisine. She even found time to produce some exceptional books for children, a specialization that has been accomplishment enough for many another author.

Through my representation of Babs, I also acquired partial representation of her husband, an economist and former *Life* and *Fortune* editor, who was than Henry Luce's political adviser at Time-Life. Eliot Janeway would write an occasional article for other magazines. He telephoned me one morning and said that he wanted to do a profile of a senator for *The Saturday Evening Post*. Would I please call Ben Hibbs, the editor in chief, and get him the assignment?

It was just before lunch when Eliot and I talked. I didn't want to tell him that I didn't know Ben Hibbs, and I was pretty sure that Ben Hibbs had never heard of me. After we hung up I became obsessed by the thought that I would call Philadelphia, not be able to get through to Mr. Hibbs and blow the assignment for Eliot.

My luncheon date that day was with a book editor who loved his martinis. How many he had I don't know, but I had two, the traditional ignition level. It was a gesture of desperation—either the martinis would fortify my courage or make me fall on my face. I became very courageous and self-confident.

I strode back to the office and placed that first call to Mr. Hibbs, who would in time become a very good business friend. He gave me the assignment for Eliot, but without the help of a bit of gin it might never have happened. The experience was a helpful one. I learned that the bigger the executive, the more accessible he is. Years later I would have some trouble with certain modern executives who believed that the opposite was true, that making oneself inaccessible was the sole qualification for accreditation of artistic leadership.

I must have needed a refresher course to reinforce that lesson, because I got just that a short time later when Abe Lastfogel asked me to place a call to David O. Selznick. I don't recall what it was about and it doesn't really matter, but instead of calling Selznick, I telephoned his story editor, Elsa Neuberger. I knew Elsa from school. Whether I was in awe of the great Selznick or simply tripped up by my own innate shyness and seeking refuge in the ear of an old friend, I don't know.

I reported back to Mr. Lastfogel that I had discussed the matter with Elsa. He didn't lose his temper. He was a gentleman and a gentle man, but annoyance and displeasure flashed in his eyes. He took time to explain that I had missed an opportunity to establish a contact of prime importance in the entertainment business. If I had handled the matter by calling Selznick, rather than Elsa, he would have known who I was the next time I had to deal with him, and the next time that difference could be critical to the interests of my client. It was always more advantageous to deal with the "head man."

Lastfogel, the man responsible for directing the great success of the agency, is known in the business as "Honest Abe." From the beginning he allowed me to work autonomously. He backed that up frequently. I worked as an extra company within a company. If anyone in the company objected, Lastfogel would reiterate, "Leave her alone, it's working."

From the beginning, although I know he did not bother with the details of my placing books for publication or selling material to magazines or my strange machinations with putting plays together and my unorthodox thinking about sales to motion pictures, there was a great feeling of mutual respect and I learned many lessons from him.

Early in my career in the agency I went to a meeting of a number of important executives at the Metro-Goldwyn-Mayer offices in New York. I admit I was impressed with the power in the motion picture industry these men had. After the meeting, I was less impressed with their cleverness and more impressed with Abe Lastfogel. The executives talked a great deal, it took hours to get to the point, but in the last few minutes of the meeting it was Lastfogel who very astutely summed up the confused conversations, and an agreement was reached. By his dignified and soft-spoken example, I learned to listen to everybody but say only what is pertinent and constructive.

Large agencies and studios are addicted to departmental meetings. These are attended by department heads and key staff personnel who are forced to state conclusions before they have begun any research and tell what they have done before they have attempted to do it. Perhaps it is just that they figure if they can sustain it long enough for everyone to become thoroughly bored and confused, the questions will stop.

We had some meetings like that and were required by certain producing clients to attend others. I used to sit in on them and say that all of it could have been handled in five minutes over the telephone. I love to talk on the telephone, though I don't like to talk long to any one person or on any one subject. Business gets done on the telephone, while too often meetings drag on to justify (or at least *tie*) the time spent in transit.

During my twenty-three years with the Morris Agency, only once did I think that I was being discriminated against by Abe Lastfogel, the chairman of the board. He was in the habit of calling executive meetings at strange hours, and this particular one was on an Election Day and at six o'clock in the evening. He was late and the other executives, all men, and I were waiting for him in his outer office.

He bustled in, calling out, "Come on in, fellers."

I cheerily piped, "I'm here, too."

He turned, loooking hurt. "When have I not treated you as one of the fellers?" It was the ultimate compliment. The only other female to become a top executive in the company was Ruth Morris White, whose father founded the agency.

At meetings in many places, I've heard the tired phrase "How does it feel to be in a smoke-filled room?" I enjoyed it and I could hold my own. Generally I found the conversation politely guarded in my presence and appreciated the respect, though I knew all the words.

Perhaps the agency, a privately owned corporation, was too paternal, but it was the model of dignity and respectability by which the hustlers were measured and unfavorably compared. I was treated like a lady, but it was also good to be considered one of the "fellers."

Abe and his wife, Frances, were to be much closer to me in future years, but initially our encounters were few, because he was then in charge of USO-Camp Shows, a monumental devotion for which he was awarded the Medal of Freedom for outstanding service. Otherwise, he was on the West Coast, not only directing the careers of the many personalities the agency represented, but always dedicated to developing new talent and extending old careers through new ideas.

When I joined the agency he was in from the coast, and one day he called to ask if I would have lunch with him on a Saturday. He, too, chided me. "Well, if you wanted to come with the agency, why didn't you come directly to me and ask?"

I smiled as the familiar lines echoed. "I don't ask for jobs. Anyway, I'm here now."

For a number of years I had enjoyed the friendship, encouragement and good will of a fabulous Broadway character who was genuinely adored by those he touched. He was Irving Hoffman. For more than twenty years, off and on, he had been a columnist and theater critic for *The Hollywood Reporter.* Sassy and succinct, Hoffman's style was typified by his summation of *Strange Fruit*— "a lemon!" He had a smile like a flashcaster, but also had conical corneas and could scarcely see, squinting at the world through spectacles that looked like paired crystal ashtrays. Yet when wounded Broadway producers argued that his impaired vision disqualified him from commenting upon their wares, he sassed, "But there's nothing wrong with my nose!"

Informed, witty, he was a brilliant caricaturist, having illustrated Walter Winchell's "Beau Broadway" column for the *Morning Telegraph*. He had ridden the dawn-patrol police beat with Winchell and was a cherished friend of an unstratified band of buddies which included Picasso, Wendell Willkie, the Maharani of Baroda, Polly Adler, every entertainment columnist writing in every language anywhere in the world, prostitutes and priests, J. Edgar Hoover and a Runyonesque assortment of Broadway types over whom he towered, quite literally and figuratively.

Using an oversized typewriter with headline-high characters, he dispatched hundreds of letters per week to friends all over the world, a grapevine of tips, gossips, congratulations and well-wishes and boosts for those he decided to sponsor. These cherished epistles were covered with ribbons, official seals, holiday ornaments, sundry stick-ons, illuminated proclamations and lavishly detailed ink-and-pastel artwork. Attached would be clippings of interest from faraway newspapers or correspondence from cronies, which he placed in circulation.

To facilitate the volume of correspondence that had earned him the title of "The Human Mailbox," Hoffman had printed reams of forms he headed "Irving Hoffman's Handy-Dandy Little Giant Nervous Breakdown Avoider and Mail Answering Form." The form contained a hundred phrases which Irving would check or emblazon with gold stars or scarlet dots. Lines like "Too bad," "Excuse my brevity, but . . . I sat on my glasses," "Naturally I want to hear your side of the story, it's undoubtedly the true one," "Please enclose blood specimens with subpoenas in all paternity suits," "Out to lunch" or "Lunch is out."

While he was foremost a personality and a catalyst, increasingly given to world travel and the spreading of gypsy good will, Irving's primary occupation was that of press agent. He had represented Coca-Cola and Bulova, movies and Mafiosi, books and doll buggies, even King Zog of Albania.

At one time or another, Irving provided employment and opportunity to bright young writers who would go on to become some of the sharpest radio and television comedy writers, playwrights and producers. Ernest Lehman and Nat Hiken were among his protégés. Hoffman was credited with saving Coney Island, making stars and hits. He was a pushover for talent and one of its most zealous pushers. One of the wonders of the man, the time and the place was just how he managed to survive.

Despite the wonderful things Irving did for people, he never asked for anything in return. For years while I was at Paramount, he had sent me to producers, recommended me in his galloping chain letters. He also dispatched books and precocious authors to me. I got more job offers I didn't want through Irving and met more good writers I was in little position to nurture and help.

It was through Irving that I had been given the opportunity to work for Samuel Goldwyn. I was called to be interviewed for the position as Goldwyn's New York story editor by Jim Mulvey, Goldwyn's general manager. Mr. Goldwyn terrified me, but I was flattered to have been asked. I became aware that there were a number of men being considered for the same post, and since I knew several of them, I quickly discovered that the money quoted to them for the job was five hundred dollars a week. But the salary offered to me was only two hundred and fifty!

I was already beginning to tire of the movie business and had set my sights on a career as an agent, but I was confident enough to feel that if I really wanted the assignment, I would get that five hundred dollars. The decision was not mine, and it turned out to be no one else's either. We were interviewed on the eve of the Japanese attack on Pearl Harbor. Priorities were quickly reordered, while Hollywood, too, geared for war—realigning its forces in anticipation of the mustering of many of its men into khaki and scrapping current film projects in favor of those serving the war effort and morale.

I had met Irving Hoffman through Billy Friedberg, one of his writing apprentices and my lifelong friend. I had grown up with Billy, played marbles with him as a kid. Our fathers had been good friends. Billy's mother was Lorenz Hart's cousin. That had been Billy's open sesame into show business. As William Friedberg, Billy would later work with Nat Hiken on Hiken's *Sergeant Bilko* television series and would collaborate with that brightest of comedy writing talents from the early years of television, Neil Simon, on many scripts.

As an old friend, Billy was also a Helen Strauss booster, but at a price. He kidded me unmercifully. He delighted in spreading the story all over New York that I would rush home from work, have dinner, put on my flannel nightgown and read manuscripts. It got to be a standing joke. If we were out, I'd start insisting that I had to get home, and Billy would be off: "Oh, what she really does is, she goes home, sits in bed in her flannel nightgown and stays up all night reading. Men she's really not into, only *man*uscripts."

When I told Billy that I was going to become an agent, he arranged for me to meet Bob Sylvester of the *New York Daily News*. Bob was then represented by a very well-known, very fancy agent named George Bye, who hadn't produced much for him. Bye was highly successful, with his name in brass letters and an impressive client list that included most of the big political figures of the era.

When Billy introduced me to Bob, Bob's only comment was: "Well, you can't be any worse that George Bye." While I understood Bob's discouragement, I also knew Bye had great stature as an agent. When I started in the business, I could only hope to become as successful as he.

Bob's first short story provided me with my very first sale. It was a short-short story titled "City Dog," about a little pooch he had. I sold it to *Collier's* for five hundred dollars, the going rate for short-shorts. Bob was off in the war, somewhere in the Pacific with Gene Tunney, and I spent all of the fifty-dollar commission on cables trying to reach him.

Ultimately, Bob was so pleased that he sent me a pair of two-hundred-dollar gift certificates, one for my mother and one for me, to buy hats at John Fredericks. That didn't leave enough for taxes.

Bob wrote an unsuccessful play, *Dream Street*, and at my urging he then wrote it as a novel. My copy of that novel is inscribed "You really wrote this, I didn't." The title was to prevail as the banner for Bob's continuing column in the *Daily News*.

He was one of my most disciplined writers, regularly grinding out column deadlines, features, special articles, short stories and books. Some time later one of his books brought me into a new clash with the Goldwyns.

For some reason Goldwyn decided that he had to have one of Bob's books for film development. I was convinced that it would not adapt well and that in the long run Bob would be penalized for Mr. Goldwyn's poor judgment if we took the chance and it failed. It would be wiser to wait out a better entry. I had not tried to sell the book. They were trying to buy it.

It was Frances, not Sam, Goldwyn who took the offensive. It may well be that Frances would never have attained the power she had in the operation of that studio had she not married the boss, but given that special opportunity, she was a formidable and effective force behind its successes. Bright, strong-willed, she was at the studio every day, always accompanying Sam on business trips, patching up misunderstandings, charming associates.

She was highly annoyed when she called about the Sylvester book. "What is this?" she demanded. "I don't understand. Are you pulling some sort of coquettish Leland Hayward tactic?"

I explained, quite sincerely, "I simply don't think it can make a good movie."

"I just don't understand," she repeated, and hung up.

Bob frequented a bar not far from the *Daily News*, on Third Avenue, Tim Costello's. It was a newspaperman's bar, a hangout for staff members from *The New Yorker*. There were James Thurber drawings along the walls and many a famous by-liner at the tables. Among the latter were a number of bright young men who had gained note as wartime contributors to *Yank, The Army Weekly* and *Stars and Stripes*.

It was at Tim Costello's that Bob first introduced me to Dave Golding, then the editor of *Stars and Stripes*. David was and is a rabid Anglophile and in recent years has been fortunate enough to work in London. But in that final year of the Second World War, David, like many of the men from *Stars and Stripes* and *Yank* whom I would soon be meeting, was anticipating a return to civilian life and a career as a professional writer.

I am afraid that I responded to David's writing dreams with a candor he requested but had not wished. I told him I thought it would be an unwise course for him to pursue. I'm not sure whether he ever forgave me for that, but he enthusiastically determined to introduce me to all the *Stars and Stripes* and *Yank* writers he could. Whenever I see Dave, I remind him that he is the one who really got me going in the business, and he always beams.

So began a regular series of weekday and Sunday meetings, the beginnings of a number of lifelong friendships and the launching or redirection of several prominent careers.

I met most of these young men when they were in town on leaves. Though they were readying for their return to civilian life, they hadn't disbanded yet. Most, I'm sure, felt that they had the great war novel gestating within them. More than a few were to discover that their true strength lay in continued reporting and in specialized nonfiction efforts.

That was true of Herbert Mitgang, who came to me from *Yank*, burning to make his name as a novelist. Eventually he gravitated to *The New York Times*, where his talent for reportage and analysis found its best forum. Later he applied those skills to historical subjects with a reconstructive eyewitness technique and wrote such nonfiction works as *Lincoln As They Saw Him* and *The Man Who Rode the Tiger*, a colorful biography of Judge Samuel Seabury.

Perhaps many of today's struggling novelists might take encouragement from the determination and staying power of Ralph G. Martin, another *Yank* postgrad, in whom the seeds of success had one of their longest and leanest incubation periods. Ralph never made a substantial living or tasted success until the publication in 1969 of *Jennie*, his two-volume life of Lady Randolph Churchill, nearly twenty-five years after our first meeting, years during which he was sustained through magazine assignments and occasional "quiet" books.

Saul Levitt, who later wrote the screenplay of *The Andersonville Trial*, was another early recruit. I quickly secured a contract for him to do his first book for Little, Brown.

Joe McCarthy, no relation to the infamous senator from Wisconsin, had been the chief editor for all seventeen editions of *Yank* and was the first GI to enter Athens during the war. He is properly grouped with these veterans of battlefront journalism, though in fact I did not meet him until after he had returned from the war and become the editor of *Cosmopolitan* magazine. He, in turn, brought me to two of the most famous *Yank* alumni, Marion Hargrove and the Pulitzer Prize-winner Bill Mauldin.

I met Joe in the course of my dealings as an agent. I had sold him several stories on behalf of clients. In time I became his agent, and when he tired of being an editor I sold him to *Life* magazine on a yearly basis. Then I started to secure some book contracts for him. He eventually wrote the first book on the Kennedy clan, *The Remarkable Kennedys,* and I sold the magazine rights for that to *Look,* thus beginning the almost constant attention that magazine focused upon the family until the publication folded.

I think the occasion which brought Joe and me closer together and allowed us to become the very good friends we have been for these many years was when I shared with him an extraordinary manuscript that arrived at my desk after its author had already tried without success to interest some half-dozen publishers in it. It proved to be one of the few great books to come out of the war. It is still being discovered today, and history may yet prove it to be the very best to have emerged from World War II.

The highly original novel was *The Gallery,* by John Horne Burns, who was not one of the wartime journalists, but a former military intelligence officer, Harvard graduate, musician and teacher, an Irish Catholic from a large and highly independent family ruled by a shanty Irish father and a lace-curtain Irish mother.

A fine pianist, he had returned to teach music at the Loomis boys' preparatory school. We collected at least ten rejections before I finally sold the book to Harper. Its initial reception was slow, but a delayed critical response eventually spawned a Burns cult. It was never a popular success.

Joe McCarthy sent the book to his friend Herbert Lyons, another *Yank* alumnus, who was by then in charge of the book section of *The New York Times.* I don't remember who did that review in the *Times,* but it was the first superlative one and drew others to give the book the attention it merited. Perhaps the most rhapsodic was the belated notice Edmund Wilson gave the book almost six months later in *The New Yorker.* In his essays Gore Vidal has continued to champion Burns as his personal favorite among authors who appeared after the war. Burns then wrote *Lu-*

cifer with a Book and *A Cry of Children,* but never matched *The Gallery* again.

On the dust jacket of *The Gallery* John described his impressions upon landing in Italy in 1944, the time and place in which were crystallized the powerful and often surreal images of his first novel: "My laughter shifted to the other side of my face and finally died away altogether. For the first time in my life I became touched, concerned, moved . . . I experienced an annihilation of myself and a rebirth in that tragic but four-dimensional country."

Nine years later, passing through time and torment toward that shore again, John Burns surrendered totally to it. On August 11, 1953, his body was mysteriously washed up on the beach at Leghorn, Italy. The facts were vague, and those who had loved him were not swift to seek any evidence beyond the sad fact that he was gone.

Grateful for the attention he had given John Horne Burns' book, I called Herbert Lyons to express my appreciation—and began a pleasant, continuing friendship. He had been in charge of the book section under Lester Markel at the *Times,* but got caught in one of the political shuffles at the paper and found himself on the street. He seized the opportunity to write a rather devastating novel titled *The Rest They Need* and he asked me to represent it for him.

Getting the book into print proved to be a herculean effort, quite out of proportion to the book's eventual impact. Rumors circulated that the book was a gauzily fictionalized version of goings-on in Markel's department. The very same tongue-clackers hinted that Markel was making every effort wherever he could to keep this smudged-finger preview of a form soon to be claimed by Jacqueline Susann from ever being published. How true the rumors were, I do not know. The book did get published and died in its sleep. That's too bad because it was a very interesting book.

Bill Mauldin and Marion Hargrove returned from the war famous and already very successfully published, but both were unhappy with their agency representation and in the market for a new office. In the months since I had inaugurated the Morris literary department, I was also establishing a reputation and beginning to have successful but dissatisfied authors referred to me by editors, publishers and other authors whose respect I had earned. It was Joe McCarthy who sent two of the most famous wartime writers to me. A third, George Baker, creator of "Sad Sack," was already handled by the Morris office in Hollywood for film and radio rights.

Druing his training days at Fort Bragg, Marion Hargrove had written a series of sketches on Army life for his hometown Charlotte (N.C.) *News* and these had been welded into book form as *See Here, Private Hargrove,* the nonfiction best seller (some three million copies sold) of 1942. By the time Marion arrived at my office he had already seen himself portrayed by the late Robert Walker in the hit 1944 film version of the book, been elevated to the rank of sergeant and further distinguished himself as *Yank's* China correspondent. Such early celebrity might easily have turned a twenty-five-year-old writer into a rather difficult young man. In Marion's case, it did.

I sold *The Girl He Left Behind* and *Something's Got to Give* for him and kept him in free-lance magazine assignments, but his ample talent was never sufficiently disciplined. Like many authors, he found it too easy to talk about writing, to think about and discuss his ideas rather than sit down and work them out at the writing desk. I sold one of his books to the movies for over $200,000, which was a very good price at the time, contingent upon its becoming a book club selection. The Literary Guild was interested, but requested a minor deletion from the text. On what seemed like principle at the time, Marion balked, refusing to discuss the matter, and the club selection and the movie option collapsed.

He went to Hollywood, and in the beginning he sometimes produced as many headaches as script pages. *Forty Pounds of Trouble* has been outlived now and a mellower Marion won a Writers Guild award for his screen adaptation of *The Music Man,* the prickles of precocity long worn away.

I am the godmother of one of his children and should probably admit that I have not done the best job with that assignment.

What impressed me about Bill Mauldin was that the economy and realistic humor of his cartoon commentary was echoed in his easy, low-keyed prose. I worked happily with Bill from the day he walked into my office until the day I exited. I presume that I handled *A Sort of a Saga,* the first of an autobiographical series which continued through the recent *The Brass Ring,* and I know that there were once files of contracts tracing the dealings. But it was easy and it was pleasant and results in barely a squeak of copy now.

I represented another of the World War II writers, probably the most perversely controversial and erratic. I suspect that I never regretted that he was the one who got away. Norman Mailer, while still in the Army and stationed at a camp down South, sent in some material. I was impressed by its forcefulness and set out to sell it. In the meantime Norman needed money, so the agency advanced him cash on the basis of my faith in his future and the submissions we had and could sell.

After I sold the first story I tactfully asked Norman if we should deduct his debt, which we had carried for some time. He screamed at me. He raged like a wounded bobcat. The future author of *The Naked and the Dead* parted company with the Morris Agency— en route to new and better grudges that would later be belabored in print. At that, I suppose, it was still our loss.

Another early client, Nancy Shores, who wrote for the slicks, also played a key role in my early acquisition of clients, and directly or indirectly led me to several of the most prestigious clients and revered friendships of my career. First she sent me Edward Harris Heth, who had been handled by Brandt and Brandt. I sold many of his short stories to magazines and then began to get book contracts for him. His most famous novel was *Any Number Can Play,* which was made into a movie starring Clark Gable.

I learned something else from that book. I was still new in the field, willing to bend to voices of experience even when my instincts played a contrary tune. When I read the manuscript I was convinced that it needed some work. Everyone looked at me as if I were a little mad. Because I still hadn't earned all of my stripes in the business, I relented and sent it to Edward Aswell, who was then editor in chief of Harper and the man who had become Thomas Wolfe's editor after Maxwell Perkins. He was accepted as one of the deans of editors. Aswell read it, then called me to say, "This is a perfect manuscript. We'll send it off to the printer's." And on he went to more pressing considerations.

How could I quarrel with Ed Aswell? And yet I am certain that if the manuscript had been rewritten, the book would have been not the moderate success it was, critically and financially, but a big best seller.

Heth told his friend Frank MacGregor about me, and MacGregor called to say that he would like to meet me. MacGregor was a tall, distinguished, very handsome man who had been graduated from Harvard and started as a book salesman for Houghton Mifflin, moving to Harper in the textbook department and working his way up to chairman of the board of directors.

At our first meeting he had taken me to the Ritz Bar. I remember that I kept calling him *Mr.* MacGregor, as I have always rejected the easy familiarity that is prevalent in so much of the business world. If my dealings were to be based upon mutual respect, I reasoned, they should begin with respectful—not awed—form. I think it was John Crosby who used to write complaining about people who didn't know him well enough to call him "Mr. Crosby."

Midway in our conversation that day Frank MacGregor interrupted me, saying, "I think it is safe to say that you and I are going to be friends. You may as well begin to call me Mac." He became, in fact, one of my dearest friends.

But I still scarcely knew him when he sent me Glenway Wescott. Glenway was a writers' writer, esteemed by his colleagues almost from the publication of his first book of poems, *The Bitterns*, in 1920, when he was just nineteen. A writer of uncompromising taste, restraint and discipline, his fame had grown from the publication of *The Grandmothers* in 1927. A sprawling three-generation Wisconsin family chronicle spanning ninety-five years without slipping into nostalgic or sentimental traps, the novel had won the Harper Prize and a place among the classics of American literature. He was a darling of highbrow journals and served as vice-president of the National Institute of Arts and Letters. I was then reading his fourth novel, *Apartment in Athens*.

I knew that *McCall's* was looking for a book that had something to do with the war, and felt that Glenway's novel, a psychological study of the occupation and its stresses upon a once well-to-do Greek family and a guilt-obsessed Nazi, might satisfy their need, particularly since it could be considered a mother's story as well. Glenway was the recipient of more living eulogies than hard royalties, and when I sold *McCall's* the serialization rights for the book, it was for more money than he had seen throughout his career. Unfortunately, he was never a prolific writer, and in the years which followed he found that he could earn more with greater ease through such tangential activities as lecturing to devotees of literature.

But Glenway was so pleased with what I had done for him that he arranged for me to meet his friend Somerset Maugham, with the idea that I could improve Mr. Maugham's financial status as well, since Maugham's agent at the time was generally suspected of rather careless bookkeeping on one hand and rather too zealous deductions for expenses on the other.

Maugham listened to Glenway's praise for my efforts and eyed me intensely. Then, in that halting stutter of his, he said to me, bemusedly, "I'm sure that you are all of the things that Glenway says you are. But I think I shall stay with my present agent, because I have so much fun checking out his statements." And I never saw Mr. Maugham again.

I had a good friend, Muriel Fuller, who held an editorial job at *Redbook* magazine. An unknown writer had submitted some work to the magazine and his material found its way to Muriel's desk. World War II was on and he was working at the Ford plant in River Rouge, Michigan, desperately trying to make a living for his family without sacrificing his ambition to become a writer.

He had been born in Georgia, was black, but despite the humiliating race prejudice he encountered from his childhood on, by sheer determination he had managed to get a very good education, first at Haines Institute and Paine College in his native city of Augusta. When he was twenty-one he received a Master of Arts degree from Fisk University in Nashville, Tennessee, and proceeded to the University of Chicago.

Frank Yerby's only published material when he approached *Redbook* was some poetry which had appeared in "little" magazines. The work he submitted to *Redbook* was unsuitable for the magazine, but one story, "Health Card," so impressed Muriel—a lady who was both kind-hearted and avidly interested in new writing talent—that she sent the story to *Harper's*. Its publication in *Harper's* provided the boost and reassurance Frank needed, as it won a special award in the O. Henry collection for 1944.

It was in February of that year that I became a literary agent. I needed clients. Frank needed an agent. He had just moved his family to Long Island and was working twelve hours a day in a war plant. Muriel arranged an appointment for me to meet him. He came to my office about eight o'clock one night after work, tired and sorely in need of encouragement in his writing. He left me the manuscript of a novel. While not publishable, it presented a vivid picture of the anguish and despair of his race. It had flashes of great storytelling, but had been so carelessly put together that no amount of revision would cure its inadequacies.

Still, I did offer it to many publishers, saying that here was a new writer who would one day write a best seller. All he needed was a contract and a little money to give him the boost to go on with his writing and improve.

The seventeenth publisher to see Frank's novel was my old friend George Joel, who ran Dial Press. He had the same instinct about Frank's writing and asked to meet him. Frank's only day off from the war plant was Sunday, and George, who loved to entertain at his home, suggested that I bring Frank and his wife to a cocktail party he was giving the following Sunday.

It was a large gathering and the Yerbys were not enjoying themselves. Frank and I sat in a corner and he told me about a book he wanted to do. It sounded exciting. I pulled George over to listen, and he immediately advised Frank to start writing it.

The following morning, I telephoned George and asked whether he would gamble the huge sum of $250 for Frank to produce fifty pages. If the first part was promising, he would give Frank a contract and advance against royalties. He agreed. The novel became *The Foxes of Harrow*. It became a best seller all over the world. The movie rights were sold to Fox for what was then an enormous price, $150,000, and Frank became a rich man. He remained a prodigious worker, writing a best seller a year, and I represented twenty-three of his books.

Following is an excerpt from a letter from Frank to me:

It's a pleasure, Dear. Only my memory is lousy, too. Why don't you write about our first conference at George Joel's, you walking around, *as usual*, with your shoes off while we (all three of us) decided to kill the prize-fighter steel mill novel and do "Foxes"?

Or you can quote me to the effect that you paid my intelligence (such as it is!) the supreme tribute of being the *meanest, roughest, hardest hitting* critic I ever encountered, mentioning that I still haven't dared publish two novels you bent my ears back over, or even write one whose plot outline you thought stunk. (It did, but since I'm egoist enough to think I could write a good novel on the basis of the multiplication tables, that hardly matters!)

Beyond that, what can I remind you of? That you were a good friend, an honest agent and a grand person? That you're living proof that cigarettes don't cause cancer nor Scotch corrode the liver? That for all the times I've wanted to hit you over the head with the nearest blunt instrument, I love you dearly? That the only thing I ever held against you was your getting tired and quitting the Racket (the Agency)? But that was your right.

Frank

The day Frank delivered the final manuscript of *Foxes*, he came directly from the aircraft factory, still in his working clothes. I recall at the time looking at him and saying, "You're going to make a lot of money from this book." He looked at me quite skeptically, but perhaps a year later, when he had made almost a quarter of a million dollars, I reminded him that I'd told him so.

"I knew it would," he answered confidently in retrospect. We both had to smile. We were both learning.

The book he chose to dedicate to me was *Floodtide*. I'd learned my lesson with Heth's *Any Number Can Play*, so when I insisted upon the rewrite I knew it needed even though the publisher was ready to give the go-ahead to the original version, Frank was furious. But I screamed, "Over my dead body!" or something similarly eloquent. He stalked off and wouldn't speak to me for about a month. He finally agreed to rewrite it—and the dedication to me was his way of letting me know that I had been right. The Yerbys also bestowed another godmother role on me.

Frank has not enjoyed the respect of black critics, largely because he staked out his claim on the costume drama he handled so successfully and was not writing the tracts others might have felt he should have been producing. His own attitude about prejudice is quite fatalistic, and his family, in addition to having almost uniformly attained heights in scholarship, government and business, is uncommonly cosmopolitan and highly individualistic.

He did suffer a great deal of abuse when he first moved into a white neighborhood on Long Island. His children's toys were broken. "Nigger!" was scrawled across a fence. The Welcome Wagon didn't call. But the moment *The Foxes of Harrow* came out, he was embraced as the local celebrity. The irony wasn't lost. For some years he chose to live in Spain.

He already was the most successful black author and had published nearly a dozen best sellers when a national news magazine belatedly acknowledged that he was black. Actually, they christened him the Modern Dumas, and book-review readers rushed to their encyclopedias to figure it out, making two discoveries in the process. People don't change as much as the thinking of those around them does.

I was Gerold Frank's agent for a number of years. He was and is both a fine investigative reporter and a collaborator on personality biographies—a master of that very special art, which is almost ninety percent ego-salving patience. The last book I represented for Gerry was *The Boston Strangler*. The autographed copy of the book he gave me was inscribed "For Helen—Agent, psychiatrist-in-residence and dear friend—Affectionately . . ."

The inscription pleased me and seemed a neat statement of the unstated credo by which I tried to function as an agent in the best interests of my clients.

To describe the function, one might best analyze that particular statement. I had negotiated a very good contract for the publication rights. I had sold not only the American publishing rights but had made separate contracts for many foreign book publication rights to increase Gerold's guarantee.

From the time he began his research for the book, we obtained legal releases from all persons and officials who would be included in the coverage. Without having secured those in advance, a movie sale would have been impossible. Once a movie company gets involved, every incidental character in the story gets a glaze of dollar signs on his eyes, and no studio would have the money or lawyers' time to play games with all of them. Without the releases, they wouldn't risk the nuisance invasion-of-privacy suits.

So we were able to sell the rights to Twentieth Century–Fox for just under a quarter of a million dollars. I can't give an exact figure because of the complicated nature of the contract. The material was there, ready for reduction into a script and filming. Being a well-promoted smash only sweetened the prospects.

As for that "psychiatrist-in-residence," I refer to another Gerold Frank book, *The Deed*. Gerry has given me permission to quote a letter he wrote me, which described my part in its delivery.

Dear Helen:

The salient fact about THE DEED is that I would not have written it without your encouragement. As I remember it and your important role: in 1961, casting about for my next book (I had written several with Hollywood backgrounds and wanted to get away from them), I mentioned something of the story of Eliahu Hakim and Eliahu Bet-Zouri to you: the two Jewish boys in Palestine who, in 1944, as members of the secret Stern Group, stole into Cairo in disguise and assassinated Lord Moyne, the British Minister Resident in the Middle East, as part of their struggle for independence. I covered their trial for *The Nation* and other publications. I was fascinated and moved by their story, by the moral dilemma it posed, by the struggle between means and end: these two boys, belonging to a people with such a tragic history as victims of violence, turning to violence. They—their lives—how they went to their deaths, all made an extraordinary story.

Now, seventeen years later, I wanted to write it. You were enthusiastic. Write an outline for a publisher, you said. I sat down, and couldn't write it. I tried an outline, a summary, a treatment—impossible. Not for a publisher or editor. Before the enormity of the emotion it caused to well up in me, I was helpless. Even thinking of it made me act like an adolescent. The skin of my forehead prickled, when I tried to talk about it I lost my voice, when I tried to sum up what I wanted to say, I struggled for words, I felt I'd dissolve shamefully and idiotically into tears. A real hangup, although the word wasn't known in 1961. Then I found a way. I wouldn't write an outline or synopsis: I'd simply confide the story to you, and so I did. I wrote you a letter, which went on for nearly 3,000 words. Whatever magic emanated from you, whatever empathy and assurance you were able to establish (and I suppose that's the essence of a true literary agent, judge, confidant and catalyzer), I felt you'd understand, get hold of it, and do justice to it, and so I was able to talk to you about it. The dam broke and I was able to get it down on paper for you with an eloquence I never thought I could reach. My memory is that you forwarded it, as it was, to Joe Barnes at Simon & Schuster and within days their advance was in my pocket and I was on a plane to Jerusalem picking up my research where I'd left off— unknowingly—seventeen years before.

The book was finished some two years later. When I had to write a preface, explaining how I felt about the book and why I wrote it, the best I could do was turn to my letter to you. Much of that became A Note to the Reader in THE DEED.

Again, I don't know how to describe precisely what special attribute of a literary agent this points to, but whatever it is, I'm eternally grateful to you.

As ever,

Gerold Frank

Of course, if Simon and Schuster and Joe Barnes had not had the confidence in Gerold Frank and in me, I could never have obtained the advance and the contract on the strength of Gerry's letter alone. But that relates to the advice given me by Alan Marple and Herbert Mayes—followed with conviction until I could earn the trust to merit confidence in my professional judgment as an agent. It explains, too, why I could not handle anyone I did not like and respect professionally. I could deal only with someone who could, in fact, become—and accept me as—a loyal friend.

When Margaret Landon completed her manuscript for *Anna and the King of Siam*, she sent it to her friend Muriel Fuller, who had helped place it for publication with John Day & Company. It was already in galleys and set for a summer release the year I became an agent. The idea for the book had germinated in 1930. Mrs. Landon, then on a tour of missionary service with her husband, Kenneth, in the country which would later be rechristened Thailand, had read *The English Governess at the Siamese Court*, Anna Leonowens' story of her five years as governess to the children of King Mongkut in the nineteenth century, and become intrigued by it.

Muriel, who had been Margaret's college roommate and friend, was the first to suggest that her friend direct her research toward rewriting the story so that it would have more general appeal. After seven more years of intensive documentation, Mrs. Landon had completed the manuscript on the afternoon of July 23, 1943, just twelve hours before the birth of her fourth child, Kenneth, Jr., two labors of love realized.

The book was contracted as a selection of the Literary Guild, guaranteeing a sale of not less than three hundred thousand copies. Though it had been submitted to the major studios for a movie sale prior to its publication, and despite the fact that it became a best seller, there had been no interest forthcoming from Hollywood. Muriel suggested to Margaret that perhaps I might be able to get it produced as a play.

I offered it to Lawrence Langner, who was head of the Theatre Guild, the large play production company which then enjoyed a huge subscription audience not only in New York but in most of the major cities in the eastern part of the country. The Guild became interested in the dramatic rights, agreeing that it would make a good play. Since Mrs. Landon was not a dramatist and had no intention of attempting to become one, Langner cast about for several months trying to find a suitable adapter.

At the same time, Mary Martin had become interested in the project and was eager to play Anna. Cheryl Crawford, one-time casting director for the Theatre Guild and a founding member of the Group Theatre and the Actors Studio before becoming a producer, was equally anxious to produce it with Mary.

To this point there were no contracts and no money had changed hands. Neither producer had found a dramatist. The book was selling well. It would eventually sell three quarters of a million copies in English and be translated into editions in Swedish, Danish, Norwegian, Finnish, Spanish, Portuguese, Italian, French, German, Czechoslovakian, Hungarian and Dutch. But at that moment, with four children, the first of whom was fast approaching college age, Mrs. Landon was anxious to provide for their maximum future security.

While waiting for something to materialize for Broadway, I cautioned her that even if the show was produced, after the predictable delay to secure the best possible dramatic adaptation, there was no guarantee that it would be successful, hence profitable. I suggested that I should now pursue the sale of motion picture rights. "You can always have a play later," I reassured her.

While the book was unusual and inspirational, it was not material that studios were wildly enthusiastic about that season. Its exotic locale required lavish and expensive treatment. Twentieth Century-Fox was the only company interested. And so I made my first movie sale my first year in the business. The price was $67,500, a considerable amount in those days, if not spectacular. John Cromwell directed Rex Harrison, Irene Dunne and Linda Darnell in the film.

When the studio a few years ago produced a television series based on the film, I received a call from Kenneth Landon, asking if his wife would receive compensation for this electronic revival. Surprisingly, I discovered that my original contract had anticipated the possibility. It was not the highly sophisticated sort of contract that would evolve later, involving retention of subsidiary and unforeseen rights, or percentages and weekly fees, but it did provide a flat-fee payment for the use of the source. It was still unusual, since studios customarily locked up all subsequent rights then.

After the film sale was completed, I reminded Mrs. Landon once more, "You can still have a play some day." And she did. But that would come six years later, the more spectacular for the wait.

Another film sale taught me a lesson that I would apply in my dealings with clients throughout the balance of my career as an agent. While I was still with Paramount, I had befriended a young writer, and when I became convinced that her agent was not doing an adequate job for her, I put her together with one who proved to be much better.

When I became an agent, she called to congratulate me and restate her gratitude. "Now," she added, "since you put me with this agent, can you tell me what I should do to leave her and come with you? What would you suggest?"

"Well," I responded. "You're happy there, so I think you should stay. I'm not in the bandit business."

"Okay, then I have a friend who is writing. Her name is Ramona Stewart. May I ask her to submit her manuscript to you? She's good."

The manuscript arrived. I read it over one weekend and became highly enthusiastic. By the time I reached the office on Monday morning, I was bubbling with confidence and crazy with the elation of discovery. I dashed off a telegram to Ramona: "*Confident* I can sell your manuscript as a serial, a book and a movie!"

Shortly after lunch my stomach cramped and my grin crashed toward my chin. How could I do a thing like that? I'll *try*, sure. I'll *hope*, without question, but what arrogance, what naïveté had inspired me to be *confident* of wrapping up not one, not two, but *three* key rights— a heavenly trinity—for a new writer, then trumpeting it into print? They used to stitch it up in samplers: "A promise made is a debt unpaid." I rushed to the telephone to balance my boasts.

The novel, *Desert Town*, appeared first as a serial in *Collier's*. I then sold it to Morrow for publication in hard cover. Hal Wallis made the film for Paramount, benevolently retitled *Desert Fury* and starring Burt Lancaster and Lizabeth Scott. I had extricated my foot from my mouth.

I had also learned a lesson in caution. Seldom again would I confide my best hope to anyone. I'd go for the very best, even the most innovative deal possible, while preparing the client for the more realistic and conservative possibility. It made for pleasantly surprised and satisfied writers.

A friend of mine told me years ago that I had to get over being a twenty-five-dollar-a-week stenographer at heart, and it was true. Maybe that is why I think I have never been discriminated against.

Everything good that happens to me is always a great surprise and I find myself facing the rest with an isn't-it-marvelous attitude. I'm not naïve. By most standards, I maintain a healthy pessimism, but I've had a lot of very pleasant surprises and have known a strong, good faith to be rewarded.

I had been with the Morris Agency for only ten months when Christmas 1944 came around. I received a call to report to the treasurer's office. Nat Lefkowitz, who was then treasurer, handed me a check for six weeks' salary.

"What's this for?"

"Oh, it's a Christmas bonus, but you'll probably get more next year."

All I could do was stand there and cry. Don't think that didn't become one of the bigger laughs around the office. But I had been conditioned to a far different order during those years with Paramount, where the executives gobbled up enormous bonuses and tossed the rank and file a grudging little fifty dollars or seventy-five dollars and only when you had been there at least a year. So I was frankly shocked by the good faith and generosity at Morris.

The next month, January 1945, I celebrated my first year there, and without a word the company gave me a raise of fifty dollars per week. There would be many more as my department grew in billings and importance. When business was good I'd get enormous bonuses, and the literary department went well from its inception. After I had been with the agency a few years, Abe Lastfogel allowed me to buy some stock. I was so naïve I didn't even know that the company was privately owned, that this was very unusual, or that I was one of the first employees to be offered the option. I didn't know what it was worth until I left the company and had to sell it back to them.

Living with my parents continued to produce as many advantages as it did problems. In a business that can allow one to become tough and unstable, they were to be a stabilizing influence in my life. I suppose in many ways it was as if I were still their little girl, but after days of dealing aggressively on behalf of clients and sharing many of the disasters in their personal lives, days during which it was essential to keep a stiff guard up against challenges to the rights of those clients and my own position of strength, it could be a healthy retreat at the end of a day.

I learned to live with it and I learned to use it to my advantage. It came in very handy at the many parties I had to go to. At some appropriate moment I'd conspicuously peer at my watch, asking at the same time, "Oh! What time is it? I *must* get home."

Invariably, someone would challenge, "Why? What difference does it make? If you got home at three in the morning, would your family throw you out?"

"No."

"Well, what are you making this big fuss about, then?"

If they pressed too hard or too long, I'd willingly admit the truth. "Frankly, I've had enough of this party." But having to get home was always a more acceptable excuse than merely *wanting* to get home. I never visited people for the weekend, didn't believe in getting too close to publishers, editors or authors. Later I would amend that rule, but for years I'd excuse myself by explaining, "So sorry, but my family has made plans." When I wanted to get away for a weekend or stay out till three, of course I did.

My father's counsel to put away some "go-to-hell" money had continued throughout the years until it became instinct. One night I was absent from the family circle and my mother sought me out in my room.

"What are you doing in here?" she asked as she entered the room and found me huddled over my desk.

"I'm counting my money," I answered.

"Nonsense! You don't have any money," she countered with typical finality.

"Oh yes. Yes indeed. Let me see, I have twenty-one thousand dollars."

"Nonsense! Where would you get twenty-one thousand dollars?" asked the woman who lived by the credo that money was for spending.

I explained, "I've been putting it in the bank for years."

A short time later, my father, by then very successful again, partnered with an engineer for Germany's Krupp Works in an electrical hardware manufacturing company, and anticipating the retirement which would shorten his life, bought my mother a mink coat. As she was not infrequently contrary, we were not completely surprised when she refused to wear it unless I, too, bought one to wear with her.

I went to the bank and drew enough money out. Wandering back along the street, I bumped into Nat Lefkowitz.

"Helen," he said, "why in the world are you crying?"

Snuffling, I finally managed to respond, "I just took money out of the bank . . . to buy . . . a mink coat!"

"Aren't you lucky that you have enough money in the bank to buy a mink coat?" he consoled.

"It's dreadful!" I snapped. "No girl should have to buy her own mink coat!"

The joke was double-gaited. In fact, I had never been able to accept gifts from gentlemen friends and had offended a few by having covered my own needs for jewelry, furs and the sort of baubles men might have liked to charge to their accounts.

My parents loved to travel and we went together most of the time. One of our earliest odd trios was occasioned by a vacation we took in Bermuda. As might be anticipated, the division of time—theirs, ours and mine—was never easy and often not fair. I happened to meet during that sojourn James A. Mollison, the World War I British flying ace who had made a headline disappearance during that conflict. He was then basking in the limelight after a spectacular solo transcontinental flight between Portmarnock, Ireland, and New Brunswick. A guest at the same hotel, he took a fancy to me.

We were sitting in the bar one night, and Jimmy was not atypically tipsy when my mother and father approached our table. Unsteadily, Jimmy rose to ask if they would join us for a drink.

My mother never had to be asked for her opinions. She could not often be restrained from volunteering them. Anyone she considered worthy of insult, she insulted. She eyed him coldly for a moment, looked past him, cropping him from her frame of reference, and spoke directly to me. "If you are not particular about the people you associate with, just remember we are." So saying, she and my father flounced out of the bar.

She did not speak to me on the voyage home from that holiday, though it had nothing to do with Jimmy Mollison. She suspected me of some sort of hanky-panky with the hotel's orchestra leader. I was not guilty, but I had disappeared for a day, and while they were searching for me, I was off in a sailboat having a marvelous time with the conductor.

It was nothing serious. I did not want to get married again, and friends who enjoyed dabbling in parlor analysis were constantly accusing me of always getting involved with men I couldn't or wouldn't marry. It made for improbable, never-lengthy alliances, prospects I wasn't likely to get serious about.

My mother had stressed so endlessly that I was attractive but not glamorous, likable but possessed of intelligence that often disconcerted the romantic male, that I never really trusted the interests of suitors, couldn't be sure what it was they found appealing in me. So I relaxed, laughed a lot and enjoyed myself, never letting anyone get too close and seldom believing extravagant claims of devotion. The latter, in retrospect, still seems a healthily realistic attitude.

It was an attitude, however, which for a long time made me very uneasy and skeptical whenever someone would bestow a compliment upon me. From a seemingly unlikely source, I was to learn an important and lasting lesson about compliments.

I was having dinner at the Oak Room in the Plaza Hotel in New York with some friends one spring night. I had purchased one of those extravagantly flowered hats that flourished so profusely in New York at the time. I was self-conscious wearing it even though I knew it was flattering. I suppose I was self-conscious specifically *because* I knew it to be flattering.

Milton Berle was there, dining at another table across the room. After I had been seated, he got up from his table, came to mine and told me how pretty I looked. In my discomfort, I made some silly sort of crack like "No, I don't! It's the hat!"

Milton started to leave, then turned sharply. "Why can't you take a compliment? I wouldn't leave my table to come over here to tell you how pretty you look if I didn't mean it. What would the point be? It probably never occurred to you to say 'Thank you, Milton.' You were too busy questioning yourself and my motives."

I was humiliated, but he was right. I was making others uncomfortable, making others pay for my uneasiness. I began to learn to accept compliments graciously, even to appreciate them.

Actually, though I was too often suspicious of flattery and too shy and self-critical, only once in my memory did a man put into words the doubts I had. Edward R. Murrow was turning on the charm, and it seemed so patently transparent to me that I denied him the girlish blush which would have been acceptable and reacted with a smart crack that probably was not ill-aimed. His response to the witty parry hit where it hurt.

"Girls who look like you shouldn't have brains," he snapped.

In time, my mother became more subtle at intervening in my private life. Just as she had imposed her will between quotation marks attributed to my father when I was a girl, she developed even more indirect means of detonating torpedoes upon my adult follies. It might have been a crueler technique, but it did make me supply the ruder self-questioning.

I was infatuated with another CBS radio correspondent during the later part of World War II. He was very romantic, handsome, amusingly good-natured, irresponsible, and he drank too much. He was also married, though he was ready to obtain a divorce. Beyond that, he made an extraordinary effort to make my parents like and accept him.

My mother raised no open objections. But she coolly slipped in questions. "Oh, wasn't he married to a *Powers model?*" she'd ask idly. Then, days later, while fidgeting with something, she would toss out a line as if it were something she was merely thinking. "You know, you're not a Powers model."

While the affair raged and she sat watching in what seemed utmost tolerance, she'd query, "Did you tell me he was a Baptist?"

"Why, yes," I responded.

"A Baptist from the South?"

"Yes, Mother."

"Oh, really? What about his family?" She offered no clarification. Did she mean the family that raised him in the South or the family born out of his marriage? I was left to ponder both possibilities and consequences. She worked on me. But she never said no.

Thus undermined, the relationship crumbled. It was fun while it lasted. It was best ended. Certainly, if we had married, it couldn't have lasted more than six months, but I didn't even have a chance to make that mistake.

As my work on behalf of clients for the Morris Agency took me with increasing frequency to California, my parents regularly rode the shuttle with me. I've been told I was an idiot never to have learned to pad or exploit my expense account, but we were always meticulous at prorating all expenses to the penny, billing one-third to William Morris business expense and two-thirds to my father. My parents loved their trips to the movie capital. Everyone aided in pampering and spoiling them. They came to expect it and were impressed with nothing short of the full treatment.

On one such trip we arrived while my client Joe McCarthy was in town on assignment from *Life* magazine to do a profile on Paul Douglas, then filming *A Letter to Three Wives*. I used to date Paul before he married Jan Sterling, so he and Joe arrived at the Beverly Wilshire Hotel, where we were staying, to extend their hospitality.

Paul told my mother and father that he would be pleased to have them as his guests for lunch at the studio. My father listened to the package offered to him and responded without hesitation, "Why should I bother going to the studio and seeing you? I know you from New York."

On another visit, I had arranged a tour of MGM for him. They were filming *The Magnificent Yankee* at the time, but in an effort to include as much as possible on the tour, friends had arranged for him to meet young Leslie Caron, who had been imported for *An American in Paris* and *Lili*. My father, who was beginning to say increasingly outrageous things, had a chat with her and was heard to say as she returned to the set, "She's really not very pretty. I still prefer Jeanette MacDonald." Among those who heard him was Miss Caron.

He was intrigued by only one of my clients, and that was Marlene Dietrich. He was unhappy that he never met her. I wish he had. She had called the apartment in New York one night, and though he hated to answer the phone, he had taken her message and spent the rest of the night frantically attempting to catch me all over town to get me to return the call. When I finally did, it was during regular office hours and he felt he had missed his opportunity to aid a lady in distress and receive her thanks.

•　　•　　•

I was leaving the house one morning when I remembered that I would not be home that night.

"I won't be home for dinner tonight," I advised my mother, starting for the door once again.

"And with whom are you having dinner?" my mother called out after me.

"With Cecil Beaton," I responded, my hand extending for the doorknob.

"Where?" my mother asked as she joined me in the entryway.

"At the Plaza," I added, releasing the knob.

"Which room?" She was facing me now.

"In his suite at the Plaza."

"In his suite?"

"Yes, you know, he's redecorated a number of suites at the hotel."

"Yes?"

"And I hear that they are quite fabulous. I'm anxious to see them."

"In his suite? Helen, is that nice?"

"Cecil Beaton isn't about to . . . I mean, Cecil Beaton isn't really that interested, you know . . ."

"Oh, with you these days, all the men you know aren't interested!" said my mother, opening the door for me.

One of my associates at the William Morris Agency was a lovable character named George Wood, who had a wickedly exaggerated sense of humor and was very generous in sharing important contacts with me in my early years at the company. One day I was in the elevator on my way to lunch. George got in with another man who had been with the agency for some years. George and I chatted on the descent. When we reached the lobby, I hurried ahead but happened to hear the other man ask George how it was that I seemed to know so many people in the publishing, political and entertainment worlds.

George laughed heartily, his answer echoing through the lobby. "Didn't you know? She was one of Polly Adler's most popular 'girls.' At one time or another, every famous man visited Polly's place! Helen met them *all!*"

His impromptu explanation so delighted him that he repeated it whenever an appropriate opportunity arose and teased me about it constantly.

Thinking the story was hilariously funny, I repeated it to my mother one evening. She just stared at me and said, "Who *is* Polly Adler?"

It was George Wood who engineered Frank Sinatra's dramatic comeback in the early fifties, selling Frank to Columbia's Harry Cohn for the role of Maggio in *From Here to Eternity*. George took me to the Waldorf one afternoon to meet Sinatra. Ava Gardner had recently abandoned him, and he was several months from the physical and emotional collapse which would hospitalize him, yet he was extremely gracious to me and would remain so throughout the years that followed. In that moment he was never more gentle or pathetic.

Wood's celebrity introduction service included some names that were more infamous and not limited to the entertainment pages of the daily newspapers. I resisted George's introduction of one Frank Costello, only to be ribbed by George when Costello emerged as a featured guest star in a popular Senate television series.

"Meet a celebrity," said George, escorting Umberto (Albert) Anastasia into my office. The next time I saw Anastasia, he was plastered on the front pages of all the tabloids, having succumbed to a closer shave than he bargained for in the Park Sheraton's tonsorial parlor.

In time, of course, I became wary whenever George announced that he wanted me to meet someone. But remembering my early lesson from Lastfogel about taking advantage of any opportunity to meet the men at the top, I seized the chance to meet Harry Cohn, founder and head of Columbia Pictures, when George announced that he was in town.

He made an appointment and escorted me to Columbia's New York office at 729 Seventh Avenue. As soon as George brought me before Cohn's desk, he very suspiciously found an excuse to dash away, leaving me alone with the legendary and terrifying mogul.

"Okay, what do you want to sell me on?" said Cohn impatiently.

"Nothing."

"I don't understand. Then what are you here to see me about?"

"Mr. Cohn, I simply wanted the opportunity to meet you, so that you would know me when I do have a property for which you might have some interest," I explained.

Cohn was used to the hard-sell, fast-talking Hollywood agents. He shook his head. "You're not like any agent I ever met. What's a nice girl like you doing in the agency business, anyway? I really just don't understand."

"I'm sorry," I said. "But that's the way it is. Thank you very much for seeing me." I turned to leave.

"Wait a minute! Where do you live?"

"On East 66th."

"Well, wait, I'll take you home." I started to answer, but he continued, "What are you doing for dinner?"

"I'm sorry. I have an appointment." I was lying. I was going home for dinner with my parents.

He took a defensive tack. "I can assure you it's very respectable." Neither of us wholly believed that.

"Do you know Judge Irving Kaufman and his wife Helen?" he asked. I nodded that I did. "Well, the dinner is with them and it is at '21' and there's no reason why you can't go." He started to gather up papers from his desk, presuming no further objections.

"I'm awfully sorry, but I do have an appointment," I argued, conjuring images to match the gossip of starlet 'hell weeks' suffered under his regime.

"Okay, but I am going to take you home if you only live on 66th Street."

"Thank you very much, but no, I'm quite used to taking taxis. I'll just take a taxi."

"Well, I'll be *damned*," said Harry Cohn.

My next meeting with the man who had built Columbia from a Poverty Row enterprise to one of the major Hollywood studios was within the bounds of his feudal kingdom. I arrived in Hollywood on business, which I completed earlier than I had anticipated. I placed a call to Columbia, asking Cohn if I might see him.

"Of course, of course" his voice came through the receiver. To my surprise, he ordered a studio car sent to pick me up, and I was spared the lengthy wait in his outer office, a technique devised to properly intimidate many an agent and producer.

The office had been inspired by Cohn's earlier infatuation with Benito Mussolini's trappings of power and was contrived to shrivel the confidence of all who entered therein. Cohn sat behind a knobless electrically controlled door, at the end of a thickly carpeted, enervatingly long and narrow office, behind an imposingly elevated circular desk, silhouetted before the glare of banks of Academy Award statuettes.

I had a few advantages. I was not there to sell anything. In time, I knew or maintained the conviction that Cohn needed me for good properties less than I needed him in a competitive market. He was tough and could skewer a pinpoint hint of weakness in any joust. He always played fair with me.

Harry Cohn stood up to greet me. "What are you going to try to sell me today?"

"There's nothing I can think of at the moment that you might want," I responded. "But I thought it would be nice to see you."

Very soon we would have plenty to negotiate, but that afternoon we simply relaxed, chatted briefly and exchanged pleasant goodbyes. He was not a man of great wit or subtlety, but unlike most who dealt with him, I did find him to have a sense of humor and charm when he cared to reveal them.

Shortly thereafter he offered me a job. I'm convinced that one of the prime reasons for the offer was that he simply didn't understand me, and that was a challenge. He offered me an escalating five-year contract, starting at $50,000 a year—a very big salary for the time.

I did not consider the offer long or very seriously, but it was well worth some thought. While the financial terms were specific, the job offered latitude if I chose to define it. In effect, I could do anything I wanted to do there.

I explained to him that I liked what I was doing and had no real desire to work in the movie business. As I've said before, my mother would have protested any job that might have required me to move to the West Coast, though it is conceivable that I could have worked out of Columbia's New York office had I been interested. I was not.

"What's nice about being an agent?" Cohn challenged.

"Well, the way I'm an agent, it's very nice." I finally convinced him that I didn't want the job, though I appreciated the offer. He accepted what I said, but I don't think he could ever understand.

I had not mentioned the offer to Abe Lastfogel, and word of it reached him by the rumor mill. He arrived in town on business and came directly to my office.

"Why didn't you tell me that Harry Cohn had offered you a job?" he asked,

"I didn't want it. I didn't seriously consider it. What was there to tell you?" Nothing more was said.

Not having worked for Polly Adler during her days as a "Madam," I felt no compulsion to stand up for her when she bundled up her ledgers and packed off to night school to reorder her life and recount her experiences in lay sociology in *A House Is Not a Home*. It was a professional consideration rather than some shock of D.A.R. distaste which prompted me to refuse to handle her memoir, though of course I was turning down a spectacular best seller and the cozy commissions it would have brought to the William Morris Agency.

She complained bitterly to Abe Lastfogel when I declined to represent her. Once again Lastfogel backed me up when I explained that Miss Adler would add no prestige to my growing list of full-time writers.

The literary department had been a success from the year I established it. At the end of that first year it was becoming fashionable for certain authors, feeling their oats and hungering for a heftier scoop in their bags, to become disenchanted with their agents and gravitate to the Morris office on the recommendation of our satisfied new clients.

Under Lastfogel's leadership, the Morris Agency, unlike many of its large competitors, had never believed in simply signing up voluminous lists of clients to a degree that it could not guide their careers, let alone remember which individual names were listed in their files. I could afford to be selective and successful at the same time.

I was very proud of my writers, their credentials for their craft and the diversity of their styles and interests. While Miss Adler's book was one of the better confessionals of its type and may well have provided valuable research and documentation for psychiatrists, social workers and law-enforcement personnel, they were not, of course, the readership which made the book a success.

Her book now towers above the literally hundreds of tell-all and how-to exploitations by amateurs which were to be spawned in its wake. Overly zealous editors would be mocking up fantasy exposés by house staff writers and hiring models to pose on talk shows as the confessor of the month, while the general fiction market suffered and waned. That may have been the future of the book business, but it was not mine, nor did I wish a part in it. I preferred to leave it to the peddlers of dime-store chocolates and concentrate on authors with more than one book under their belts, books that could be written sitting up.

As my own memoir unfolds, it will be noted than few women made their way to my client rolls. Women can be particularly effective agents for men by virtue of their patience and their willingness to worry about and take care of problems that are at best only tangential to the immediate concerns of manuscripts, contracts and deadlines. The male client may frequently feel less uncomfortable exposing his frustrations and weaknesses before a sympathetic woman representative. Ideally, the female agent can be stronger, less devious, more devoted. Not always, but in the appropriate relationships.

For the most part, the women I handled were those who generally bridled at the prospect of dealing with the stereotypical woman in business. Others may have felt more comfortable under the protective wing of a seemingly strong man. I hate to generalize. Surely it is just as possible that many a shrewd and forceful lady author has found a weak male agent to bully into her bidding. However many possibilities there are, I did find it generally true that women were not comfortable dealing with another woman. For one thing, it is particularly difficult for them to take the severely honest criticism required between author and agent. At one time a woman might ask another if her make-up was flattering, but she ultimately only gave a damn what a *man* thought.

Novelist Taylor Caldwell confided to occult researcher Jess Stearn that she had known scarcely a single day of happiness in her life. As best I can determine, it did not occur during the very brief period that I represented that talented and unhappy lady. She came to me in 1950. I promptly secured a $40,000 contract for her with the *Woman's Home Companion* for the serial rights to *The Balance Wheel*. I think we had had enough of each other in less than a year. Her husband was then acting as her business manager, which made for a very sticky and meddlesome family affair that was simply too great a nuisance for what it was worth.

Helen Eustis came to me after she had written *The Horizontal Man*. I sold her novel, *The Fool Killer*, to the films, and that relationship is memorable only because the movie that was made from the book was one of the most ignominious disasters of a generally chaotic period in the film business. At one time or another, almost everyone worked on the film—including future Academy Award-winning director William Friedkin—then the film was passed from one distributor to the next, none of whom seemed anxious to foist it upon the public.

Lucille Fletcher came to me in the wake of the acclaim that followed her radio classic, *Sorry, Wrong Number,* and after she had contributed the libretto to the opera *Wuthering Heights,* composed by Bernard Herrmann, her husband at the time. Lucille proved to be one of my ideal clients and is still a dear friend. I handled her books and screenwriting assignments for some years, found her receptive and responsive to constructive criticism, which made both of our jobs easier. We talked, she sent it in, I sold it.

I passed on the opportunity to handle one of the most successful lady writers of our time, though she did not cash in finally until I was already in the process of departing the agency business. It probably would have been a very pleasant alliance. In truth, it remained a pleasing acquaintance even though I did not represent her. Whenever Jacqueline Susann and her husband, Irving Mansfield, were in Los Angeles promoting her latest best seller or making one of those astronomical movie deals, we would inevitably find ourselves thrown together at one of those A-list brawls at someone's Beverly Hills acropolis.

On such occasions Irving could always be depended upon to entertain all demi-immortals within earshot with huzzahs for the role I played in goosing Jackie's career. According to Irving, it was Helen Strauss who first encouraged his wife to begin writing, at a rate which would average about ten dollars a word. But then, the Mansfields were always charming and generous with me.

This was long before Jackie had written a homage to her poodle, graduated to shrewdly promoted "guess who?" novels and won the volunteer press agentry of such giants of modern literary criticism as Rex Reed. It was before she acutely assessed her audience and raised to a high art the business of marketing her wares. In the process of becoming an almost omnipresent media personality, she never overestimated her literary pretensions, preferring to take pride in spinning a good simple morality tale about a bundle of juicy riddles.

I had just begun as an agent when Bob Sylvester sent Jackie to see me. I knew her husband was a very successful and highly paid executive at the Columbia Broadcasting System, and I could see that Jackie was too bright and ambitious not to aspire to earning her own satisfaction and celebrity. She placed her manuscript in my hands and I read it. It may well be that what I said that day had the effect of encouraging her to pursue her writing, but she and Irving colored the recollection rather too generously. What I remember saying, as I lifted my eyes from the final line of her submitted prose, was, "Oh, Jackie, aren't you lucky you're married to Irving."

That line has a patronizing echo in retrospect, but its content is unimpeachable fact. Any encouragement Jackie might possibly have needed, he supplied.

If I represented relatively few woman and had excellent or uneasy relationships with about an equal number, none of those commitments ever offered the discomforts that a few of the male clients could create.

With one notable exception, a "charity account" I handled throughout his career despite my objection to unprofessional antics which the agency found it politic to tolerate, I did not keep a client I did not like, nor one who created troubles his talent and his output could not justify.

Some very prolific and scintillating male writers turned out to be dirty old men who wouldn't settle down to the conduct of business. A few others—whose kinks should have been their own concern—promised to get into more trouble than I would ultimately be able to throw a carpet over, and I was happy to turn the headache and the extracurricular police detail over to some other agency. I was equally willing to "fire" one otherwise respected American barrister on the basis of his words, not his actions.

I handled Morris L. Ernst no longer than a month. His offices were close by and he found it amusing to call frequently, commanding, "Come over to my office." The long-time champion of civil liberties found it funnier still to be represented by a woman agent and to greet her whenever she entered his office with chortled phrases like, "When were you laid last?". . ."Getting any?" and similar bits of grizzled humor.

I suppose it was some attempt on his part to put me at ease and show his acceptance by liberally peppering his conversation with obscenities and rude nuzzlings into my private affairs. It struck me as something less than the respect appropriate to a healthy client-agent association. So I "fired" him.

In the agency business, it is important to specialize. I did not, for example, represent Paul Bowles for his music. The Morris Agency had a television department, a play department, an office on the West Coast which knew the studio routine best. Lastfogel had eased the office out of its unprofitable band business and had groomed specialists in the guidance of personalities' careers.

The agency represented screenwriters who were not my concern. Some had come East to make assaults on the novel market or Broadway, usually without success. I represented authors in print. Still, with greater frequency and with Lastfogel's full support, I was allowed to cross whatever departmental lines of demarcation existed rather than turn over my writers to strangers when they ventured into other fields. I found that I could not relinquish my responsibility to them, nor could I always trust them to the mercy of agents to whom their style, strengths and sensitivities were alien.

I'm sure that my covetousness often angered associates in the West Coast offices when I insisted upon handling the film rights

for all of my clients' properties or when I insisted upon representing Archibald MacLeish in his television excursions. My unorthodox methods probably infuriated them most because they so often
worked. At best, a détente of mutual distrust existed between the
Hollywood Morris agents and myself and between *my* clients and
theirs. I let them blow a few deals, but no more.

My stance was frozen out of bitter experience. Early in my ca-
reer I handled a young writer named Paddy Chayefsky. He started
writing stories for magazines. He wrote a novelette that I sold to
Cosmopolitan. I was then able to sell the film rights to Fox for
$25,000. It became a vehicle for Monty Woolley under the title of
As Young As You Feel. It was the film that Fox rushed Marilyn
Monroe into after her impact in *All About Eve*.

Paddy's consuming desire, however, was to establish himself as a
dramatist. Specifically, he was excited by the potential that the
emerging television medium offered the young writer. I did everything that I could to facilitate his dream. I made all of the preparations. Paddy would go to Hollywood. I told the Beverly Hills office
that Paddy had a great deal of talent, ambition and promise, and
placed his future in their hands. Paddy was set.

He arrived in Hollywood and promptly got the "nobody" brush-
off. He couldn't get in to see anyone at the Morris office. Everyone
was too busy. Naturally, he immediately left the agency, which lost
an important share in the Golden Age of Television and the subsequent plays and films that he was to write. I didn't blame him. He
knew what he wanted. He found it elsewhere.

PART
THREE

WRITER, scholar, diplomat, Bucks County squire, connoisseur of art and music, patron, man of reason and concern, thinker and doer, sports enthusiast, but above all, gentleman. This is James A. Michener.

Nancy Shores, an eccentric woman who was one of my first clients and a writer for the large-circulation women's magazines, was responsible for my meeting Jim Michener. When I first saw her in 1944 she was a faded blonde, but she still bore the traces of youthful beauty, although too much drink and living had leached her classic features.

She was not an ideal client, being constantly the victim in troubles of her own making. Sometimes her woes were imaginary. And she had an irritating habit of telephoning in the middle of the night, then forgetting completely with the new dawn that she had called.

Though she was always reluctant to discuss her background, I got the impression from bits and pieces of idle conversations that she had a better than average education and came from a good Middle Western family.

The first year that I handled her, I sold many of Nancy's short stories to *Ladies' Home Journal, McCall's, The Saturday Evening Post, Collier's* and *American*. They were stories about clean, upright, foursquare American families who believed in the sanctity of the home, had well-scrubbed, obedient children, and lived in homes erected according to the blueprint of the American dream. Nancy, who pursued different dreams, was not without writing talent.

The first year that I represented her, she made enough money to buy herself a private brownstone house in what was then a good section of Greenwich Village. She converted it to apartments. World War II had just ended, apartments were scarce, and the property should have ensured her security.

But Nancy was not an astute businesswoman and chose her tenants as one might make up a list for a party to shock the squares. They had to be congenial and amusing, preferably eccentric or talented. Apparently they did not have to be good financial risks, reliable, upright or sober.

Jim Michener had enlisted in the Navy during the final year of the war, and served as a senior historical officer attached to the office of an admiral in the South Pacific. When he returned from service he resumed his job as a textbook editor at Macmillan.

Jim was, relatively speaking, a late starter as an author for general publication, by his own admission having reached his mid-thirties before he attempted any creative writing. And it was while he was in the service that he wrote a number of short stories, first published in *The Saturday Evening Post*, which were to form the core of *Tales of the South Pacific*. Yet he had been in print before. As a history professor, first at the state teachers college at Greeley, Colorado, later at Harvard and Swarthmore, he had published *The Unit in Social Studies*, and he was justly proud that his essay, *The Beginning Teacher*, was chosen as the introduction to the Tenth Year Book of the National Council of Social Studies.

Back in civilian life, Jim became Nancy's prize tenant—very likely the only one who paid his rent. While he lived in the house in Greenwich Village only briefly, he developed a continuing interest in Nancy and maintained an affection of sorts for her. He once claimed that it was gratitude he felt for her because she had introduced us.

Nancy's drinking parties and the strays she managed to collect about her increasingly interfered with her writing. Her money dwindled, and I've reason to believe that Jim often extended a helping hand when Nancy needed it. Later, when Jim started doing extensive traveling to research his books, he always told me that I was to notify him immediately if she was in trouble.

When Nancy stopped writing, I lost contact with her. A couple of years later the police department in Newark, New Jersey, notified me that she had died, alone and without a penny, in some ramshackle rooming house. They had found my name and address among her few belongings. Jim was in Honolulu, writing *Hawaii*. I cabled the news to him there. His immediate response was that he would pay for anything necessary.

I've never really been certain whether or not Nancy thought I'd be a good candidate as Jim's next wife, or whether she thought I should become his literary agent. Nancy was so determined that I meet Jim, no political campaign manager could have done a better job. Since Nancy wrote glossy fiction, it was typical of her to describe me to him as having the beauty of Helen of Troy and the wisdom of Socrates. Knowing Nancy's machinations, I was embarrassed.

It was Jim who eventually telephoned me, saying Nancy had insisted we get together. I suggested he come to my office. I knew little about him then, only that he had been an officer in the Navy, had been in the Pacific and was back at his old job at the publishing house.

Our first meeting was not a comfortable one. At that time I had no idea what Nancy had told Jim about me and my work. To make the meeting more perplexing, Jim, after a few minutes of pleasantries, asked me to attend the Metropolitan Opera with him in two weeks. I have never been an opera enthusiast. Also, I've always kept my appointments flexible because I never know what I might want to do socially from day to day. I didn't accept that invitation and it was quite some time until I saw him again.

However, that meeting in my office at the William Morris Agency in Radio City in 1946 was the beginning of a rare friendship of mutual respect and trust, which has considerably enriched my life. My impression of him that day, and it has remained the same all these years, is that he is, above all, a gentleman. Later I was to realize he is one of the great intellects of our time.

Success has not changed him—and he's never taken it seriously, as so many others have. One might be put off by his reticence, but his modesty and humility are genuine, especially for anyone who has attained such world-wide fame. Yet he is not an easy person to understand.

One must always remember that he is a man of many moods and a loner, and his interests are varied. Some of his Quaker upbringing is apparent in his mode of living. His attitude toward money is baffling. He has a great ambivalence about it. He relishes his success but spends little money on himself. He lives modestly. His personal material needs are simple. He has helped many people in many ways—artists, writers, people with financial problems—and, of course, he certainly helped me professionally. I know of no one who is less interested in status.

Even when traveling on some company's expense account, he is economical. He is so lacking in ostentation that if one meets him without knowing who he is, the first impression would be that perhaps he is a college professor or a clergyman who has no real interest in wearing apparel other than that it's functional, whose income is modest and who lives in some Middle Western university town.

Months after the initial meeting Jim asked me to dinner. In the forties early-autumn New York nights were magical. The air was crisp and fresh and the stately Park Avenue buildings had the charm of what New York used to be. Jim had asked me to meet him at the Crillion, which has since been replaced by an enormous skyscraper office building. The Crillion at that time still retained a faded elegance and a European atmosphere.

The evening was memorable. I knew I was being appraised. Jim told me, prophetically, that I'd be successful. It was not what most people thought. Jim asked to escort me home, but had mentioned something about playing handball at the Y.M.C.A. if we finished dinner early enough, and being an accommodating young woman who would never think of interfering with a good game of handball, I took a cab by myself.

Jim must have believed his own prognostication, for in the ensuing months he recommended me to writers and publishers, and his recommendations were most helpful. One day I read in the newspaper that he had been a speaker at a forum sponsored by the *Herald-Tribune* and that he had highly praised two of my young writer clients, John Horne Burns and Marc Brandel.

I telephoned Jim to thank him. We made an appointment, but this time it was to lunch at Sardi's, a rendezvous of the theatrical profession on West 44th Street. *Tales of the South Pacific* had been published by Macmillan, but no one could anticipate what would result for this volume of short stories, since nine of the ten major book reviewing agencies had completely ignored it. It was not even a matter of record in *Time, Newsweek* and *Saturday Review*. Jim has always said that that was a lucky break which kept him from getting a swelled head.

Jim confided to me that Rodgers and Hammerstein were interested in the book for a Broadway musical. I asked if they had offered a contract or option money. So far they had not, Jim told me. I was new to the agency business, and contracts for Broadway shows were still a mystery to me, so when Jim suggested tentatively that I might be of some help, I was emphatic that this was one area of business I had not yet learned. Jim asked me about another agent, Harold Freedman, then the dean of play agents. It was he who negotiated the contract with Rodgers and Hammerstein, but the deal was not consummated until Jim was awarded the Pulitzer Prize. Still, Rodgers and Hammerstein paid the handsome advance against royalties of five hundred dollars! Who could have known what a bonanza was being launched on that bargain?

The Pulitzer was announced just as the paperback edition came out, so additional hardcover sales were lost. The award proved to be highly controversial, some critics editorializing that the content of the book was trivial. *Tales* had not been one of those considered a likely contender. But time would confirm the stature of the book and the wisdom of its selection. For years to come, Jim's royalties for *Tales of the South Pacific* continued to be equal to the amount he earned from the initial hardcover release.

In retrospect, if I had suggested representing *Tales of the South Pacific* and, lacking in experience, had botched the negotiations I would have lost a friend and a prospective client. Eventually, of course, there were big commissions to be made on the *South Pacific* musical, but from that time on I'm certain Jim always had complete confidence in my credibility and in the high priority assigned to his best interests. I earned his trust.

Still, I came to the realization that it was lack of confidence rather than of ability that kept me from negotiating that Broadway sale. I was not the opportunist some thought me to be. As shrewd as Rodgers and Hammerstein could be at the bargaining table, I know I would have made no worse a deal than Freedman's and am convinced that I would have foreseen and protected more of Jim's interests. Freedman sold all rights to the book, though Rodgers and Hammerstein and Joshua Logan, who directed and co-adapted the musical, used only two of the stories, "Our Heroine" and "Fo' Dolla'."

When I became Jim's agent, I used to make an annual trip to the Rodgers and Hammerstein offices to try to get them to release their hold on the rights to the other stories in the book. They never would, nor were they inspired to make any further use of the material themselves.

Like all other musicals, months went by before *Tales of the South Pacfic* became *South Pacific* on Broadway. During this time Jim remained in his editorial job at Macmillan, not quite certain he would have any substantial income from the play or that he could support himself entirely by his writing. After *South Pacific* opened, Jim and I had another lunch at Sardi's. Jim asked me whether or not I thought he could earn his living by writing.

At that luncheon I told Jim I was sure I could get him magazine assignments which would compensate him more than his pay as an editor. Having won the Pulitzer Prize, he was a recognized name as far as the literary world was concerned. I asked whether he'd like to revisit the South Pacific and do an article on it. He looked at me rather incredulously and said it was most unlikely a magazine would send him there! It was not false modesty—it is just the way he is.

After I returned to my office I telephoned *Holiday*, which was beginning to be a great magazine. Ted Patrick was editor in chief and Harry Sions was editorial director. Both believed in publishing only first-rate writing by first-rate writers. I suggested to Harry that Jim write for their magazine and that he would be the ideal choice to write about the South Pacific. Ted Patrick and Harry Sions agreed, and I negotiated a deal for Jim to write a series of articles on that part of the world. Jim resigned from Macmillan.

The results of that luncheon proved very lucrative for many—Jim Michener, *Holiday*, Random House and me.

When I was officially committed as Jim's agent, I overstated my credo on agent-client relationships—as I was inclined to do, as it seemed fair to do, and as it was with so many others quite necessary to do: "I'm always available if it's business. You can always reach me on the phone, but I don't have a house in the country. If I did, you wouldn't be invited. Don't expect to be entertained on weekends."

I was attempting to ease a warmly developing friendship into a wholly professional working association. It turned out to be something else, of course, and a very special relationship. I did get the house in the country after my parents died. I did have guests and on rare occasions I would be a houseguest. I think my clients discovered that they had to be auditioned and then had to put up with my idiosyncrasies too.

Jim, whose research, travel, quest for philosophic points of view and writing consume most of his life, was my most prolific and profitable client, as well as my good friend.

I had become Jim's agent with the *Holiday* articles, which eventually became his third book, *Return to Paradise.* His second book, the autobiographically flavored *The Fires of Spring,* was reputedly completed before *Tales of the South Pacific,* though I could never get him to admit that.

Regarding *The Fires of Spring,* it is a moot point whether Macmillan rejected it or whether Jim wanted it to be published by Random House because of his admiration for Saxe Cummins, who was considered one of the great editors in publishing. His list of authors included such luminaries as William Faulkner and John O'Hara. At any rate, *The Fires of Spring* became a Random House publication, so it seemed logical to offer *Return to Paradise* to them.

When I made the agreement for the articles with *Holiday,* I retained all rights to them for Jim, other than their initial publication in the magazine. I had the foresight to realize that perhaps they might make a book or perhaps there were motion picture possibilities. The articles were a great success in *Holiday* and for a number of years he wrote for that magazine and was thus enabled to continue his travels around the world.

It was after the *Holiday* assignments that he started to contribute regularly to the *Reader's Digest,* which gave him the opportunity to write with greater latitude about people, places, art and foreign politics.

I then had the idea that the *Holiday* articles could be made into a fine and publishable book. Jim was pleased with the suggestion, but he had an even better conception of what it could be. In addition to the factual pieces that had appeared in the magazine, he came up with some short fiction stories that matched the locales of the articles. But getting *Return to Paradise* published as a book was not easy.

Bennett Cerf was the president of Random House. In the years that followed we became good friends, but when I offered *Return to Paradise* to Bennett, I had one of the classic sizzler arguments of my career. To say that Bennett put me down was an understatement. I was informed that I didn't know the slightest bit about publishing—collections of articles and fiction were dismal failures as books and no publisher in his right mind would undertake a book of this kind, according to Bennett. He lost his temper and sense of humor. So did I. But I wouldn't be discouraged. I was determined I'd get the book published and equally confident it would sell well.

Knowing that LeBaron Barker of Doubleday had enthusiasm for Jim's writing, I called him and told him what I had to offer. Having the authority to take on the book, Lee advised me within a couple of days that Doubleday would give us a contract and an advance. Lee was a good editor and the firm was noted for its promotion and advertising. I was excited and pleased that Lee Barker and Doubleday had the courage and imagination to back us.

Morally, I had no obligation to go back to Bennett and inform him of Doubleday's offer. It was pride. I wanted to prove to Bennett I was not the idiot he implied I was. Implied, hell! He had shouted it. Bennett realized if Doubleday published the collection, Jim might then stay with that firm for subsequent books. Random House did not want to lose Jim. He was not a dilettante writer—it looked even then as if there was going to be profitable longevity in publishing Jim Michener.

So in the end Bennett talked Jim and me out of letting Doubleday publish *Return to Paradise*. Random House had no real enthusiasm for it, and I think it was a pleasant surprise to them when it became a Book-of-the-Month Club selection and a best seller in hardcover as well as in paperback.

I liked Bennett Cerf. He was an amusing personality. but each time I made contracts for authors with Random House, and there were many beside Jim Michener—Justice William O. Douglas,

Robert Penn Warren, Garson Kanin, Paul Bowles, Ralph Ellison, Maurice Edelman, Lucille Fletcher, Aubrey Menen, Oliver Statler and others—I had to mention tactfully, as tactfully as I could, that Bennett was the "star" of Random House.

I was able to sell only two stories out of the book to the movies: "Mr. Morgan," which later became *Return to Paradise* with Gary Cooper, and "Until They Sail," which Robert Wise made with Paul Newman. The money paid for both of the stories was minimal. Not until Jim wrote *The Bridges at Toko-ri*, *Sayonara*, *Hawaii* and *Caravans* was I able to make sales of the motion picture rights for prices which startled the industry.

Selling *The Bridges at Toko-ri* was exciting, the sale of *Hawaii* the most spectacular. The biggest headache came with the sale of *Sayonara*. The easiest sale was *Caravans*. I had a theory, nevertheless. I never sold anything. All of these novels were *bought!*

The reason *The Bridges at Toko-Ri* was the most fun in all respects is best expressed by Jim.

Personal relationships with you could not have been more congenial. I was at ease with you. I respected your judgment. I liked your approach. I felt that the advice you gave me was constantly of the highest order both ethically and economically, and to my advantage. I remember once when I returned from the South Pacific and told you a brief outline of a story I had in mind, on your own responsibility, and with considerable agility of mind and procedure, you approached *Life* magazine with the idea. It was solely the result of this overture on your part that I wrote and published *The Bridges at Toko-Ri*, which, in some respects, is the best single piece of writing I have done. The work from inception to completion required only a short period of time because I was totally immersed in the subject matter. But I suspect that I might never have put it on paper had it not been for your strong urgings in that direction.

I frequently would go over with you a score of ideas which had been collecting in the back of my mind, for I have been cursed with a very prolific imagination and always have eight or ten books on the back of the fire, most of which never materialize. I would suppose in your papers there would be found discussions of not less than a score of books that I did not write, but talking their prospects over with you was often an impetus to discard those which seemed to have no promise or fulfillment.

Aside from the acknowledgment from Jim for my contribution, it was an exciting adventure from the beginning to end.

Jim and I had lunch. Usually we did our best work over a meal. He told me something about the locale, the time and the characters he had in mind. His only quandary was deciding which branch of the service would recruit his characters. Would they be in the Marine Corps, the Army or the Navy?

I asked Jim how long it would be. That was before he started writing long novels. He estimated it could be short. *Life* magazine had published Ernest Hemingway's *The Old Man and the Sea* and I asked Jim if his story might be approximately the same length. If it was, I might be able to sell it to *Life*.

Immediately after lunch, I called Jay Gold, who was text editor, and told him the idea for the story, which he told to Ed Thompson, who was editor in chief. *Life* was interested, and a few days later Jim and I had a meeting with the editorial staff of *Life*. They agreed the story might be good for them and made plans to publish it in an issue which would be out around the Fourth of July.

These conversations took place in January, and in order for *Life* to publish in July they had to have a finished manuscript in May. I negotiated a price of $30,000—in those days a good price for a story that would be about 30,000 words. An integral part of the agreement was that *Life* would only have the right to publish in the magazine; all other rights would be retained by the author.

I also insisted there would be no advance publicity. I knew each of us had our own conception of what the story was and if, as it happens sometimes, the finished work was not publishable in *Life*, I didn't want Jim to have "egg on his face."

Jim completed the manuscript before his deadline, as he always does, and *Life* was very pleased. It was then that I alerted Bennett Cerf and sent him a copy of the manuscript. Bennett was furious with me for not telling him about the novel before, but Random House was delighted to publish it and the book came out simultaneously with the publication in *Life*.

Before publication, the movie companies heard about it. This was the era during which the major motion picture studios were in great competition with each other for story material, stars, directors and writers. The system then in selling story material was to prepare many copies and send them to all the companies simultaneously, and if there was great interest, to set a price.

The Bridges at Toko-ri seemed to me excellent movie material, but I decided not to submit it to anyone, and I requested *Life* and Random House not to give advance material to any motion picture company representatives. Whether or not they complied with my request, I'll never know. When the movie representatives asked to see it, I told each of them to buy a copy of *Life* on the newsstands in a couple of weeks. This method of operation hardly endeared me to the movie people. David O. Selznick sent me one of his classic telegrams, threatening to have me fired because I had not had the story submitted to him. Paramount eventually bought it for $100,000 and the movie with Bill Holden was a big success. The book was a best seller all over the world.

The writer is always in a vulnerable position. He deals in ideas born out of experience and imagination. Naturally, the same ideas have bobbed in the heads of others with similar experience or imagination. The writer brings it forth whole. The others cannot or do not do it first. Inevitably there are suits brought by people who claim an *idea* was stolen, when the differences between a generalized idea and an actualized book are indivisible. More than that, the writer constantly dips into the same wellsprings of his mind, re-forms the same experience, turns his point of view 180 degrees, casts it in a different time and place and situation. In that sense, a writer could be said to be in the process of constantly stealing from himself, an original source, his own raw material. And he does not always know when he is doing it. Others may too readily decide when they think he has done just that.

Prior to writing *The Bridges at Toko-ri*, Jim wrote a fact piece for *The Saturday Evening Post* drawn from similar observations, the source reference, certain kinds of men in a specific period in a special field of combat. It was titled *Forgotten Heroes of Korea* and it was purchased by MGM for development into a film. The price was modest, only $25,000, but then we viewed it as a bonus that a film company had been able to spot the dramatic potential in Jim's factual battle-zone documentation.

The amount of money involved was small, but the amount of work I had to do on it was staggering. I had to secure some ninety-three releases from naval personnel whose personalities and functions were depicted in the essay, so that the studio could proceed with the film (to be retitled *Men of the Fighting Lady*) without the threat and additional cost of invasion-of-privacy suits.

It was one of those rare occasions when I had allowed the Morris office on the Coast to handle the contracts. Foolishly, they had given MGM sequel rights to the material. If *Men of the Fighting Lady* had proved to be a surprising success, it would have been advantageous for the studio to grind out Returns of, Sons of, Children of the Men of the Fighting Lady Striking Again, having gotten the initial rights cheap and the sequels for a token. Television series, kiddie uniforms might have followed. Probably not, but I bristled at the idea of selling Jim short.

I urged Jim to let the deal go. "God knows you might want to do your own sequel one day."

Jim was certain that he would never return to a Korean War setting. Of course, as you surmise, his next book was *The Bridges at Toko-ri*. MGM contended that it was obviously the war and warriors they had contracted for. In the threatened suits and snickers which followed, MGM agreed tentatively to drop their claim to the *Toko-ri* film rights on the condition that they get the first look at Jim's next book. The next book was *Sayonara*, which had enough entanglements without that minor one.

Sayonara from beginning to end was trouble. After I read the first draft and both Jim and I agreed it needed revisions, he asked me to send it to his editor at Random House, Saxe Cummins, with the word that he was eager to have his opinion and wanted to do whatever rewriting was necessary. Jim rewrites when necessary and regards editors with respect as people who know their jobs.

After Saxe read the manuscript of *Sayonara* he telephoned me saying the manuscript was going to the printer and when I queried him about revisions, he said none would be necessary! This was very upsetting. I had no doubt whatsoever that the novel had a great potential as a book, a magazine serial and as a movie, but I also had no doubts about its needing more work done on it and that Jim had relied implicitly on Saxe to do this with him.

I was audacious enough then to tell Saxe that if this first draft of the book was published, it would hurt Jim's reputation as a writer and from the publisher's standpoint, it would not sell. I couldn't understand Saxe's attitude, until suddenly I realized Saxe was on in years and his attitude toward new writers had changed. He was too busy with John O'Hara and William Faulkner, and perhaps, to him, Jim was a "Johnny-Come-Lately."

A few days later Jim and I went to the theater. During intermission I got the courage to tell Jim his editor's reaction. Jim wasn't angry, but I got the impression he was hurt and disappointed. I offered to go to Random House to discuss the problem.

I confronted Bennett, and he called in his partner, Donald Klopfer. It became a "palace revolution," and neither Bennett nor Donald thought I made much sense when I insisted they assign another editor for Jim. Of course, I knew that underneath all the furor about this particular situation was the fact that I had touched on just about the most delicate nerve in publishing. Even lesser editors become prima donnas at the very thought that one of their authors would want to change his editor. Furthermore, I was only an agent, and I had the effrontery to be critical of Saxe, who was *the* great editor!

But I went ahead doggedly and made the suggestion that Albert Erskine become Jim's editor. Bennett figuratively hit the ceiling. Donald in his usual calm way became the arbiter. I threatened to have Jim's contract canceled unless they agreed. Perhaps all this does not seem very important, but most writers need editorial help and frequently a good book can be hurt by careless editing and a good book can become a much better one if the author and editor work together.

It was finally agreed to make the switch, and Albert Erskine became Jim's editor, and is to this day. (It is probably the best thing I did for his career, because with Albert and, later, Bert Krantz, his copy editor, Jim got the editorial help he always wanted.) Jim and Albert worked closely together on *Sayonara* and it became a best seller. I was also able to sell the serial rights to

McCall's; the reprint rights brought a very good price; and it was a Book-of-the-Month Club selection.

I told Jim I thought the story had motion picture possibilities, and we agreed to let the studios read it. The reactions were all enthusiastic. Film-rights prices had not as yet skyrocketed, but there was plenty of gold being scattered about for everything to do with films—story material, stars, writers, directors and, of course, producers. A producer is the man who used to be in an exalted position, who reported to the head of the studio, who in turn gave the producer the authority to spend money as if it had gone out of style. But it didn't matter then. Everybody went to the movies and most pictures made money. As a result, there were plenty of instant millionaires, as there are today.

After careful consideration, I told Jim that a price of $150,000 plus a percentage of the profits seemed reasonable to me. Percentages then were not usual, but I was never one to adhere to usual practices.

With Jim's approval, shortly thereafter a telegram outlining what rights were available, including the purchase price, was sent to all the major movie companies, requesting each to make a decision whether or not the offer was acceptable. In this telegram it was stated that acceptances had to be made no later than Friday of that week, and that if more than one company accepted, Jim had the right to choose which studio could buy *Sayonara.*

The telegram was sent on Monday. The die was cast! That's what I thought.

I knew that between Monday and Friday would be nervous time for me, but I didn't anticipate the events that subsequently occurred. Thursday night, while I was listening to the eleven-o'clock news, content that nothing startling had happened to the world in general and that the next day I'd know about the sale of *Sayonara,* the phone rang. It was Jim.

The fact he called at all at that time of night was a great surprise. He had been to the theater, alone, which was not unusual. Jim did this sort of thing sporadically. He had wandered into Sardi's, where Josh Logan, who directed *South Pacific,* was having supper after a rehearsal of *Kind Sir,* which was to open on Broadway with Mary Martin and Charles Boyer. Jim asked me to take a cab and come over to Sardi's. He seemed excited.

The idea of dashing over to Sardi's might have been a pleasant idea for someone else, but the next day was "D-day" for *Sayonara*. Then Jim added that Josh had a wonderful idea—he wanted to make the book into a musical for Broadway. Josh got on the phone to confirm Jim's statement, then Jim got on the phone again and said he wanted Josh to produce *Sayonara* as a Broadway show.

I gasped. I knew it wasn't very wise to explain at that moment that the creative thinking was four days too late, so I suggested we talk the next day. Jim repeated how thrilled he was with Josh's interest. Josh, by the way, had not read the manuscript.

The lunch bunch the next day included Josh Logan, his financial adviser and one of the attorneys who represented Josh, plus Nat Lefkowitz, who was treasurer of the William Morris Agency. Josh had a limited amount of time because of his rehearsals, but kept reiterating that he had to have *Sayonara*, whatever the cost. He would not take me seriously when I told him that it could only be bought under the terms and conditions put forth in the telegram which had been sent to the studios, that time was of the essence. We had to have an acceptance by telegram by five o'clock.

After Josh left the lunch table his attorney told me that he would make a bid on behalf of Mr. Logan, but if no studio accepted our terms, Logan would make a counter offer. The telegram was sent, but it was not the deal we had requested. Three companies—Metro-Goldwyn-Mayer, Twentieth Century–Fox and William Goetz—accepted. The Logan bid included dramatic rights and a clause stating that if no company accepted our proposal, Logan could withdraw.

But Jim wanted Josh Logan to have *Sayonara*, and the interested companies were notified. The three of them banded together, hired a very influential attorney, Sam Rosenman, and a lawsuit was instigated. For a couple of years testimonies were the order of the day and I spent many hours in examinations before trial. Judges often chided me for remembering too many details. Jim Michener, Josh Logan and the Morris Agency were to be sued for restraint of trade and damages. The suit got as far as the Supreme Court of New York, and finally a settlement was reached.

Jim Michener received $250,000 instead of $150,000, but no percentage. Bill Goetz was awarded *Sayonara*, which Warner Brothers released. In one of those settlements in which everyone seems to win and everyone owes something to someone, Josh Logan directed the picture for Goetz, agreed to direct *Bus Stop* for Twentieth and tentatively agreed to do penance on the Metro lot if and when it could be arranged. The film of *Sayonara* was a smash, the flurry of lawsuits created work for everyone, and perhaps someone was happy.

Josh Logan's Broadway musical version of *Sayonara* becomes a footnote in this quizzical history. Irving Berlin was to write the score. Michener might have debuted as a librettist.

I suspect one of the reasons Jim has developed such concentration and goes into isolation for such long periods when he is on a project—beyond his basic dedication and professionalism—is that he can get himself into trouble so easily by trying to be agreeable. It's the soft spot in his Quaker indoctrination.

Jim tried his hand at drama and screenwriting, found he liked neither and returned to his own province. First, however, he again got me in Dutch with Samuel Goldwyn.

Goldwyn, one of the few studio heads to have been greatly in awe of writers, could pursue them as other producers sprinted after starlets. He called me to say that he had to have Jim do a screenplay. He had just the property, an untitled moss-covered Somerset Maugham story that had been waiting on the shelf for just this opportunity.

"I'm not sure about that," I said, trying to back out graciously. "I think it would be a disservice to Michener and to you. He isn't a screenwriter and hasn't any passion to try it."

"Well, may I meet him anyway?" said Goldwyn, easing me aside.

I called Jim, told him that the legendary Sam wanted to meet him. For lunch.

"You'd better come along," Jim answered.

"He doesn't *want* me along."

"Frankly, I'm not interested in doing a screenplay, but it would be interesting to meet the man." So Jim went.

Returning from lunch, Jim crept into my office. "I think I did something wrong," he hinted.

"Like promising that you were going to do a screenplay for Mr. Goldwyn?"

"Yes. I guess you'd better get me out of it, if you can."

So I called Mr. Goldwyn and said, "I'm terribly sorry, but there's been some misunderstanding."

Mr. Goldwyn *screamed.*

"You were so convincing that he forgot for a moment what would be involved and at this time he is very busy . . ."

Mr. Goldwyn *yelled.* He asked me if I thought I was God. Where did I come off? Michener said he would. How could I say my own client couldn't write a screenplay? He continued to exercise his anger.

"Mr. Goldwyn," I tried to interrupt. "I don't have to take this from you. I'm sorry." And I hung up. I knew that he was going to pick up his phone and call Lastfogel. I knew he would try to get me fired.

Three days later I went to lunch at the Barberry Room, then a very popular sport for broadcasting executives and publishing people. I spotted Lastfogel across the room and he walked its length toward me.

"Congratulations, Helen," he began. "I guess you're the first person who ever hung up on Sam Goldwyn."

Years later, when I met Frances Goldwyn in Hollywood, I reminded her that she had sent me flowers that week, with a note that began: "I'd like to explain Sam to you . . ."

The Bridge at Andau was an exciting triumph—an example of how a good book could be written and published in record time. Hobart Lewis, who was then an editor at *Reader's Digest*, telephoned me late one night and asked whether Jim would report on the Hungarian revolt in 1956. At the time, Jim was on his way home from an extended trip to Italy and Spain but was stopping off in Amsterdam. Hobe cabled him, I cabled, and he took off for Andau. A few weeks later Jim arrived at the airport in New York with the last chapter of a manuscript he had been mailing in a chapter at a time. It appeared in the *Digest* and was subsequently published by Random House. Always the professional!

When Jim told me he was going to write a novel called *Hawaii*, I told him I thought the title was poor. Everyone would think it was another travel book. I was wrong. Hundreds of thousands of copies were sold in the hardcover edition, as well as in paperback, in the United States and Canada. It was a Book-of-the-Month Club selection, a Reader's Digest Book Club selection. I sold the first section of the book to *Life* magazine. It was another worldwide best seller.

Hawaii was the occasion for yet another showdown with the celebrity president of Random House. Again Bennett Cerf received a proposal of mine as a heretic assault upon the tenets of publishing.

"You have made a great deal of money on James Michener," I said when I was brought before Cerf, fully aware that what I considered a reasonable, well-deserved and long-overdue demand was about to inflict a wound which would be blamed upon a mad revolutionary in the general's camp. "And you have made a great deal more on subsidiary rights, particularly paperback reprint rights. The paperback book business is exploding and I no longer think that it is fair for Random House to continue to claim fifty percent of Jim's income from paperback editions."

Bennett Cerf was stricken. "You are going to put us out of business!" he flustered.

Indeed, the major publishing houses had always maintained a fifty-fifty split with the author on the subsequent paperback reprints. It was a standard maintained from an era when sales of original and subsequent low-cost hardcover books represented the bulk of a book's revenue. As the paperback business soared and the rising cost of producing hardcover books whittled away at the break-even figure, the paperback revenue claimed by the hardcover publisher often represented the difference between profit and public service. From a paternalistic vantage, the publisher could argue that the bonus from the sale of paperback rights would not exist but for his initial gamble.

I understood Bennett's interest and his position. To yield on the issue in favor of Michener would provide an opening for renegotiations with every other writer in the Random House camp who was in a position to bargain.

But Jim Michener's interests were my business and I believed that Bennett's only gamble at this stage in our dealings was deciding how large the initial printing would be for a new Michener book. Bennett knew that as well, so we negotiated. What resulted was, in fact, a revolutionary breakthrough in expanding the share the writer can retain in his works.

It was finally settled, with Jim Michener taking sixty-six and two-thirds percent of the added reprint income, the remaining third of the paperback bonanza going to Random House. Additionally, I secured a contract clause stating that I was to be consulted and had to approve any paperback deal which came through the publisher and I would ever after impose this writer approval clause whenever I had the leverage to do so.

The selling of the motion picture rights to *Hawaii* was a great event. After I read the finished manuscript, I called Jim, who was still living in Honolulu, where he had taken up residence while he researched and wrote *Hawaii*. I was very excited about the book's potential in every area and I was sure there'd be a movie sale. Jim, as usual, in his very quiet, polite way, thanked me for my enthusiasm and volunteered no suggestions. I was on my own. Whatever happened from here on was my responsibility.

This was an unusual novel. It was not an easy one to adapt for the screen and it needed a superb director to ensure its success as a film. I spent many hours going over in my mind pictures I had seen, carefully sorting out the directors who had impressed me most.

Finally I concluded that if Fred Zinnemann, who directed *From Here to Eternity, High Noon* and *The Nun's Story,* could be interested, the chances for success would be enormous. I sent the manuscript to Zinnemann, whom I knew. Freddie was a client of the Morris Agency and in those days was represented with tender, loving care by Abe Lastfogel.

After Freddie read *Hawaii,* I got a call from Abe telling me Freddie wanted to buy the movie rights. Large theatrical agencies like to get their director clients story material. It means a special service to the directors and in many cases it assures jobs. Freddie, of course, was greatly in demand by the studios, so that didn't apply to him. Lastfogel asked me what I thought it was worth and

I said not less than $600,000 against ten percent of the picture's gross business.

I think I startled Abe Lastfogel because I told him Freddie couldn't afford this, I knew, but it seemed like a good idea to sell both *Hawaii* and Zinnemann together—a package. I also added that I could not in any way prejudice my client, and if some studios wanted *Hawaii* without Zinnemann, if they agreed to my price, and had counter suggestions for the director of the movie, I would, of course, have to consider what was best for Jim.

I was requested to come to California immediately and explain how I expected to work a sale of this kind. It was really quite complicated. The price, of course, was astronomical for the motion picture rights to a novel, and ten percent of the picture's gross receipts was unheard of. Fred Zinnemann was a very important motion picture director and a long-time client of the agency. We not only had to consult with Freddie as to whether this *modus operandi* of attempting to sell his services as director along with *Hawaii* suited him, we also had to consult his attorney, Leon Kaplan.

A price for Zinnemann's services was agreed upon—$375,000 plus twenty-five percent of the picture's *profits*, and it was understood that if studios only wanted to purchase *Hawaii* without Zinnemann, Jim could sell the motion picture rights to any interested studio he chose.

After the meetings I left for a quick trip to Honolulu to see Jim. I explained what I hoped to accomplish, and it was agreeable to Jim. That was only the beginning. I returned to New York and had more conferences with attorneys to put into legal language the offer to the motion picture companies, stating what rights in *Hawaii* would be acquired by the purchaser, the terms under which Fred Zinnemann would direct the motion picture, and the fact that a studio could buy *Hawaii* without the director.

The proposal was put into the form of a letter which was sent to all the major studios that had expressed interest in *Hawaii*. The document outlined in detail what the deal was. The original price for the novel was $600,000 against ten percent of the picture's *gross*. The purchaser would acquire all rights, excepting publication and dramatic stage rights. With a ten percent of the motion picture's gross, Jim would receive ten percent of the gross receipts of whatever was made of the material, remake, or television—in perpetuity.

To coordinate the details and timing of what would be an unprecedented as well as unorthodox film sale, I often found myself in flight, racing my own airmail communiqués. Legal and ethical propriety created an operation that was becoming more and more like some monstrous battle plan.

I was returning to Los Angeles, shortly after the letters had been dispatched to all the major production companies. I was relaxed for the first time in some weeks, pleased that during the flight at least I would be isolated from the machinations which had been consuming my time and thought. I leaned back, letting my thoughts drift through other times and concerns.

But I could not for long ignore the man and woman who were seated in front of me. I could not hear what they were discussing, but I saw a letter in his hand. My letter. But who was the man? I did not recognize him, and I knew the men who had received the *Hawaii* directive.

The letter he held had been sent to Max E. Youngstein, general vice-president of United Artists, but he was not Youngstein. I contained my curiosity as long as I could. Finally I lunged forward. "Oh my God! That *is* my letter."

The gentleman turned to me and said, "Well, then I'd better introduce myself. I'm Arthur B. Krim." And that was how I met the man who was then the president of United Artists; it was the beginning of a friendship and a professional association which would continue and grow more important in the years to come. At that moment Jim Michener's book had prompted him, too, to boost the airline's stock.

All of the studios were interested in the book. A few cringed at the price and terms. A deadline was set for the companies to respond as to whether or not they would accept the proposal. On that final day, in a countdown as dramatic in fact to those involved as it must sound melodramatic in the recounting, two lawyer-couriers arrived late in the afternoon at the William Morris offices in Beverly Hills.

One was from United Artists, representing the Mirisch Company. The other represented Warner Brothers. It was Harold Mirisch who accepted the proposal without qualification. Warner Brothers accepted, but threw in a clause specifying how many pages of the book it could use for advertising and promotional pieces. They were disqualified. Other studios bid below the quoted price.

The sale was made to the Mirisch Company, with United Artists financing. They voluntarily escalated the payment to $750,000. Harold Mirisch celebrated the acquisition with a party at his home. Circulating through the turnout of studio chiefs and executives making chagrined toasts to the record film-purchase price and the promise of an epic film-to-be, I encountered Spyros Skouras, whom Herman Wobber had introduced me to in New York years before. Buddy Adler, the head of production at Twentieth, had refused the *Hawaii* deal, and Skouras, now president of the company, also felt that the price was beyond all reason.

"We'll never spend that kind of money," said the man whose star would crash under the weight of the *Cleopatra* disaster in just a few more years. He complained bitterly about the money Michener, Zinnemann and the Morris Agency were guaranteed, reminding me that there would still have to be stars and star fees to match the importance of the project, and millions more for the production itself. Could the film be successful enough to repay that investment?

"They'll never be able to get it produced," he concluded. Confusing the Mirisch brothers with the Wright brothers, he sounded like a man on the sidelines at Kitty Hawk, North Carolina, clucking his tongue and wheezing, "They'll never get it off the ground."

"Wanna bet?" I snapped confidently.

"A thousand dollars!"

"All right, on the day the film begins production, send your check for a thousand dollars to the committee for retarded children that I have been working with."

Skouras would later acknowledge that he lost the bet, but he went to his grave with that debt unpaid.

After several false starts, and disagreements between Zinnemann and United Artists in proportion to the epic, the picture was taken over by director George Roy Hill, who subsequently had his own falling-out with the company and did not complete final editing. The scars showed and it was not really a good movie. Still, it grossed about $25,000,000.

The film opened while I was working in London. Months later, after I returned to New York, I went to see it with Jim Michener. He had not gone to the opening. Any other writer might have been eager to attend. But Jim was busy. When I was highly critical of the film, Jim simply chided me that I always expect too much. He is one author who can leave the moviemaking to the moviemakers without crying "Foul!"

Twice after *South Pacific*, he had been involved with plans for contributing to Broadway musicals that were stillborn. He tried his hand at the libretto and it was not his form. He tried doing an original screenplay, which was neither satisfying nor satisfactory, and received an even cruder rewrite salvage at other hands. After an attempt or two, he decided he preferred seeing plays to writing them. He is a novelist, he writes books—books always born out of extensive research and always founded on some basic theme resulting from his concern for human truths. In recent years that sharp reportorial and social aspect of Jim's writing has been even more obvious in the nonfiction inquiries he has written.

But Jim did make one spectacularly successful venture outside of his own field, and it proved to be even more profitable for all concerned than *Hawaii* had been. The ABC television network was interested in series which broke away from the Hollywood soundstages and New York stages to exploit exotic locales and escapist plots.

Jim wrote an excellent presentation outlining the course and potential for a series utilizing the South Pacific islands and settings he knew so well. ABC-TV seized the opportunity and the series *Adventures in Paradise*, produced by Martin Manulis for Twentieth, was headed for its 1959 season of new shows. Other hands—and a few feet—took over from that point. The magic of Michener's name and the location coverage resulted in more publicity than television schedules and talents could hope to justify.

Despite stilted acting and some Victorian melodrama plotting, the series survived for three seasons and lived on in syndication around the world for many, many more.

It made for a very cozy holiday at the William Morris Agency that Christmas. From Michener and others participating in the series, the agency had taken in over a million and a half dollars in commissions, and it was still coming in. They didn't know what to do with it all, so there were snowstorms of Christmas bonus checks falling on every desk.

I had very little prior knowledge of *The Source.* Jim had visited Israel and become fascinated with the history of the locale and the people, but we had never discussed his doing a book about it. I saw him when he was preparing to leave for Israel—where he lived for nearly two years while exploring, documenting and researching that country, with long excursions into surrounding Arab countries—and it was only then that I asked him what his next book would be about.

It would be a novel, he explained, but it would really be nothing short of the story of civilization, and it would be his most complex work structurally and thematically, framed by the story of a group of archaeologists thrown together during an excavation in the Holy Land.

Because he was in residence in Israel during the long preparation for that book, I had to meet him there for any business we had to conduct. That included the signing of the contracts for *Caravans.*

Caravans was a novel that Jim himself had never considered important. He had visited Afghanistan several times and was intrigued by it. The novel that resulted was disappointing and was notable only for some vivid descriptions of the scenery and customs. But the book did become a best seller and a Book-of-the-Month Club selection. Prior to its publication I offered it for sale to motion picture companies and the reception had been cool. Such interest as existed was attracted by Michener's name and the prospect of the book's making the best-seller lists.

Metro-Goldwyn-Mayer, once the giant among studios, had suffered for want of the sort of strong direction it had in a different era when Louis B. Mayer had built the company to its eminence. Changes in the film business, the damage done by television, periodic reorganizations had dimmed the image. Robert O'Brien, who had just risen to the post of president and chief executive officer at

Metro, hoped to play a part in restoring the luster. He wanted story material of "name value" and with the benefit of a "pre-sold" audience.

Since there had been no clamor from the studios for *Caravans,* I had never set a price tag on it. Bob O'Brien asked me to come to his office and expressed an interest in purchasing the book. He asked me to set a price, but I suggested that he think it over and decide what he felt to be fair. With that, I left.

I must admit that I was treated by Bob O'Brien in a manner unlike that he might have employed with another agent. He was a good friend of Justice William O. Douglas, my client and friend, who had introduced me to O'Brien. The effect of that association was to make me a member of the club, never a peddler with wares to show by appointment. My relationship with O'Brien was, therefore, a source of some consternation for Olin Clark, the Metro story editor and another old friend, who felt his role short-circuited in these dealings.

Shortly after my meeting with O'Brien, I received a telephone call from Olin. He quoted a purchase price of $350,000 and a percentage of the profits. Jim was off in the hills somewhere in Israel. I made several unsuccessful attempts to get a call through to him.

Despite my challenge to Spyros Skouras, I have never been a gambler, but I gambled with my next step in these negotiations. I knew that no producer at the studio had volunteered an interest in making *Caravans*. Production plans in general at the studio were vague, cautious, cancelable. I told MGM that I wanted $500,000 and *no* percentage. I did it on instinct. A half million was as big a bird in hand as anyone could hope for. MGM accepted.

O'Brien had wanted a name property, something big to announce to the industry, and that much he got. I gambled and won, but I insist that I did not *sell* the book. If I had had that sort of confidence in the book, I would have made an assault with the kind of terms and conditions I employed with other Michener works. It was a bad property for films, but they wanted to *buy* it. I made the best deal I could, based upon their interest. They did not ever ask my opinion of the book or its film potential. They asked for it. They got it. Michener's reaction to the sale was one of complete surprise.

It had been a fascinating experience for me, seeing the places that Jim was writing about in *The Source* and meeting people I could not have met but for him. It was not the discovery of the roots of my religious heritage, as I might have imagined when I began the journey, but it was memorable in many other ways.

I was able to see much of the world I probably would not have visited had it not been for Jim's lengthy explorations in distant places: Hawaii, Israel, Spain and Turkey; Colorado, Maryland and Bucks County, Pennsylvania. I had a guide, steeped in the history of each locale and privy to special corners and personalities in each.

Yes, my role in *The Source* was minimal, but I constantly remind Jim that it is the book that finally broke my back. When he finished the manuscript, Jim arranged for me to pick it up for delivery to his publishers. He asked where I would like to meet him, in Paris or Istanbul? I'd been to Paris, so Istanbul it would be.

As I was preparing to leave, I received a call from Hobart Lewis of *Reader's Digest*. The *Digest* had been publishing Jim's articles and book condensations almost from the beginning of his career, and Hobe was anxious to meet with Jim concerning future commitments. So I was joined by him on the Pan Am flight to Istanbul.

There was at the time great interest in another television series from Jim, so plans were made that a day later we were to get together with his former TV series' producer Martin Manulis; Tom McDermott, the then head of Four Star Television; and Dominick Dunne, his associate.

We convened in Istanbul. As we drove along the shore of the Bosporus, my only thought was how very much it resembled the barren hills of Los Angeles, and the natives all looked like "Gadge" Kazan!

I took possession of the manuscript of *The Source*, distressed at learning that it was the only existing copy of the complete book. The television boys worked with Jim on the projected series, which would have involved Robert Wagner and which never came to pass. Temporarily satisfied, we boarded another plane and departed for England. I was lucky, because Martin Manulis carried the manuscript for me as far as London.

I had to make a side trip to Paris to meet Gore Vidal, so I reclaimed the many pages of that giant book. It weighed a ton. Imagine a woman described as "petite" clutching that oversized box of irreplaceable prose to her bosom, weaving and pushing along air-terminal corridors. But I made it to the plane. As I descended the ramp on arrival in Paris, however, a millennium or two in the "story of civilization" shifted. It was an earthquake, it was a tidal wave. It was also raining in Paris. My ankle corkscrewed beneath me and I went sprawling to the pavement. It shattered my pride. It loosened my heel. It sprained my ankle and broke a vertebra.

The Source rose in the list of best-selling books and stayed there for seventy weeks.

Jim has lived for many years in Bucks County, Pennsylvania. His home there is simple, like its owner—remote, situated inaccessibly high on a hill, where the atmosphere makes one feel that the decayed cities, the wars, the violence and the world of unrest are nonexistent. He works constantly. I have never stayed at his house for more than one night at a time, but each visit made me more aware of what a prodigious worker Michener is. Along with the first bird songs of early morning, one hears the click of his typewriter.

There are times when Jim is so engrossed with his own thoughts, he is really not aware that you are in the same place with him. He might not even answer your greeting. I learned that this was not rudeness, but total concentration on whatever was in his mind.

Jim's collection of modern American paintings is exciting. He has helped many promising young artists. Their pictures hang briefly and prominently in the Michener home and are then forwarded to museums for everyone to discover and appreciate.

About once a year Jim used to descend his mountaintop to take part in the Doylestown Fair in Bucks County. The specialty at his booth had nothing to do with exotic lands or their memorabilia.

He told fortunes. He told mine once, many years ago. He said that I would die the same year that he did.

"That's a fine way to keep me as your agent!" I snapped.

It was extremely rewarding being Jim's literary agent. There were, of course, large commissions to be derived from the huge sales of the books and their motion picture rights. Those went to the Morris Agency, even though they ultimately helped to pay my salary. The rewards of working with Jim were always greater.

There were books that won many readers and made huge profits—*Hawaii, The Source, Sayonara, The Bridges at Toko-ri, The Voice of Asia, Caravans, Return to Paradise.* There were others that did not. I have always believed that a writer should write what he enjoys writing, whether the profits are great or not.

Some of Jim's books on Japanese prints have not been best sellers, but he took enormous personal satisfaction in their publication. I did, too, and I have an autographed, specially bound copy of a volume of Japanese prints which is inscribed "To Helen Strauss, who makes books like this possible." Then there is the Modern Library book which will always stay in print, *The Selected Writing of James A. Michener,* which has this dedication: "For Helen Strauss, the friend of writers."

I shall always remember a special day when Jim came to my office. I had no idea that he was in the city, and after the usual pleasantries, I learned the purpose of his visit.

My office at the William Morris Agency faced north and allowed me a good view of Central Park. As Jim looked out the window, he said, without turning, "I've come to thank you."

"For what?" I asked, surprised.

"In less competent hands, it wouldn't have been that good."

Perhaps, perhaps not, but an accolade like that made up for other pleasures I might have had if I had been less dedicated to a job.

The last book I handled for Jim was *Iberia* in 1967 when I left the agency business. We are still in constant touch. It is a rare friendship with an unusual gentleman and a great human being.

PART
FOUR

C ALL me 'Red,' " said Robert Penn Warren. "My friends call me 'Red.' "

I was still in awe of the author of *All the King's Men*, a work which had grown in depth and dimension from an epic drama, *Proud Flesh*, written six years earlier. True, I am not one who presumes first-name familiarity at any rate, but I was still young to the business and no less reverent in the face of a towering talent than I am yet today. It was difficult not to continue addressing him as "Professor" Warren.

Warren was enjoying enormous critical and commercial success, but for this scholar, poet, philosopher, critic, teacher and man— whose roots burrowed deeply into his native Kentucky soil while his branches extended with compassion and cosmopolitan assurance toward the horizons of his America and the world beyond— sure and steady accomplishments had prepared him to accept and bear his celebrity with grace.

As if my enormous respect for him had not been a sufficient barrier, I had been further intimidated by the events leading up to this meeting.

I forget who recommended me to him, sometime in 1946, just as *All the King's Men* was being shipped to bookstores, but I remember that the initial call brought the first Mrs. Warren, Cinina, to my office to look me over and pass judgment or sentence.

She asked the obvious questions: what I could do for her husband and how much, and how much commission was charged, and how much Hollywood was offering for best sellers, and whether he could make the transition from scholarly quarterlies to the high-priced slick magazines without compromises—that sort of thing. Though the questions and answers were routine, her intense scrutiny of me was not. Clearly she was bright, but also as clearly, insecure, and we were not, it seemed, just discussing a simple business alliance. She was wielding the power of decision in the matter, but she carried it dangerously, with fearful unsteadiness. Her assessment would be wholly personal, focusing on me, not my reputation or my function.

At last she announced, "I think that I have nothing to be afraid of. You are the one woman I can trust Red with." I did not fully understand that remark for many years, didn't know whether it was a vote of confidence, compliment or curse, though I knew better than she that I could indeed be trusted with a client, married or not.

As with so many wives, the career of her husband, the isolating and introspective existence of the writer, was a challenge, a closed door beyond which her husband found fulfillment that she could never fully share. That, in truth, is the writer's ultimate mistress, but someone who can share those concerns, particularly if she is a woman, is always a threat, the accomplice, an imagined potential rival to any wife who is not secure within herself and who lacks a comparable fulfillment beyond a limiting role as *Mrs.* Writer.

Granted the grand housewife's seal of approval, I met Warren for lunch at Toots Shor's, found myself awed in the presence of that ever-so-*literary* knight, humbled and deferential. Robert Penn Warren is one of the most wonderful humans I have known in my life, and that luncheon provided me with insights which I was to carry and share with many another writer throughout my career.

I began to recite from my knowledge the list of his published novels. *Night Rider* in 1939, *At Heaven's Gate* in 1943 and, in that year of 1946, *All the King's Men*, for which he would be awarded the first of his two Pulitzer Prizes. Three novels.

"Eight! There were five novels before that," he corrected.

"What happened to the others, Professor Warren?"

"I learned from them. They weren't publishable. Call me 'Red.' My friends call me 'Red.' "

How many times, when working with a fresh young author discouraged by the rejection of his first pain-born volume or arrogantly refusing to shear a single lock from its empty towhead, I have recalled the example of Robert Penn Warren and the novels born of years of labor which he was willing to charge to his growth without the compulsion to inflict them upon a reading public. It takes an extraordinarily well-disciplined ego to pack one's creative offspring away and move on, informed by the experience.

He had returned for this meeting from the University of Minnesota, where he was teaching English literature. His fortunate students adored him and he was a great teacher in that particular field. He was somewhat reluctant, however, to give writing courses, a wise decision for a practicing author anyway.

Though he later taught many writing classes, he explained that he did not believe writing could be taught, that it was a talent, God-given or inborn. You either had it or you didn't. You might learn to be a better writer through the disciplines imposed in a class—simply by writing, by producing.

Though Warren was to remain a frustrated dramatist, he did head the drama department at Yale for a time and brought his inspiring gifts as a teacher to bear upon that assignment, before resuming his more important contributions to the riches of our literary legacy.

When he returned to Minnesota he sent me a longish short story, "The Circus in the Attic." I grew very excited once I had read it and promptly sent it to *Cosmopolitan*, which offered $5,000 to publish it. Before closing the sale, I grew oddly apprehensive. Warren, associated with Allen Tate, Caroline Gordon and the Kenyon school of criticism, had been respected as editor, essayist and a leader in that too convenient, heterogeneous grouping known as the New Criticism for over a decade in the pages of scholarly and prestigious little magazines. A Rhodes Scholar from Kentucky, who had attended Vanderbilt, he was associated with the Fugitive Group of poets in Nashville—Tate, John Crowe Ransom, Donald Davidson, Merrill Moore—and had encouraged the early publication of the best of a generation of new Southern-born authors in the pages of *The Southern Review*. *Cosmopolitan* seemed a big jump, but it was at that time a magazine which published writers such as Hemingway, and for no good reason except a certain ignorance of that circuit, I did not know if this commercial leap would sit well with Warren's peers, or with Warren himself.

I sent him a telegram, cautiously inquiring if it would be all right to sell his story to *Cosmo* for the $5,000. Warren, who had likely never been paid over $250 for a story, quickly responded that he had not known that such money existed for a short story. Having become a friend, he became a fan, and sent me many a promising fellow author and many a graduating student.

"The Circus in the Attic" became the title piece in a short-story collection which I sold to Harcourt Brace.

My next move was to switch him to a new publisher, and it proved to be a very productive realignment. His good friend Albert Erskine, born in Memphis, was an editor at Random House. Warren had not been happy with the treatment at his original publishing house, and we felt that Erskine would be more attuned to a fellow Southerner, would understand his temperament, style and background.

Warren always came to me with every project he planned. While there is often a danger that the writer can talk out his idea and lose it before it is committed to type, I never had that fear with Red. When he came to me I knew that he was already committed to the venture. He was merely keeping me informed and checking in for my approval.

At work, he proved to be as disorganized, as instinctive and emotional in his battles with theme and characters as Jim Michener and Gerold Frank were meticulously organized, pre-planned and researched. The books that emerged from this chaotic agony often rambled, but I think it was Eric Bentley who once said, in acknowledging the problem resulting from Warren's combination of informed critical and raw creative power, that he would rather have Warren's passion and romantic genius with its faults over the output of "a dozen petty perfectionists," Each work involved a protracted dredging of the soul and ruthless self-questioning. Many joined the unpublished novels in his trunk. A poem might be abandoned, to take focus years later.

Warren can be the epitome of the absent-minded professor, but if daily routines and technology fight him to a draw, they are merely the impediments beyond which his clearer visions of mankind project. As a very young man, he embraced the testimony of history, rejecting the fickle advances of fashion and Marxian intellectual vogues. If his first works appeared at a certain time and in a certain place, he was inevitably grouped in someone's convenient column, forcibly enrolled in the current school of thought or style. Yet he remained independent of those labels, ever an individual.

Though his intense affair with history continues and informs all that he thinks and believes and writes, though he was very early labeled a writer of "historical" novels, he did not and does not write them in the swashbuckling sense that Frank Yerby did.

Underlying the historical detail were always more urgent and topical themes and clearly universal concerns. In a very real sense, Robert Penn Warren finds in the past problems we have carried into the present, and by identifying them, would seek to inform a better and wiser future. That impetus, that regard for social justice, of course, may often be overlooked in the success and popularity of a work that was intended to reach the largest available readership, just as it may fail on its own terms in any given attempt. But at the heart of each of those sprawling chronicles is a deep human concern, together with the wisdom of the man who has always been anxious that we learn to appreciate our differences rather than simply try to eradicate them by assuming prescribed attitudes.

If Warren's novels began in a burst of energy and incubated in extended and often paralytic agony, he did know better than most how to let them go and stand in the public gaze, whatever their faults, once he was convinced that they were the best he could make of them at the time. He knew, too, that their life beyond their publication, once they had been sold for condensation or adaptation for the screen, was beyond his control, that a movie was the work and problem of other men, who would have to succeed or fail to their own credit or disgrace.

I sold Warren's *Band of Angels* to Warner Brothers for $200,000. They cast Yvonne De Carlo, Clark Gable and Sidney Poitier in it, overproduced it as if to recapture some of the Civil War splendor of *Gone With the Wind* with an older and weary Gable, and assigned it to Raoul Walsh, a veteran director of action programmers of the thirties and forties.

When the film was completed, a Warner representative called to ask if Mr. Warren would like to see it. I called him.

"Warner would like to know if you'd care to see *Band of Angels*. I hear that it's a disaster."

"No, thanks," Warren replied. "They paid me the money. The check was good. That's all I have any right to expect of them."

It is a rare author who can refrain from viewing the damage and revealing a bit of the flagellant within him.

I was always unashamed in my continuing admiration for Warren. He took me to a party once, where he introduced me to William Faulkner, for whom he had enormous respect. Warren walked off to greet some old friends, leaving me with Faulkner.

Finally I said to Faulkner, "Red Warren thinks that you are the greatest living novelist."

There was a very long and awkward pause, and then Faulkner nailed me with a penetrating glare and said, "And what do you think, Miss Strauss?" Fortunately, Warren rescued me in a hurry.

Warren's continuing success should have provided increasing security for his first wife, Cinina. Instead, his fame and the demands it made on him aggravated and amplified her insecurity and fears, which festered into a constant and crippling emotional malaise. The breakdown and the breakup were imminent.

Remarkably, her trust in me did not waver from that first commitment when we had met in my office before Warren signed with the agency. In fact, we had become quite close. When all other buttresses to her emotional well-being had collapsed and she was committed to the psychiatric division of New York Hospital in White Plains, her doctors thought that I might have some stabilizing influence over her and she was released into my custody.

However well-intentioned I might have been, it was a foolish and futile gesture on my part. I did not have the time the assignment called for, nor the special training and knowledge which should have been required to detect danger signals and guide and redirect a healthier course for her.

As a result, and since I had managed to take custody on the day that exhaustion and the season's imported virus were taking custody of me, the experience simply brought me down, leaving two terribly but differently infirm ladies trying to prop each other up.

Ultimately, Cinina's recovery required a break from the scene of her distress and a clear and lonely path toward recovery and independence. She and Red were divorced, and in time he took a second wife, Eleanor Clark, a writer who could share his life and accept its special demands without feeling threatened.

Warren's aspirations as a dramatist remained frustrated, but like many another client, he did have a brief infatuation with the idea of writing for the motion picture screen. Fortunately, it came early and he recovered.

Warren had known Max Shulman at the University of Minnesota and seeded a continuing friendship. Shulman had by then written *The Feather Merchants* and *Barefoot Boy with Cheek*, and Warren was visiting him in Westport one weekend when they were both between projects. With nothing better to do, they toyed with the idea of writing an original screen story, a period comedy about a middle-aged tycoon who learns that he is about to die and plans an extravagant burial party for himself. The comedy was scheduled to begin when he didn't die.

Shulman's agent, Harold Matson, proved to be shrewder than I, because he generously volunteered to let the Morris Agency represent the venture for the screen's newest comedy-writing team.

I was to carry their outline to Hollywood on my next trip. The publicity suddenly got out of hand. Louella Parsons and the lesser sibyls of the movieland press corps dispatched daily communiqués on my approach toward the dream capital's moat, clutching the hilarious offspring of the literary marriage of the decade to my bosom.

The work was known by two different titles in its daily heralds, *Pickle My Bones* and *Don't Bury Me at All.* Warner Brothers, Twentieth, Paramount and Metro all put in bids for immediate adoption. Unfortunately, they wanted to see the little nipper first, and it was my sorry task to expose it. I returned to Manhattan with the well-fingered manuscript in my valise, stillborn, by which time both vacationing authors had resumed their primary interests. Shulman's trip to Hollywood was delayed for a time, until he settled in for a long run with Dobie Gillis on television.

In an era in which people are labeled by the buttons they wear and the fashionable attitudes they pin on, Robert Penn Warren towers as a true liberal, one of open heart and mind. He has all of the social virtues and grace of his Southern heritage. His love of history might easily have served to document the expedient notion of maintaining traditions and resisting the perils of change, had that same history not strengthened his conviction that each man must be free to realize his destiny while understanding the forces which challenge him. Warren could have become a selectively informed and comfortably sequestered bigot, but he did not.

Removed by thousands of miles from his native soil, studying at Oxford, he had written an essay, included in the Southern Agrarian book *I'll Take My Stand* in 1930, which was an intellectual defense of segregation, based in large part upon the unlikely readiness of North, South, the courts and the Negro himself for integration in that year.

Back in America, and particularly when he was engaged in the more challenging soul-searching of writing the novelette *Prime Leaf*, he found not a rationalization for what was, but an insight into what justice dictates must be. *Prime Leaf*, not *I'll Take My Stand*, was the position paper from which he advanced.

Except for very special prepublication of John Hersey's *Hiroshima* in *The New Yorker* and Hemingway's *The Old Man and the Sea* in *Life*, agents had not made approaches to the major news weeklies with clients who were major novelists, "literary" figures. The beat was left to journalists, though many a novelist had spent years researching in areas of special interest and combined the novelist's descriptive prose and passion with his special knowledge as an informed reporter.

I did sell James Michener and Walter Lord to *Life*, but the fighting men in Korea of *The Bridges at Toko-Ri* and the recreation of the Pearl Harbor attack in *Day of Infamy*, which drew upon the magazine's research facilities, possessed a logic the newsmagazines could quickly grasp. And selling Robert Penn Warren to *Life* represented an even greater challenge to their imaginations.

More than that, in the spring of 1956, following the publication of *Band of Angels*, the year of Adlai Stevenson's second defeat, two years following the Supreme Court's landmark decision on school desegregation and several more before its implementation—in that year which ushered in four more cozy Eisenhower years before the shift in national tone marked by the inauguration of John F. Kennedy, Warren was placing himself in the forefront of a just-awakening new civil rights awareness, not yet "good copy" in a country still recoiling from Senator Joseph McCarthy's reign of terror and too comfortable to face speedily a reckoning too long overdue.

As a teacher, as a Southerner, Warren was finally assigned by Jay Gold of *Life* to return to the big cities and back country of the Deep South and border states to interview hundreds of citizens black and white, old and young, to try to determine the impact the Court's decision would have and the divisions and anxieties it would aggravate. It was a thorough and balanced piece of reporting that accurately gauged the whole range of attitudes soon to be challenged by change. It was published in *Life* in the summer of 1956 as "A Divided South Searches Its Soul." prior to its expanded hardcover publication as *Segregation: The Inner Conflict in the South.*

Warren returned nearly a decade later for a second nonfiction article about the civil rights issue—*Who Speaks for the Negro?*

What more is there to say, but that it was rewarding to have the continuing friendship of a man for whom I have such admiration and respect, a great human being; that I did my job well in his behalf, securing lucrative contracts and new outlets which allowed him to reach a larger audience and expose different facets of his talent and humanity; that he was fair and honest and loyal—and that it was good.

One evening in 1951, as I was getting ready for some event that seemed very important at the time, my telephone rang and the Los Angeles operator announced that Walter Wanger was calling long-distance. Wanger, his stature in the film industry intact, though his fortunes had taken a disastrous turn with the production of *Joan of Arc* and the desanctification through headlines of his star Ingrid Bergman, was suddenly in the headlines himself for a cavalier and wildly emotional act which toppled his well-buffed image as Hollywood's resident intellectual man of reason.

Assuming the chivalrous outrage of an earlier century's wounded aristocrat, he had waited in a Beverly Hills parking lot to surprise his wife, actress Joan Bennett, and the Hollywood agent he accused of alienating her affections. As they approached, Wanger took out a gun, took wild aim and shot the agent in the groin. Walter called it "poetic justice." The courts took a different view. Walter Wanger was going to jail.

He spoke hurriedly, running through a list of things he wanted me to do, to check out, to secure during his confinement. I raised no objections, though my tone may have been abrupt, as I had my own deadlines and was briefly annoyed by the presumption on my time. It seemed as if he were dictating a clean-up list to someone who was still running his New York office, an office closed out more than a decade before.

My mother, unnoticed until that moment, had followed my end of the conversation closely. She rose now and spoke firmly. "You are going to do whatever he asks."

She understood, as probably no one else ever did, how infatuated I had been with Wanger. He was the only man I met in business that I adored. Though he had initially been interested and that had been flattering, in my youthful fear and by my own rigidly imposed professional code, I had optioned for a longer-running deep personal friendship. I had learned much from and been inspired by him and enjoyed many opportunities born of his confidence in me.

My mother reminded me, although she really need not have done so, that he called in that hour because he knew he could trust me and that I would not let him down. I knew that I could not.

Ernest Lehman was working for Irving Hoffman when he entered my life. I was working in the story department at Paramount. He was weary of Broadway press agentry and anxious to write, and had decided to pursue a job with the movies. His father happened to know Adolph Zukor. Not surprisingly, by the process of elimination common to the studio system, the resulting referral was passed from office to office until, at last, Ernie arrived at my desk.

After he spread his credentials before me and we had traded exotic tales from the life and times of Irving Hoffman, I asked him what he really wanted to do.

"I want to *write*," he said, with that painful emphasis that distinguishes the young author.

"If you want to write," I cautioned, "you'd better not take the job that is available here, because you'll never write. Worse than that, in your frustration, you will come to resent and antagonize the writers it would be your job to help and encourage."

Lehman listened to my considered advice, fretted a bit, seemed to absorb it with obvious discomfort, then promptly went away, hating my guts.

He resurfaced several years later, after I became an agent. He had, indeed, begun to write while working as a copy editor on Wall Street, had secured an agent and been published in such magazines as *Esquire, Liberty, Good Housekeeping,* Street and Smith Publications, *Cosmopolitan* and *Collier's.*

Ernie can be lovable and maddening—probably one of the most neurotic clients I ever handled. Decisions are agony for him. The irony is that Ernie, a writer who needs tender and patient care and reassurance, should have risen eventually to the roles of producer and director, which require the most decisive postures.

When we met again, he wanted to leave his agent and join my roster at the William Morris Agency. Maybe. I did not push it and apparently he could not. It took him nearly two years to make up his mind, in pain and coquetry.

The decision made at last, he confessed that he was anxious to make his assault upon Hollywood. Perhaps *assault* is not the most appropriate word to use in association with Ernie. Though he was and remains a tight bundle of frayed nerve endings, eternally put upon, he had a sharp ear for dialogue and his stories were tough, peopled with swiftly yet sharply sketched characters in the sort of melodramatic situations that were the substance of some of the best movies.

One of his stories was bought by Republic and became the Allan Dwan film *The Inside Story.* Much later director John Frankenheimer staged his story "The Comedian," with Mickey Rooney, on the old *Playhouse 90,* and it created as much of a stir as a "guess who?" game as it did for its flashy techniques, production and performances. Lehman and Clifford Odets adapted Lehman's "Sweet Smell of Success" for a critically praised and publicly ignored 1957 film. Yet Ernie's stock in the movie business would build as an adapter of other men's works. I had initially thought of him in terms of original screenplays when I first tried to sell him to Hollywood.

The Morris Agency bought out the healthy Berg Allenberg Agency shortly after the outbreak of the Korean War. Among their prized clients was the writer-producer-director Joseph L. Mankiewicz, then at his very peak, with *A Letter to Three Wives* and the upcoming *All About Eve* and the premature yet powerful racial drama *No Way Out* following.

Mankiewicz was the particular pride of Bert Allenberg, head of the newly acquired agency. I had already scheduled a trip to Hollywood to meet with Allenberg, so I packed a folio of Lehman's work to take with me, hoping to excite Bert's interest in a talent I considered comparable.

Allenberg stood several inches over six feet, a bushy-headed man taller than any agent in town, and seemed all the taller to me, since Lastfogel, Lefkowitz and most of the men at the Morris office were slight and short men. I asked Allenberg whether he would try to sell Ernie Lehman to the studios. I told him that I was convinced that Ernie would make as much money and was ultimately more talented than Mankiewicz.

Allenberg reached down, placing his hand squarely atop my head and laughed for a full minute. "My dear country cousin, you don't know what you're talking about. Nobody, but nobody is going to buy Ernie Lehman!"

I burned under the pat of that patronizing palm. I bristled at the challenge. "Well then, you won't mind at all if I just go out and do it myself?"

He smiled benignly. "You *can't!*" He might as well have said, "Godspeed."

I returned to New York, went promptly to the New York offices of Paramount and negotiated a contract for Ernest Lehman. He was set to move to Hollywood and begin writing that string of original screen hits, or so it seemed at the time. Getting there wasn't going to be half the fun. It was no fun at all.

For one thing, Ernie was and is terrified of airplanes. The thought of "winging to tinseltown," as they say in the trade-paper travel columns, was enough to make him want to chuck the whole deal. If the conveyance inspired panic, it was aggravated by a sudden rush of fearful second thoughts, all the terror any established New Yorker can feel at the threat of being displaced, all the horror stories of fiction and fact about the West coast. The possibilities could unnerve any man, but they could send Ernie into a fit of hysteria. We settled for the train.

Even as the Twentieth Century pulled out of Manhattan, Ernie was calling my office. He still wasn't sure that he had made the right decision. He had started his ride down to the western slope, but sounded ready to jump off. He kept calling for reassurance until the train's telephones were finally disconnected and the state's suburbs began falling behind him.

When he arrived at Paramount, naturally they gave him another man's work to adapt. It had already been adapted by another hand or two, and, not surprisingly, it was due to be mauled by several other contractees when Lehman was pushed to other busy work.

Though he was to collaborate with Billy Wilder on the adaptation for *Sabrina*, Lehman's tenure at Paramount was not happy. It was not until he adapted *Executive Suite* for Robert Wise's successful MGM film that he became in fact the "hot property" I had kept predicting.

With the major exception of *North By Northwest*, an original script which inevitably must pay credit to director Alfred Hitchcock for at least a part of its conception and design, Lehman was to become known as the best bet to entrust with the adaptation of big-budgeted acquisitions from the stage and the top of the best-seller lists. Certainly his taste and his ability to reduce the essence of sprawling works from another medium are a credit to his talent, but those who understand screenwriting will also acknowledge that every screenplay is an original screenplay for all practical purposes, and to transpose beloved works without bruises is a harder task than it seems. *The King and I, West Side Story* and *Who's Afraid of Virginia Woolf?* pretty well typed Lehman, made him very rich and opened the doors to production and direction.

When I was safely out of the agency business and when studios were still throwing money about as if it were their own and not borrowed, I asked a major-studio executive just how they could manage and justify paying Ernie those truly astronomical fees for adaptations.

"Simple, my dear," the executive responded. "*Other* writers might change them, and that's not why we bought those properties. Ernie is worth the money and the percentage because he doesn't screw up the properties we buy."

Ernie and I have resumed our friendship after a number of years. I think the reason for our final estrangement was that when I heard he planned to adapt, produce and direct *Portnoy's Complaint*, I called to warn him of the folly of assuming too many hats and risking them all on a bad film gamble. I told him frankly that I thought he was a fool to do so. Unfortunately, he was a fool to do so, as only time would prove; and adding to the general failure of the film were the cruel accusations which smoldered for months in the press, accusing him of a tasteless anti-Semitic joke. Happily, Ernie and I survived my predictions.

While launching Ernie's career, I managed to get involved tangentially with Mr. Allenberg's best of breed, Joseph L. Mankiewicz.

To be an agent means that you will of necessity spend many of your days in court. Michener's kindly and agreeable nature and his almost pathological disinclination to offend sent us packing into courtrooms throughout our association, to extricate him from deals he would be bullied into by shrewder men who would not accept "no" from a man who could not say "no."

Lesser authors, stricken with simultaneous inspirations, are always there to be contended with. More often there are the disreputables who postdate similar ideas based upon the inspiration provided by your client's latest successes.

I kept records and maintained expert legal counsel and followed all the proper procedures relating to copyrights and registration, but more often my call to the courtroom dock succeeded by virtue of the very good memory with which I was blessed. Often enough I was able to present the proper defense weapons before a case ever had to come to trial. In fact, a judge once threw me out of his courtroom for remembering too much detail too well.

Joseph L. Mankiewicz had become a Morris client with the acquisition of the Berg Allenberg Agency. In October of 1954 his film *The Barefoot Contessa* had opened, and a woman immediately brought charges that Mankiewicz had plagiarized her idea for the film story.

We were all summoned to court and I was accused of having received the lady's manuscript and slipping it to Joe, who allegedly stole it for his own purposes. The suit came to trial and it was beginning to look very bad for all of us. In circumstances such as this, it often seems that one is guilty until he can prove his innocence, and since it seemed to us that there were no facts to substantiate the charge, it was just as difficult to challenge it. Sometimes you get so involved with the legal details, you overlook the obvious.

During a court recess I turned to the attorney and suddenly asked, "When did Joe come with the William Morris Agency?" He checked and gave me the date, which I don't remember now. But Joe had made the deal with United Artists through his own production company before the Morris Agency had acquired the Berg Allenberg clients.

"Well, what are we doing here, then?" I snapped. "This lady is claiming that I gave some manuscript to Joe before I ever knew him and after he'd already sold the picture." We were out of court and back to our respective jobs in no time flat.

It is a far stickier business when the agent has to become involved in a litigation which threatens to bring two different clients of the same agency into opposition in court. The likelihood is that everyone will lose, the agency most of all. Nonetheless, I precipitated just such a showdown.

Walter Lord, who had worked solo for nearly twenty-seven years researching the tragedy of the *Titanic* sinking for *A Night to Remember*, was swept into my office by the gust of success that detailed historical reportage brought him. He carried with him his love affair for research and Americana, and I remember that he was an upright foursquare citizen who contributed many thousands of hours to working with the Boy Scouts of America.

His sights were than aimed at an epic re-creation of the events leading up to and encompassing the Japanese attack at Pearl Harbor on December 7, 1941.

I thought if it took him twenty-seven years to investigate the sinking of a single luxury liner, what would it take for him to document the holocaust in the Pacific? The problem was to satisfy his insistence upon ferreting out every minute detail of the events while speeding the processing. *Life* magazine satisfied both requirements handsomely.

Life commissioned the project and made available its news bureaus and massive libraries with their readier access to eyewitness accounts. This accessibility made it possible for the researching of the book *Day of Infamy* to be completed in one year. Portions of the book, based upon interviews and questionnaire responses gathered by Lord and *Life* correspondents from 850 Americans living in Pearl Harbor at the time of the attack, were printed in the magazine prior to the 1957 publication by Holt, Rinehart and Winston.

Between scout troop meetings and retreats or whatever they call those things that drag fathers huffing into the wilds, Walter jumped back through four decades to document *The Good Years*, a panorama of the fads, follies and forward leaps of the years 1900–1914, the so-called good old days of innocence. His eyewitness approach to history then focused on the siege at the Alamo in *A Time to Stand*.

Making his own forward movement in the entertainment hierarchy in the late fifties, while Walter was doing his library work, was another client of the Morris office, producer David Wolper. David had entered television in the late forties as a salesman and distributor of Superman films. A decade later he cracked the TV networks' resistance to documentaries produced outside their own news departments. He had acquired enormous libraries of vintage stock footage which enabled him to produce an exciting and award-winning series of specials which matched their premium cost in high ratings. Naturally, his prolific production unit and its many seasonal television commitments brought in considerably more commissions than the office earned from Walter Lord's lengthy research projects.

Wolper's press agents suddenly announced that he would produce a television documentary on the Pearl Harbor attack. It would carry the title "The Day of Infamy."

Wolper had the footage, and certainly Walter Lord's valuable research as collected in *Day of Infamy* was historical fact, now made handily available to all. He had no exclusive claim to that dark day in history, but since Wolper had not purchased Lord's book, yet seemed to be capitalizing upon Walter's title and the book's succcess, many would assume that the Wolper special was in fact based upon the book. I took the position, in my client's best interest, that Wolper had stolen the title of Lord's book and would have to pay for that privilege. Wolper refused.

Lord and I then decided that we would bring an injunction against the broadcast of the documentary if Wolper did not pay for the rights he had assumed. The men at the Morris Agency, with a lot more to lose in the event Wolper exited than if Lord left unhappily, shrieked their outrage. I had not consulted Abe Lastfogel on my action, nor did I ever hear reaction or complaint from him concerning what I did, though I heard all of the rumblings in the halls. I held firm to what I knew to be right, ignoring pleas to settle for what was cool and expedient.

David Wolper finally paid and the show was broadcast on schedule. Wolper and Lord, while not laying the foundation for any intra-office friendship, both stayed with the agency. The television boys had popped a gross of Gelusil in vain.

Had I still been in the business when the popular television series *All in the Family* went on the air, I would very likely have brought similar legal action to protect the title—*All in the Family*—one of Edwin O'Connor's most successful books.

I met Gore Vidal when he was nineteen years old and had just had his first novel, *Williwaw*, published. He had begun writing it in longhand in pencil in a gray accounts ledger aboard a ship on which he served as a World War II naval warrant officer in the Aleutians, and completed it at a sunny Florida coast training camp. Glenway Westcott introduced the young author to me. I recognized in him an extraordinary talent and noted with some concern that it all came too easily for him, with a facility that could discourage the discipline such a talent required to be realized.

We knew each other for a long time before he finally sought representation by the agency, and when he made that approach, it was because he wanted to write for television. I routed him to the television department and then to the theater department for the plays that followed, and to the Hollywood office for the screen-writing assignments that resulted. The new books, alas, came later. To whatever degree I exercised any influence in guiding his career, it was always more on a personal than a professional level.

As a friend, I have known another Gore Vidal—not the waspish television talk-show guest, nor the personality commentator, nor the one who does patchwork footnotes and essay collections in the manner of his friend Norman Mailer and dedicates them to his celebrity friends "Joanne and Paul."

I am not sure if I could have imposed any more influence than I did, though I might have tried to discourage what I find to be the waste of a major talent. Gore was determined to be a Renaissance man in an age of specialization and in a time when the media can bleed a personality in a few seasons of late-night parlor repartee.

Gore was one of the young men at the forefront of television's possibly overpraised golden age. He was probably not the best in a medium that passes into the air in a single evening, and the best is very likely as disposable as the rest. He wrote two commercially successful and well-made plays, but Broadway is no better for them. At his best, he was a good journeyman screenwriter or adapter, though his film activities have involved some of the most ill-conceived stinkers to blemish the screens of empty theaters.

He has been an instant political analyst in an age in which every-one with access to a camera and air time makes the same claim. He has been a frustrated political candidate. He has been a social critic, offering his view of America—from the safe vantage of a table at a sidewalk café in Rome—to director Federico Fellini. He is the darling of the social-consciousness clique beside the swim-ming pools of Beverly Hills, by his presence bestowing credibility upon charlatans of concern. Talk-show hosts encourage him to stir freeze-dried controversy between commercials by loosing an acid tongue against the midget celebrities of the day. He is book re-viewer, film and theater critic, career and marriage counselor, Pied Piper, court jester—and society's centerpiece.

His popular success *Myra Breckinridge* remains a facile, mastur-batory and cruel sex joke with which he amused himself for a few moments while squandering his time and talents. Briefly, that book afforded him the title of film producer, and there is no shame in his failure at that guise.

In none of these roles, or poses, does he reveal the depth, the gentleness and sensitivity of the Gore Vidal I have known. Only once, maybe once again, since I have known him did he invest the time and the discipline in his work that his talent demands, and approach the greatness he might have as a major novelist.

With some interruptions for plays and movies and clashes on the lecture circuit, Gore devoted almost a decade of research and hard work to his novel on the fourth-century philosopher-king Julian. He read Julian's letters and essays, read about his contemporaries, the epoch, the places, the concerns. He read what Julian read, assumed his eyes and ears and senses before he ever began to write. With the possible exception of the earliest books, in which circumstance imposed some isolation, *Julian* was the one book to totally absorb Gore's vision and ability.

Gore's book on Aaron Burr, from whom he happens to be descended, also reflects some seven or eight years of preparation. Perhaps, at last, Gore has tired of being the writer-personality at the podium, publishing his transcripts, and resumed his place as the lonely figure behind the printed word.

But then *Julian* was followed by *Washington, D.C.*, and we had a great disagreement over it. I admonished him for his frivolous course in settling for a place as a transient personality and tour guide rather than as a full-time writer. Though he can argue the point, the novel is not dead so long as he can write them as well as he can.

The one really valuable contribution that I was able to make to Gore's career involved making available his body of work. I made new publishing contracts for all of his early novels and the short-story collection *A Thirsty Evil*, allowing him to surface an underground reputation and reach the readership the books had been denied in their initial printings. The continuous printing of those works in subsequent popularly priced paperback editions has made possible a continuing discovery of Vidal on campuses by young people who would otherwise know him only as the attractively middle-aged bitch-kitty of conversation video or as a somewhat aristocratic alternative to Mort Sahl.

That latter, glib public image of Vidal has very little to do with the private man I know, a man of uncommon sensitivity and understanding who is both responsive to a need and gifted in directing his attention to it.

We carry with us long, delaying fuses which detonate reactions separated by many years from their source. My mother had died of cancer, but having been ill in childhood and survived with a sturdy constitution, I have had little to do with doctors, simply refusing to sit still for a virus or a sniffle, taking no more medication than an aspirin or a spoonful of milk of magnesia and only when some minimum balm seemed absolutely necessary.

Then, nearly seven years after my mother's death and brought about more than anything else by fatigue, I became ill. More than that, I became convinced that I had cancer, that the malignancy which had killed her was now visiting me. I grew obsessively cancerphobic, finally submitting to tests which I was sure would only substantiate, not relieve, my fears. The fear itself became the far more debilitating disease, and I was almost ready to resign myself to a verdict that had not yet been brought in and would not be.

Throughout that frightened period, no one was more concerned or more attentive than Gore, no one more willing to expose that sentimental corner of himself. He called regularly for reports not only on my condition and the tests but on my spirits as well, and with each call he managed to lift those spirits considerably. He sent flowers and sweet notes and speeded the time until fear again gave way to reason.

From the time of the publication of *Washington, D.C.*, I grew more discouraged by the course of Gore's career, and it was always in proportion to the stature of the talent he was playing with.

I suppose one can justify trying to be a popular spokesman-personality, to use the media to generate controversy and stimulate thought on pressing issues, but I don't believe that Gore is succeeding even in that role. Those mix-and-match panels and "great debates," with their interchangeable guest appearances by Bill Buckley, Norman Mailer, Jimmy Baldwin or Steve Allen, only excite the initiated claques and have become as predictable as the snob's equivalent of the wrestling matches.

When Gore or any man of his knowledge and background makes an appearance on a segment of a talk show, his social and political comments, however audacious, carry the same weight and supply just about the same fleeting entertainment programming content as the visiting movie star tittering about his bowel movements, the starlet supplying straight lines for labored jokes about her breasts or the woman from South Dakota who insists that her dog can sing "America the Beautiful." Since Gore is indisputably a true intellectual, I wonder why he should settle for playing that role for the applause of inferior if glamorous poseurs.

I took a very active interest in one screenwriting assignment that was proposed to Gore. The British film director John Schlesinger and producer Jerome Hellman were almost alone for many years in their conviction that James Leo Herlihy's book *Midnight Cowboy* could be brought to the screen. Their steadfastness and confidence extended to the conviction that Gore could and should be entrusted with the screen adaptation.

I sat in on a number of meetings they held, John describing his conception of the film, how the sensitive material could be handled acceptably, what the essence of the story would be. I thought they would surely capture Gore's imagination and challenge him to a really important piece of work for the screen, if he did in fact wish to continue film assignments.

But Gore surprised me. Again and again he broke his silence to shake his head and mutter, "No, no. It just won't work as a movie."

After a long courtship, Gore turned down *Midnight Cowboy* and wrote an awful Broadway play instead. John and Jerry continued their fight and finally made the film, which won Academy Awards for best picture and direction and for Waldo Salt's screenplay. Gore's ideas about what could work on the screen were about to change radically.

I was getting ready to leave the agency business and accept my empty executive title with Warner Brothers when Gore hurriedly completed a new manuscript. He did not seem too anxious for me to read it, though we necessarily had to submit it to Little, Brown, with whom he had his contract.

"Don't read it," he cautioned. "You'll hate it. I don't even want my name on it." The best he would predict was that it might make a very funny, quick paperback book.

Whatever other reservations Little, Brown's editors may have had about the book, whatever other aroma it emitted, they caught the scent of a best seller. To ensure that result regardless of the aesthetic cost, they finally persuaded Gore to let them keep his name on the book, *Myra Breckinridge*.

I reported to Warner, and decided that I should have a copy of the manuscript so that I would have the book covered in case anyone wanted to know what it was about or if it had potential for the screen. I had a synopsis made. Because I was certain that no one at Warner was interested in it, I called my own friend David Brown, then vice-president of Twentieth Century–Fox and extended to him the courtesy of covering the book as well.

Even as I made the gesture, I warned him that nobody would ever make a film of it anyway. David had the book read, then called me to say, "You're absolutely right. Nobody!"

In the meantime, I had received a call from Gore in Rome, asking me to tell him whatever I knew about a young director named Bud Yorkin, whom he had met in Italy. Yorkin was the partner of producer-writer Norman Lear and they had made a well-received film titled *Divorce, American Style* before their company brought *All in the Family, Maude* and *Sanford and Son* to televison. While I had great respect for Norman Lear, I really didn't know much about Yorkin, though I figured that Gore's call indicated that he had more information about Yorkin's immediate plans than I.

"He wants to do *Myra Breckinridge* with me," said the voice on the transatlantic line. I remember kidding Gore about becoming a film producer and trying to unsort his book into some kind of intelligible screenplay. I was kidding. He was serious.

He came to Hollywood to announce his plans to the press. He told them that he would co-produce this epic and write the screenplay. He charmed them out of any doubts, and they believed him, too.

Another of the final deals that I had handled as an agent was selling Broadway producer Robert Fryer to Twentieth Centu-

ry-Fox. He was already set to produce *The Boston Strangler*, Gerold Frank's book, and *The Prime of Miss Jean Brodie*. And his
third film?

Bobby came to me one day with an odd smile on his face.
"Helen, I'm going to do *Myra Breckinridge* next."

"You're crazy, Bobby. Who wants you to do it?"

"Dick Zanuck and David Brown."

"You're out of your mind, " I said, but he did it, and though the
outcome—*any* outcome—was often in doubt, he was one of the
few left standing and on speaking terms with most of the others
when that bizarre production was concluded. It was the beginning
of the end for the reign of the younger Zanuck and Brown at
Twentieth.

One night during the fallout Gore and I were on our way to
dinner at "Joanne and Paul's" when we ran into David Brown, and
I found myself trapped in a storm of accusation and recrimination.
Never have so many fallen out of favor with so many over so little.

I had moved on to Universal when Gore sent me the manuscript
of his next novel, *Two Sisters*. He asked that I comment only upon
its potential for films. I was relieved not to have to comment on its
other merits, simply reporting that it had little chance for a film
sale.

In putting together this book, with so few letters or clippings or
records to draw upon, I am continually struck by the fact that what
I remember, what all of us instinctively tend to remember about
the past, are the uncompleted and disappointing experiences, the
problem areas, the lawsuits, the noisemakers, the ones who made
waves.

For example, it seems unfair that the most important single
impression I leave about Gore Vidal is my annoyance at the diffu-
sion of a major talent. That may have been the prevailing disappointment, but the relationship itself was one of the happiest and
warmest. Things went smoothly, as they did with others, but what
can you say about the happy routine? Michener involved me in
happy deals which are noteworthy because of the complexity of
the sales or their record amounts, but I can't truly convey the

simple joy of my long friendship with Jim, and how many times could I say of him and other favorite clients that they were reliable, good friends who made the job seem easy.

I remember turning Gore Vidal over to the television department because I preferred to concentrate on the printed word and kept waiting for him to write that great and important novel that I felt he had in him. But I can't summon the details involving David Karp, a Guggenheim fellow whom I did represent for a number of television deals at a much later date. David has gone on to be a very successful Hollywood writer and an important functionary in the Writers Guild, with side excursions into slick novels. He does what he does well, so that's not a notable waste of talent, nor are the achievements chiseled in marble. David's Mystery Writers of America Award will be around longer than the television show he received it for.

I remember Hans Koningsberger and his novel *A Walk with Love and Death* only because he seemed to demand more attention than his output or personality merited.

Professor Karl Friedrich came down from Harvard in 1949 to see if I was suitable to handle his young son, Otto Friedrich, who had come to me through Jimmy Baldwin, whom he had met in Paris. Otto had sent me several novels, which he had been turning out at a rate of one every three months. He was twenty, and claimed to have written another book in three days and one in one day.

On the strength of my praise for him, Emmett Hughes, then the articles editor of *Life*, gave Otto a $600 advance for an article on Santayana. Simultaneously, he got a contract for a novel, *The Poor in Spirit*, from Little, Brown. The $600 paid for his honeymoon. *Life* rejected the article. The novel died, and by his own admission Otto wasted the next ten years of his life writing literary criticism, "and so we sort of drifted apart during the mid-fifties."

Later he wrote for *Harper's* and was managing editor of *The Saturday Evening Post* when it shuttered. That experience served him in writing *Decline and Fall*, the story of the Curtis publishing empire, which was followed by a book on Berlin in the twenties, neither of them successful.

He seems to have written all of his novels during that wildly prolific twentieth year, then settling for twenty solid years as a journalist and editor, accumulating five children along the way. I remember him as one of the most buoyant and likable of the young men who bounded through my door.

Most of all, Paul Bowles eludes me now. There were no crises, no traumas, no unmanageable successes or spectacular ones. I could not begin to re-create the many dinners we had which involved pleasant but remote and weird conversations about the absolute and mystic forms of religion. We were friends. It was an odd friendship, never touched by the apocalyptic visions which surfaced in Paul's exotic novels.

When I met him he was a New York music critic and a fine composer who had already written music for the stage. He had also written some short stories published in small literary magazines. I encouraged him to write a novel and he finally delivered *The Sheltering Sky* to me. I continued to handle all of his works, via Tangiers and Ceylon, until I left the business. He was one of the least troublesome, most gentlemanly clients I had, really a nice man. Despite our friendship, he always addressed me as "Miss Strauss."

Leon Edel was one of my most prestigious authors, the recipient of a National Book Award and the Pulitzer Prize, and I can comment upon him best in the context of answering a question which has occasionally been asked: "Who was your easiest client?" Not only was Edel the easiest, but in many ways he really didn't need me at all.

A distinguished literary scholar and biographer, Dr. Edel knew his way through that rarefied world of research grants and fellowships and academic funding. He was no hungry young author desperate for a modest advance to complete his work. And in his province he was the expert, more likely to give than to seek counsel. His biographical pursuit of Henry James, originally estimated as a three-year undertaking, grew and grew until it consumed twenty years of meticulous research and literary detective work, resulting in five volumes. He was recently selected editor of the diaries and journals of the late Edmund Wilson.

I simply secured improved contracts for the publication of his books, got him better deals than he might have had without me.

He was satisfied that I did. I was proud to represent him, and it couldn't have been easier.

I have been picking up restaurant tabs and taxi bills all my life. It doesn't bother me. It is a part of my job that I have managed to handle as discreetly as possible, forestalling any possibility of embarrassment to the chivalrous males with whom one sometimes deals in business. If there is any surprise to be had, it is in the large number of men who can hitchhike on any available expense account with a brazen incapacity for the barest twinge of embarrassment. Quite apart from feeling that they are leaving a lady to dole out the change, many have simply looked upon me as the closest available representative of some monster corporation with a bottomless kitty for subsidizing promoters.

During one of my scouting missions for a possible package deal for Broadway, I remember going to lunch with the director Josh Logan, his attorney, his business adviser, the treasurer of the William Morris Agency and a few rhinoceros birds. In effect, we were discussing the possibility of putting together a production which would eventually keep the hangers-on in feed. As the last cappuccino was being slurped and each little echo was congratulating the other on his genius at the conception, the check arrived. Over the undulating waves of hands in relay, the bill made a full, record-speed circle of the table and seemed to slide its way unaided under my last remaining spoon. It was such an agile loop that I fully expected my assembled basketball team of escorts to stand up and cheer.

Many years before, I took the president and chairman of the board of Harper to lunch at the old Ritz. When the check came I picked it up, naturally. I was startled by a sudden gasp from the next table. Seated there were an elderly lady and her husband. She had the sort of startled expression that was usually accompanied by the dropping of pince-nez into the soup in old movie comedies. She averted her eyes and clucked to her mate, "That woman's picked up the check!"

I thought in that moment that when we exited I'd whisper under my breath, "Expense account, you know."

When the moment came, however, I was seized by wickedness. Allowing the gentlemen to clear their table, I turned, winked at her and chortled, "Sure, they keep me broke, but oh, Lord— they're worth every dollar!"

Irving Stone, the biographer of the safely interred, called one day to invite me to lunch. We went to Toots Shor's. It was a familiar story. He was unhappy with his agent and was scouting a replacement. He wanted to know what I thought I could do for him. I answered his questions, though I didn't need another client and felt that I was wasting valuable time, but it was a pleasant enough luncheon. When the date he initiated was over, he pushed the check toward me, smiled and said, "The Morris Agency has more money than I have." Not at that rate.

I was riding in a taxi with the flamboyant showman Mike Todd, discussing deals that carried verbal price tags in paltry increments of hundred thousands and millions, when he suddenly ordered the driver to stop. "I'll get out here. You pay the man. The Morris men have more money than I do!"

More recently, when I had begun working for the *Reader's Digest*, my old client Ramona Stewart had a book out, *The Possession of Joel Delaney*. A producer who had been with the Morris Agency was searching for a property to produce at MGM. I thought I'd do him a favor, so I sent him my advance copy of Ramona's book.

He called the next day. "You were right. It's a great story. Listen, I'm having lunch today with the story editor, Russ Thacher. May I tell him that you liked it? It should help."

I replied, "Certainly! But I'll go further than that. I happen to be having lunch with Jim Aubrey [then the studio's production chief]. I'll tell him that I liked it."

I did as I had promised and the producer got a deal to make the film at Metro. Because it seemed that the agent for the book might jeopardize the sale, I voluntarily handled the deal for him with Ramona. Then I suggested a number of writers who could handle the adaptation at the price he could afford.

To celebrate, the happy producer invited me to lunch at the Beverly Hills Hotel. His wife joined us. Immediately, he clapped his hands and said, "Well, let's celebrate with champagne!"

I demurred. "I don't want any champagne, but you two go ahead."

He insisted that I should accept some sort of finder's fee for my role in his good fortunes.

"No, no, no," I objected. "I've been doing this all my life. If I can be of help, fine. I never take anything."

"I *insist!*" he argued. "You *must* get something."

"I've never taken anything," I responded, "though I have to admit that I've done a yeoman's amount of service on this one."

"Absolutely! You *have* to get something. I'll take care of the arrangements."

Would it surprise you to learn that he never did? It didn't surprise me. I might have felt less a fool if at some point he had even sent flowers and a handwritten thank-you note, but he never did that either. Still, you'd never do anything for anyone if you held out for thank-yous, and there is satisfaction to be had in just helping things happen, then tolerating the grandiose promises and not getting bitter about the schnorrers one helps along the way.

Nonetheless, the happy luncheon, awash in good champagne, reached its climax in a rush of rash promises and gush. That was followed by the bill.

"Darling," he whispered, "won't you put this on your expense account?"

He handed me the bill. It certainly was no business of my employer's, so I paid it myself. The man is still my friend, a technicality which causes closer friends to crown me a fool, but it is the sort of thing one gets very used to in Hollywood, where everyone still manages to eat well.

As an experienced check-plucker, I'm still in no position to make any scientific generalizations, but I have a few observations of some coincidental interest. For some reason, the Irish Catholics I knew almost never passed the tab. Edwin O'Connor never allowed me to pay a bill. I had dinner with Steve Allen and Jayne Meadows one night. I think I handled one of his early books, though I'm not even sure of that now. I do remember that it was a very pleasant evening and a fine dinner and that I had the rare honor of being treated like the honored guest. Never had a chance to sign a thing.

• • •

Shortly before Christmas, 1953, I was at the home of Edna Ferber, in a meeting concerning the musical adaptation of *Saratoga Trunk*, when I was abruptly called away with the news that my father had suffered a serious fall. I arrived home just in time to join him in the ambulance on the ride to the hospital. He had broken his hip. I was frantic. As I feared, like many his age, he did not mend. He did not get up again. Incapacitated, his aged body began to short-circuit, sector by sector, just slowly burning out. In a sense, it was an acceleration of a process which had begun a few years earlier, when he retired and surrendered so many of his interests in life.

He was hospitalized for three and a half years, and thus began the long vigil that ended with the loss of both my mother and father.

It was very difficult when my father was hospitalized, but my mother was still active and sharp-witted and we shared the burden and responsibility. Her strength was remarkable, and through it all she lost none of her hauteur and sass.

I remember that we were walking through the lobby of our apartment building on East 66th one hot summer day in 1955, when we were accosted by a woman who lived in the building and had often tried to strike up conversations with my mother. Until then my mother had managed to avoid her, but we were trapped this time.

"Oh, Mrs. Strauss," the woman whispered, eying my mother's outfit and moving her face closer and closer, "you must be very, very rich."

"Oh?" my mother snapped, doubling her stride toward the door. "Have you been counting my money?"

By summer's end my mother's strength began to decline rapidly. She entered the hospital for tests. The diagnosis was cancer. It was her last summer, and I was at her side nearly every waking moment until she died. I wanted to be and I needed to be, but she literally demanded it as well. She had seen me into the world and nursed me through lengthy illness to prepare me for life. Now I was to prepare her for death and summon all of my strength to meet her increasing claims on me. She would not and could not go gentle into that good night.

By this time my staff had grown in proportion to my list of clients. At the peak, I had 130 clients and thirteen employees. Though I continued to devote my full energies to the main core of that list, those who worked with me were able to assume greater responsibility, relieving me of much detail and busy work.

Additionally, after I had been in the business for a while and had met the players and knew their names and built my reputation so I no longer had to waste time in cocktail and dinner courtship games to get a fast, honest answer, I stopped attending those endless literary cocktail parties and publishing functions. Instead, I'd send those members of my staff that I was pushing. They would keep me posted on what was going on out there, if anything, and generally pay my respects, leaving me to attend specifically to my writers and their deals.

During that three and a half years I relied more and more on my staff, and how they did comfort me!

Most of them had started in the business with me. I take some pride in having chosen them well, and they learned with me. Lisel Eisenheimer was one, and I used to drive her mad by calling her "Eisenhower." She was and remains very devoted to me, and throughout the years she worked with me, she treated me like a star. Today she is one of the editors at *McCall's.*

Arlene Friedman came to me straight out of school, still moist from delivery out of Katherine Gibbs, brash and bright and attractive. She is currently editor of soft-cover books for Fawcett Publications.

I could be a terrible boss. I didn't care how long a job took, so long as it was completed. I didn't care if anyone took time off if she wanted to, so long as her work was finished. And, of course, I was always a stickler for keeping appointments on time, returning calls and answering correspondence promptly. But so long as the work was done, it could be a pretty loose shop.

In turn, I let them criticize me freely. I always let everyone who worked for me do that. They learned to spot the cues when I was entering or exiting a stormy romance. And they kidded me about the day that I chased a pompous Hungarian author through the halls and into the elevator because he had dared to question the ethics of the Morris Agency.

They were marvelous, and because they were, I had terrible fights with Nat Lefkowitz every year at bonus time. I'd storm into his office and scream for more money for all of them. He would finally relent, grumbling, "Well, it's coming out of your hide!" My answer was always the same. "Without them, I couldn't do the job anyway."

Jane Wilson was bright and beautiful and charming, and I'm sure she enjoyed her work. She would report to me faithfully after every swing on the cocktail-party circuit. At one party, I remember, she had met Richard Whelan, who wrote the Joe Kennedy book *The Founding Father.* They talked at considerable length about what he was writing. Later, I asked her if she had thought to ask him what he was going to do about it, only to learn that it hadn't occurred to her to ask.

Whelan was then working for *Fortune* magazine, and I suggested that it might be a wise move to call to follow up their conversation and inquire about his plans for representation. She placed the call, raised the subject, and Whelan responded, "I was just waiting for you to ask me."

We took over the representation of the book, and she had learned in the process that writers are shy creatures who have to be courted before they will do what they want you to want them to do.

It was something of a breakthrough when I added a lone male to my department. He was Herman Gollob. He had come from Texas to Hollywood, taking a job as a trainee in the mail room at MCA. He wanted desperately to work in the literary department there and he quickly grew impatient.

His opportunity came one evening when he was asked to drive Jules Stein's daughter Jean home. On the ride home she asked idly what he did, and he told her of his interest—and frustration—in taking a spot in the literary division.

Largely through her intercession, he was routed to the literary department. Once there, he found that the emphasis on movies and television in a Hollywood-based office wasn't what he wanted at all. Publishing was his interest and he wanted to be at the center of it in New York.

He went to Elliott Kastner, then an agent and soon to establish himself as a film producer, and told him that he wanted to work in New York and he wanted to work for me. He asked Elliott if he could suggest any way of getting to me. Elliott explained that he did not know me well, but suggested that Herman shouldn't waste time looking for a side door, but should simply write to me straightaway and see what would happen.

Herman took his advice to heart and I received a very amusing letter, which stated bluntly, in effect: "I want to come to New York and I want to work for you, so what do I do about it?"

I wrote back explaining that there was no job, but should he ever be in New York, I would be happy to see him. Who was that knocking at my door? He had arrived in New York.

As he walked into my office, it was one of those instantaneous things. I knew that I was going to like him and that he was going to like me. We got on famously. Everyone at the Morris Agency had teased me for some time about getting a man in my department, kidding me about running a segregated shop. Maybe this was the time to test their sympathies on minority hiring.

I asked Herman how much salary he would need and he named some outrageously low figure. "Honeybunch," I said, "nobody asks for a salary that low. You need an agent."

I set out for Nat Lefkowitz's office to sell Herman. He got the job and the right price. I got a valuable assistant. He should not have been satisfied with that, and he wasn't. He became convinced that he was still on the wrong side of the business. He began announcing at regular intervals to all who might hear and believe, "I'm going to be the greatest editor of all time."

In a couple of years he had learned much and was ready to change sides. I got him a job at Little, Brown. He proved to be a fine editor and was very influential in launching the careers of James Clavell and Donald Barthelme, who dedicated *Unspeakable Practices, Unnatural Acts* to him. Herman moved to Atheneum, then to Harper, returning again to Atheneum as editor in chief.

My salvation during that difficult period of my parents' hospitalization was Louann Cleghorn. She had worked for the Kanins before coming to work for me, and she was with me for a dozen years, first as my secretary, later as an assistant agent.

She met the planes and handled the details and took care of me with a loyalty and efficiency that are increasingly rare. I particularly would not have made it through the year of my mother's illness without her.

My mother demanded increasing attention and I had to be with her most days from early morning through dinner. Lou, who had come to know Mother very well, would join me at the hospital with the mail, messages, manuscripts and paper work, and I would go over everything with her. The hospital room became my outpost office through which all the work filtered normally, thanks to her.

She used to say that I had three distinct personalities: one for my family, one for those on my staff, and the act she thought I put on for the outside world.

During those long hours, doing work with Louann and standing vigil in the hospital, I began smoking to settle the nerves. Until then, I had only taken a cigarette occasionally. More for the hands than the throat, I grew incendiary. To this day I am one of the champion cigarette burners in the business. To my advantage, I do more lighting than smoking, sometimes having two or three cigarettes burning at once. I have managed never to smoke when I drive, but that is the only time I am safe.

I'll never forget the time I returned to the office from the hairdresser's en route to the airport for a trip to London on business. I had been at my desk for only a matter of minutes when my driver arrived. My secretary stopped him. "She'll be with you in a moment," she told him. "She's set fire to her hair again."

Those who knew me, and thus knew the relationship that existed between my mother and me, were startled that I did not cry when she died. Few would ever understand why. Very simply, I had nothing to cry about.

When most people cry on the death of a loved one, their tears are aggravated by guilt or regret at things left unsaid or responsibilities not met during the life of the departed. While death itself is final, the tears relate to all that remains and will ever remain incomplete, unsaid, undone.

My mother's final gesture was to liberate me. Though she was failing rapidly, she chose her moment and her words wisely and well. She looked up and turned to me suddenly in her hospital room. She took my hand and said that I could not have been a better daughter to her. Slowly, she then apologized for having been extremely selfish and possessive with me. We understood and accepted each other, without anger or regret, and we loved each other still.

She lapsed into a coma and died on February 29 in that leap year of 1956.

Among the messages I received in the days that followed was one dated March 12, 1956. It read:

Dear Helen Strauss:

It is only within the past few days that I've had the news of your loss. Perhaps I can understand something at least of your feeling. Your experience is so much like mine of five years ago.

It just happens that I saw you stand up magnificently under a terrific shock a few years ago. Your behaviour then makes me feel sure that you will have the fortitude to face, and triumph over, this new blow.

Yours,
Edna Ferber

My father lived until Flag Day, 1957. Although he had lost most of his faculties, I finally realized in the absence of my mother and with the perspective those months gave to me, just how much he had loved me.

My parents had been a long time dying, and while I was able to maintain my level of work, I had been effectively isolated socially and emotionally by the long watch. So it was that when they were both gone, I felt completely alone for the first time in my life. Now there was no one.

For the first time in my life—and the last—I couldn't keep appointments. I'd wake up in the morning not wanting to get out of bed, not wanting to leave the apartment, enervated by a succession of psychosomatic maladies. I couldn't face anything. I didn't want to. My doctor, who was used to long periods of neglect by me and no more than my reluctant cooperation on a minimum number of checkups, saw no need for nonsense now. As I flaunted my sniffles and vapors, he offered no hand-holding, but told me candidly that there was nothing physically wrong with me. I knew it, of course.

It was a traumatic period also for those who cared about me. Some clients became very paternal, perhaps too much so, since I didn't need to be humored. Finally, one of my bolder friends suggested that I see a psychiatrist. I responded that I would not consider it, but he had a friend, Dr. Phillip Mersky, professor of psychiatry at the University of Pittsburgh, and he prevailed upon Mersky to call me.

After we had spoken for a time, Dr. Mersky interrupted to say, "Now, I don't know you very well, but I know you well enough to know that once you started seeing a psychiatrist, you would soon be telling him what to do, rather than him telling you. You've got to get out of this yourself, and I think you know how to do it."

So I did. Every time I thought no, I can't keep that appointment, or no, I can't go to work today, I'd mentally grab myself by the shoulders and shake hard, submitting to a long introspective talk, challenging myself not to ruin, to throw away, everything that I had worked so long and hard to achieve, in a few moments of panic and indecision. I bullied myself out of what might have been a protracted and permanently damaging period of self-absorption and mourning. I sought in myself the strength that was always there, the strength that had been invested in me as a living memorial to my parents. I stood up again and got back to business. I can't kid myself. I am still adjusting to that loss. The influences remain even though their presence, which was so long a buttress to my life, is no longer there.

I never did take time for psychoanalysis, which seems to me no more than the extended approach to trying to find in yourself the strengths to carry your weaknesses.

I've known some psychiatrists who were crazier than any of their patients. I had a good friend in Beverly Hills who was a psychiatrist. Under the pressure of many demands for business decisions and the trickier need for personal ones, at the end of a long and tiring day I'd occasionally talk with him on the phone and announce suddenly, "I'm crazy. I have such a terrible time making decisions when they are personal."

He usually laughed and answered, "I don't know anyone who is more sane than you."

In my early years with the agency, my contact with Abe Lastfogel was limited not merely by the fact that he had granted me autonomy to run a separate and independent department. When I arrived, he was still very actively involved producing camp shows for the USO and staging Armed Services benefits. His home base was Los Angeles. Mine was New York. We met in transit or at the summit of crisis. For the most part, he had higher-priority crises elsewhere. He not only left me free to govern an extraterritorial island within the organization, but warned its sharks not to meddle near my shores. Nor did he often intrude.

It was after the death of my parents that Abe and his remarkable wife, the former Frances Arms, assumed a greater role in my life, and a very close role. There were many people who were of the opinion that Abe and Frances seemed to have taken the place of my parents in my life. Certainly it was more than a warm business alliance, but I believe that the growth of that relationship was no more than the inevitable blossoming of continued mutual respect and the somewhat longer process of getting to really know each other.

Abe is a man small only in physical stature. His quick mind, imagination, dignity and integrity, his lack of pretense, his uncommon gift for decision making commanded respect and had logically carried him to preeminence in his field. His fairness with me, and his confidence, inspired special trust. Ultimately it was Frances who helped me to know him better and be more responsive to him. In the process, I learned some things about myself and inherited a bit of his humility in accomplishments.

One evening after Frances and I had dinner and were walking along Broadway, savoring the crisp evening breeze, she remarked unexpectedly, with the candor that was her trademark, "You know, you're the only one at the Morris Agency who doesn't really

need the agency. You can always make a living, whatever you do."
It was not calculated to buoy my self-confidence, though it did.

We walked another block. "He may not ask," she began, "but
tell Abe what you're doing. You have to tell him once in a while."
I had appreciated and enjoyed the freedom. Frances was reminding me of one of the bills that I had not picked up.

Frances, who had been a vaudeville star on the Keith's circuit,
was a down-to-earth and thoroughly honest woman who has shared
Abe these many years with his Morris family. Throughout that
time they maintained a lifestyle so modest as to border on rebellion in a town as status-conscious as Hollywood. For forty years
they lived in a comfortable complex of rooms at the Beverly Wilshire Hotel, driving the same car year after year and accumulating
few of the expensive trophies that clutter the homes and lives of
their contemporaries. I suspect that was the influence of Frances,
who lived out of a trunk long enough to know that the things of
greatest value don't have to be packed or stored. They collected
good will instead, generously responding to numerous charitable
causes. Frances died a few years ago, and with her passing, I lost a
very good friend.

Of course I've liked a lot of married men but I've never for a
moment desired to be a home wrecker, nor have I ever been one.
I've never been involved in a scandal, and much to the chagrin of
some jealous wives of business associates, have never been involved
with a man with whom I had to deal in business. If the man tried
to kid me or himself with promises neither of us wished to keep, I
either discouraged that promptly or made a swift and graceful exit.

Sure, I've known a few publishers who have come on like Cos-
sacks. Producers have pinched. Authors have occasionally tried to
break the house rules, but if they failed to realize that—in that
regard—every hour with them was a business hour, I knew it and
was never about to forget it. If some authors' wives had realized
that at the outset, life would have been a lot easier. No such luck.
Some of them could be a pain.

Women like Betty Smith and Edna Ferber liked me *in spite of*
the fact that I am a woman, but I worked with them, not with their
husbands. But I remember the initial response or the delayed ad-

missions of authors' wives and others whose husbands I had business dealings with when they were first introduced to me—and I have to conclude that most of them really didn't want to like me.

Sometimes, of course, they did, regardless of the fact that I often knew more about their husbands than they did, that their husbands could talk to me about their careers, their hopes and their sometimes impossible dreams of success, the stock market, real estate and politics and the state of the world.

I do wish that the ladies who resented me knew that their husbands could not have been in safer hands. I wish that they had been secure enough in themselves not to cast me as a medium for their fears. I have met some bitches.

One author's wife actually threw open my clothes-closet doors and snarled, "Honey, you couldn't have bought all those on your salary!"

Another tugged at my mink coat and sassed, "If you weren't representing my husband, you couldn't afford that mink!"

When he is in town, I occasionally have dinner with the husband of one of my best friends in the business. I've known them both for years, yet he has frequently had to get up in the middle of one of those dinners to call her long-distance with a report.

Another author brought his wife to dinner to meet me one evening after I had represented him for some time. She entered the restaurant, sat down, looking at me quizzically, as if she had been hoping to see some missionary schoolmarm, then squeaked, "You're nothing like my husband told me you were. I really expected an old bag!"

I knew a publisher with whom I was very friendly, and frequently we had lunch and sometimes we shared an early dinner over business. I had met his wife and we were friendly, too. I had not seen her for some time, until one evening when I ran into them at a theater opening. She waited for the chance to speak, then: "It's so nice of my husband to take you to dinner so often, isn't it?"

I smiled and said, "Oh yes."

Lillian Frank, Gerold's wife, was totally secure, a complete woman, not the appendage of a husband. She was also the perfect, understanding author's wife. She and I could even discuss Gerry's plans for books objectively, with understanding and humor. We both disagreed independently with Gerry on *Too Much, Too Soon*. Gerry, just as independent, proved us wrong.

Barbara Masters, John's wife, was another enlightened author's wife, also delightful in her own right, as was Ed O'Connor's wife, Veniette.

How many times have I sat in on day-long meetings with men on a Saturday or Sunday, only to hear them confess that they didn't mind working at all on Saturdays and Sundays, that they weren't missing anything at home but a week's accumulation of domestic whining and neighborhood gossip?

More recently I spent an evening with the wife of a business associate. She had started with the pre-dinner cocktails early that afternoon and her tongue was thick but loosened.

"I was all wrong about you," she blubbered.

"Were you?"

"Uh-huh. I had you followed."

She had actually hired a detective to see if her husband came to my apartment or had assignations in a hotel with me.

"And what did you find?" I asked.

"Nothing!"

"You were disappointed, weren't you?"

"Yes," she sniffed, and collapsed in tears.

She's become a very trusting friend since then, but it seems the hard way to get there. Also, I can't forgive her husband for trying to bolster his reputation by implying indiscretions with me in the first place. Perhaps he had to do that to bolster his ego after I intercepted the first pass he tried.

Throughout the years I have had friends, even some in the business, who never fully understood my professional absorption, perhaps because it was alien to them. I remained to them a woman in business without becoming one of those gross caricatures of the emasculating career woman, so they persisted in the belief that if the proper match could only be made, I'd escape the business arena with my decency intact and settle down in the country and live out my days posing for gracious-living rotogravures in the Sunday supplements.

These were the friends who never could understand the very close relationships I enjoyed with many of my clients and foolishly presumed that a deep understanding and affectionate regard were necessarily just a two-step away from his-and-hers linens and a shared roof. In fact, that domestic package was beyond any imaginable fantasies.

Yes, I really did adore most of my clients. I can even say I loved many of them. I loved them as I loved my work. More so, perhaps, because writers are the crucible and the factory, the substance and product, the inquiring mind and the means and urge to communicate. They are the ore, the foundry and the craftsmen, fashioning monuments from bits of memory, senses and flesh. They are vulnerable, often precious, as tolerable as the depth of talent allows. They are, above all, human beings whom you must understand in order to be able to help. In the process, after respect and understanding, often comes love.

Edwin O'Connor could be childishly arrogant, and would refuse to allow a line or a single punctuation mark of a cherished completed manuscript to be touched by an editor, even when the work cried to be cinched and polished. He neither asked for nor accepted suggestions. I admired him for the joy he took in the success he finally grasped, though it often seemed to clutch him too securely as he reveled in the embrace of the Boston "elite" and squandered increasing time as a cultural table decoration for the Kennedys, the Schlesingers and their coterie.

When *The Last Hurrah*, already honored as the $5,000 Atlantic Monthly–Little, Brown novel contest winner and soon to win the National Brotherhood Media Award, rose to the third position on the list of the best-selling novels of 1956, Nat Lefkowitz suddenly took an interest and asked how long we had been representing O'Connor. He had been with me for the greater part of a decade by then.

He had been a writer-producer for the Yankee radio network in Boston and had been writing for the "Accent on Living" section of the *Atlantic Monthly* when *Atlantic's* editor, Charles Morton, told him that he should come to see me. Charlie was quick to warn Ed that the Morris Agency had been founded initially and primarily for variety artists during the heyday of vaudeville.

"You go see her," Charlie told Ed, "but don't be surprised if they make you sit next to the midgets in the reception room!"

I liked Ed immediately. Like most young writers of his era, he wanted desperately to go to Europe. The first thing I did for him was to arrange an assignment for *Life* which would take him to London for an extended period of research for a magazine article on the operation of the British Broadcasting Corporation.

He was tall, with bright blue eyes and chestnut-colored curly hair, and everyone found him very handsome, the more so for a lovely, lovely sense of humor. Success, of course, increased his charm, and the most glamorous women of the time gravitated to him in a crowded room.

He was a very devout Catholic and I always believed that he had wanted to be a priest. Much of that feeling I gathered from his most deeply felt novel, the Pulitzer Prize-winning *The Edge of Sadness*, whose central character was a priest.

His father, a doctor, had strongly disapproved when Ed became a journalist and broadcaster, and felt that his son would be wasting his life. The lengthy hand-to-mouth existence that accompanied his earliest writings only aggravated his father's sense of betrayal.

One of the things which we had in common and which brought us closer in the beginning was that both Ed and I had enormous attachments to our families. Fortunately, his father lived to see the publication of *The Last Hurrah*, vindication that his son had not wasted his life. His father's pride seemed to double Ed's own.

In the beginning, of course, Ed was poor. Still, he would not write letters. He hated to write them, so practicality be damned, he would always call me long-distance. He had a furnished room on Marlborough Street in Boston. To reach him by phone, I had to place the call to a telephone in the downstairs hallway, and then his landlady would have to go upstairs to call him down, while I waited. We've all seen it in a hundred movies, and there isn't a romantic ounce to it in real life.

I did not think that *Benjy* ever should have been published and was not alone among those urging Ed to let it go. He had every right to write a juvenile book, though its timing would have been unwise at any rate, but *Benjy* wasn't really for the juvenile market, or any other. It was an unpleasant little story about a nasty little boy named Benjy. I believed that Ed wrote it simply to drain away whatever venom he had about certain kinds of nasty little boys, and he wrote it venomously. Then he should have packed it away. He would not.

He wrote *I Was Dancing* initially as a play, allowed himself to be flattered into having it produced largely on the strength of his name and success, and when it failed, he still persisted in rewriting it as a novel to salvage the script, when its weaknesses should already have been apparent to him. But he had certainly earned the right to try to capitalize on the success he had made.

In 1951, Harper published Ed's first novel, *The Oracle*. Getting it published was no easy matter, but it took no effort for the public to ignore it. There was a lapse of almost five years before Ed saw his next book in print, and while *The Oracle* had exerted influence in no other way, it rose in stature as an obstacle to his future.

Then Ed began to write *The Last Hurrah*, and I submitted a portion of it to Harper. Their response was rude but swift. They slammed the door on it. They had already taken their O'Connor gamble, thank you. Doubleday, in turn, saw no reason to tread where Harper had hesitated.

It was Ed who suggested that I take the snippet of the new book to Little, Brown. It seemed poetic justice to return to the Atlantic Monthly–Little, Brown family where he and we had begun. They accepted it, but I had trouble getting Ed an advance that would permit him the time to finish the book. Like all the other publishers I talked with, Little, Brown preferred to see a completed manuscript. Fortunately, the Atlantic novel prize of $5,000 in 1955 finally allowed Ed to finish the work. As usual, the Morris Agency made no claims upon such grants and prize monies.

While the novel was still in galley proofs, I submitted it to Harry Cohn at Columbia. I told him I thought he would like it, and he knew me well enough to know that I would not submit anything to him that wasn't suitable to his needs. I don't know if he read it. I doubt that he did. He wasn't the sort to let paper work interfere with his snap instincts.

In less time than it would have taken him to say *The Last Hurrah*, he called me. "Okay. I'll buy it," said Cohn. "One hundred and fifty thousand dollars," he announced, savoring each word in the phrase.

"Mr. Cohn," I interjected. "It's worth a quarter of a million."

His enunciation quickened. "Hundredfiftythou! Take it or leave it! And by noon, Monday!" It was Friday.

"Mmmm," I responded offhandedly. "I'll think about it. I'll discuss it with the author." I hung up the phone, lifted it again and placed a call to O'Connor in Boston.

"Ed, I can sell *The Last Hurrah* to Columbia for a hundred and fifty thousand dollars."

"Well, what's wrong with a hundred and fifty thousand?"

"It's a very good gamble, but the novel is a Book-of-the-Month Club selection and I think it's going to be a leading best seller when it reaches the market. That would make it worth every bit of a quarter of a million dollars. It's up to you. A hundred and fifty thousand is a healthy bird in hand. Two hundred and fifty thousand involves taking a chance that my confidence is matched by the reviewers and the public, and it is subject to all the unforeseen risks tomorrow might bring."

We decided to accept Harry Cohn's offer. His studio was riding high and its stature with book people had soared with the successful realization of *From Here to Eternity* on the screen three years earlier.

The Morris Agency was then representing Spencer Tracy, who wanted to play the role of Mayor Skeffington, a character very reminiscent of James Michael Curley, the old-time Boston mayor and political boss who many saw as the prototype for the book. Cohn wasn't buying Tracy. He had other ideas, and they involved a star who would either cost less or guarantee better insurance for the box office in what would necessarily be a very expensive film.

The agency sent me on a pilgrimage to convince Cohn that Tracy, and Tracy alone, was the right actor to create Skeffington. By then my mother had died, and as if to bleach out my mourning, I had suddenly become what my mother would have called "embarrassingly blond." It was a transformation she would never have sanctioned while she lived.

Looking like the stand-in for his studio's *Blondie* series, I sashayed into Harry Cohn's office. He looked up in shock.

"One of the best qualities you have," said Cohn, lecturing as he rose imposingly from behind his platformed desk "is that you're a lady. You know what you look like now? Do you? You look like any Hollywood tramp! Get out of here and go back and dye your hair back to its original color!"

And by God, I obeyed.

I returned to plead the case for Spencer Tracy's casting. Cohn assented, at which point Abe Lastfogel moved in to close the deal. Cohn turned the picture over to his old friend, director John Ford, and construction was begun on the Columbia ranch lot in Burbank on the largest set to be erected in Hollywood for many years, practically an entire precinct of Boston brownstones.

Problems beset the production from the start. There were delays. There were script problems. Ford cast the many juicy character roles in the film with most of his beloved Irish cronies, many of them long absent from the screen and most preserved by a familiar pickling process. There probably never was assembled a larger and more inflammable bunch of hundred-proof carousers. No surprise, then, when fire broke out, consuming a great portion of the set and requiring additional time for rebuilding. Costs soared, and by the time the film finally opened to disastrous business, Harry Cohn had been in his grave for nearly eight months, his energies finally spent.

With his long-delayed success upon him, O'Connor may have seemed to grow more obstinate, but I believe that his paternal hold on his prose had always been present and that the few inadvisable ventures he insisted we pursue were a part of the same strong will and the sense of adventure that had kept him going until *The Last Hurrah* and those that followed. Those side trips, except for the time they robbed him of, did not do all that much harm.

With success and strengthened confidence, Ed also found a woman who was both attractive and intelligent. Like him, she too was a devout Catholic, and since her first husband had been a non-Catholic and she had been able to have the marriage annulled, she and Ed were able to be married in a cathedral in Boston, with Cardinal Cushing officiating in a ceremony that befitted their very happy and mature alliance.

I was not able to attend their wedding, because I was then in the midst of attending to my mother and father in their final days, but Ed and Veniette and I would spend many, many happy evenings together in New England and in New York and in the country.

The last night I saw Ed, I had just returned from my sojourn in London, and he and Veniette came down from Boston to welcome me home. We were all staying at the same hotel and were joined by Abe Burrows and his wife and Arthur Schlesinger, Jr. It was a memorable evening with Ed, the spoiled priest who did not drink but kept us all up and laughing until four in the morning. He still did not approve of my criticism of the surviving Kennedys, but he permitted it, and as the night wore on, we became convinced that we had managed to solved most of the outstanding problems of the world.

I took the job with Warner Brothers and it eventually forced me to move to the Coast. I had forgotten or had yet to let all my friends in the East know that I was out there. On the morning of March 24, 1968, many of those friends were trying to reach me, to prepare me, as I turned on the radio to listen to the eight o'clock news. Edwin O'Connor, Pulitzer Prize winning novelist, who wrote with special understanding of the Irish in America, was dead at forty-nine. Big, strapping, bursting with life Ed O'Connor—dead.

Shaken, the only person I could think of calling at that hour was Arthur Thornhill, Sr., chairman of the board of Little, Brown & Company. It was Arthur who had presented me with the leatherbound set of Ed's books on the shelf before me, that short span which would now and always be the complete works of Edwin O'Connor.

Arthur lived in Duxbury, Massachusetts. The phone rang. What did I say? What could I say? The obvious words, the necessary words, though little needed to be said about Ed O'Connor between Arthur and me. And then I asked, "How did it happpen?"

"We had a lunch date. He was on his way to lunch with me."

The two friends had been meeting for lunch once a week for years, usually at the Ritz in Boston. As Ed was leaving the house, he turned and said to Veniette, "I don't feel well."

He collapsed, a stroke, and he died that afternoon—with work yet to be done and the taste of success still fresh.

PART
FIVE

My parents were always interested in politics and world affairs. They embraced the concept of the two-party system from opposite flanks but under the same roof. They were avid readers of newspapers, periodicals and books, the contents filtered through the bifocular bias of their respective political preferences. They did not actively participate in the group political process, but our home was a campaign platform for many spectacular clashes.

In later years these ideological confrontations became so violent that my father, a staunch and starchy Republican, accused my mother, a Democrat, of being a Communist sympathizer. She, in turn, would hurl charges that he had leanings toward Fascism. Reason, logic and fair play had little part in these debates whose pig-bladder polemic more often took a form reminiscent of classic vaudeville comedy routines.

I cast my first vote for Herbert Hoover, my own, generally independent political attitudes not yet crystallized, my father's influence having been the stronger that year. With him, I was devastated when Franklin Delano Roosevelt won the election. With him, I was convinced that the country would rapidly go to the dogs. I didn't know any better. I hadn't been paying much attention. I was growing up on other fronts. My political maturation came later.

I emerged an avid Democrat, with frequent lapses of independence. I personally collected $14,000 to contribute to the first Adlai Stevenson presidential campaign. I still believe that Harry Truman was one of the great Presidents. And the impressionable young woman who blithely voted the Republican ticket in that crucial 1932 election found herself associated almost exclusively with liberal Democratic figures for more than two decades as a literary agent.

While I tried to facilitate the literary aspirations of many engaged in public service and elective office, a number of the authors I represented were driven by their social and political convictions to seek elective office. In those pursuits beyond their primary occupation, I could be of no help, and each of them needed plenty.

Bill Mauldin ran for Congress on the Democratic ticket in New York's Republican Rockland County. Gore Vidal, the grandson of former Senator Thomas P. Gore of Oklahoma, eventually manifested his political heritage, running for office in Dutchess County. He, too, is a Democrat. He, too, raised his lance in Republican territory. He, too, fell. My third Democratic Quixote was James Michener, the Pennsylvania squire, who placed his congressional bid from Bucks County—and could do no better than place in the race. My professional politicians were to have far better success in their assaults on the literary best-seller lists.

My first political client was Judge Jerome N. Frank, one of the early participants in FDR's "brain trust" and thus one of the architects of the New Deal economy. In those years of dynamic changes he had risen to the chairmanship of the Securities and Exchange administration and was then serving as a judge for the U.S. Court of Appeals for the 2nd Circuit, where he remained until his death.

We were introduced at a party given by Elizabeth and Eliot Janeway at their penthouse apartment. He was one of the most erudite and enlightened men I ever had the pleasure of meeting. Sometime during the evening, as we chatted, he mentioned that he had written a magazine article concerning women lawyers. The judge was a leader for his time in his outspoken conviction that women should be accepted and treated as equals in the professions and business. He would have been catnip to the Women's Libbers had he lived today.

Shortly thereafter the judge sent me his manuscript. I read it and decided that it might be suitable for *Good Housekeeping*. Herbert Mayes, who ran that magazine, bought the article for $500. It was a short piece which Jerome's former agent had been unable to place for publication, so he was doubly pleased with the sale. He introduced me to many of his contemporaries and eventually encouraged my happiest political alliance.

Any son would have been unlikely to live up to the achievements and charismatic appeal of Franklin Delano Roosevelt, the only President to a generation. No less intimidating would be the living legend of Eleanor Roosevelt, who, for all of her detractors, eventually became the most respected woman in the world. Unfortunately, the Roosevelt sons were generally not equipped to rise to the heritage. One might have. One had the charm and the concern, though his political star waned and personal headlines further tarnished his promise.

Jimmy Roosevelt was one of my first political clients, and at the time I represented him the public seemed anxious to transfer its affection and support to him, even as he evidenced the integrity and personality to reward the trust. He came to me shortly after the death of his father. He was lean, had a pace-setter's stride and a broad smile that seemed wholly able to illuminate the arena.

I remember walking along the streets with him, and people passing would stop, thrusting out their hands to shake his, with smiles that seemed to acknowledge him as the true heir. Many spoke of his father with tears in their eyes.

I secured a contract for him to do a biography of FDR. He was given a $100,000 advance, but he decided against the revelations or ruses the work seemed likely to impose upon him and he canceled the contract. He managed to return the entire advance, though many another political youth might have settled for only partial return.

Throughout the years he would resurface at my office, enthused by some new idea for a book, but nothing ever came of the initial excitements. He never seemed ready to risk enough. He remained as gracious as he had always been, but in time he faded away.

My introduction to the Harry S. Truman administration was steeped in honor and was ultimately of little consequence. The next time it involved my client Joe Alex Morris and it almost resulted in my representing a major presidential biography. As it turned out, Mr. Truman was not ready yet to sit for his memoirs; he would have, had he not defeated Tom Dewey.

I was surprised to receive a summons from President Truman to participate in a conference of communications executives in

Washington, D.C. The others so honored were major administrators of the broadcasting services, publishers and newspaper and magazine managing editors. My representation of writers might have seemed only tangential in that company of men who made the decisions that determined what was broadcast and printed in the country. My role was closer to that of broker or liaison. I was also the only woman chosen to attend.

Ben Hibbs, the editor in chief at *The Saturday Evening Post*, served as something of an anchor man for the conference and it was he who had suggested that my point of view might complement the proceedings. It was a three-day affair, awash in complimentary booze and an avalanche of catered cuisine, moving through a series of smoke-filled rooms and the cloakroom conversation of dynamic men away from home, hard-working in the daily sessions, lonely, adventurous and footloose at each adjournment.

It was good experience and practice for me, learning to hold my own with men but without competing on terms other than my own. In retrospect, I realize that I used certain wiles, knew how to gain attention, knew how to stress my opinion or defer to others when necessary. I have been accused of coquetry. I have been accused of being an actress, assuming different roles on different stages to direct my own denouements.

I had seen women who barge in and bang on tables, transforming themselves into gross caricatures of men. I've seen others who become equally caricatured as females, playing their own pimp and prostitute in the absence of any other negotiable talent in their fields. Sure, there are moments, but only brief moments, when it is shrewd to know when to go limp and helpless, to widen your eyes in awe, to flatter and smooth the lapels of some cavalier come to your aid. But there is no purpose to the help unless you know how and where to apply it once the moment has passed and you get back to business. While I have analyzed it since then, my actions were always largely instinctive, inspired by the situation and the moment.

One of those participating in the conference was Dan Mich, the managing director of *Look*. One afternoon, during a break, he turned to me and whispered, "You're really not very naïve, though you try to act that way, but you're also not very tough. You know what to ask when you want to ask it, and how." I smiled, lowered my eyelids, genuinely flattered and complimented, as I smoothed his lapel.

I did not meet President Truman while I was there, but I did meet Averell Harriman and several other statesmen I respected. I had a wonderful time. There is always some value when men and women in a common field of endeavor get together, but I imagine that after the testimony and proposals and sharing of mutual problems had been aired and tucked back into briefcases and carried home, the conference probably didn't accomplish any more than such working holidays ever do.

Joe Alex Morris was the managing editor of *Collier's* when I met him. He had a joyous sense of humor and we established a fine rapport. In a nice way, he found me a little daffy. Our calls were brief and seemed to brighten his afternoons. I could always depend upon him for a direct and swift response to any idea.

I would call him, saying, "Joe, do you think that this is a good idea for *Collier's* ?" I'd quickly sketch the author's approach to some topic, wait a moment while Joe processed it in his head, and brace myself.

He'd respond, "It stinks!" Or he'd say, "Yes, it's a great idea. Now what are you going to do about it? When? How much?"

One of those reorganizations which helped to diffuse the image and style of *Collier's* in the postwar years deposited Joe in the street. I had heard the rumors of a shake-up, and many of those fingered for firing had been discussed along with many who survived that purge.

I was in a meeting when Joe placed a call to me and I could not talk to him immediately. When I picked up his message from my secretary, I was surprised. I was asked to call him at home. "On a *Monday?*" I muttered.

When he answered my call, I immediately blurted, "Joe, were you fired?" He confirmed this, and I asked, "What are you going to do?"

"I don't know, but I'd like to talk to you about it," he responded. I asked him to come right over. Our office was then in the RKO Building on Sixth Avenue between 50th and 51st. When he arrived, I took Joe around to Toots Shor's for a drink.

The same approach that can be effectively blunt can be gauche when I've failed to brief myself properly. Stupidly I opened the conversation by lamenting, "Too bad you don't write."

"I guess you haven't read anything that I've written," he said with unconcealed disappointment.

I knew that he had been foreign editor for the *Herald-Tribune* and represented United Press in Europe during the war, and was also head of the UP bureau in Washington for a time. "What else did you do?"

"I've done a lot of stuff for *This Week* and I've written for *The Saturday Evening Post*."

"Well then, why don't you just call up Ben Hibbs and let him know that you're available. They'll jump at the—"

"I couldn't do it that way," he admitted proudly.

"So you want *me* to?"

"Will you?"

"Why didn't you just say that? But if I call, you'll probably be stuck with me as an agent."

He smiled. "What's wrong with that?"

I called the *Post*. They were delighted and Joe was assigned to do an eight-part serial on the distribution and content of the incoming mails at the White House. That first assignment grossed $20,000 for Joe and was almost as much as his yearly salary at *Collier's*.

On my suggestion, Joe expanded the material from the *Post* serial and it was published in hardcover under the title of *Dear Mr. President*. During the years that I represented Joe, he wrote the biography of General Mark Clark; *Deadline Every Minute*, the story of the United Press; *What a Year*, a chronicle of 1929; *The Private Papers of Senator Vandenberg*; and *Those Rockefeller Brothers*. One of my last gestures as an agent was to secure a commitment for him with the *Reader's Digest* to contribute a specified number of articles on a yearly basis.

Following the book on the White House correspondence, Joe's stock at the White House and at *The Saturday Evening Post* soared. He was enjoying a satisfaction and recognition he had known in his previous years of distinguished reporting.

The election year of 1948 erupted. President Truman's personal style and man-in-the-street image were uncomfortably different from those of the flamboyant and charismatic man from whom the mantle of office had descended after enough years for it to seem to be his by mass fiat. Truman was judged an underdog from the start. The political obituaries had begun so early, echoed in editorials by so many newspapers calling for a change in favor of the Republican party, that his expected defeat promised to be an anticlimax, a footnote to a postwar withdrawal into a new isolationism.

I received a call from Ben Hibbs. *The Saturday Evening Post* had made a crafty deal with President Truman. Despite Mr. Truman's confidence, in the face of a nearly unanimous skeptical press and the cocky Cassandras of the public opinion polls, the President was playing the odds and had placed a bet of his own on the possibility of an opposition victory. If he was defeated, he would agree to have his autobiography published in the *Post*, and further that Joe would handle the incidental detail of its writing. Ben arranged that Joe and I would meet him at the *Post*'s offices in Philadelphia on the morning following election night. No contract could be signed before the outcome of the election, and we were sworn to secrecy.

Most of the country went to bed on election night believing that Tom Dewey would be the eventual winner. Headlines were set to scream his victory. Unfortunately, a few of those headlines prematurely hit the stands.

Joe and I were on the train, pulling in toward Philadelphia, very early on the appointed morning, going over such details as we had and working out our approach to the deal. The porter entered our car, and as he passed he beamed. "Truman's been elected!"

We had lunch with Ben Hibbs anyway, talking more about the upset election than our aborted deal. I remember that as we were leaving Ben Hibbs called out, "Sorry I wasted your time. But isn't it nice that we won't have to have John Foster Dulles!"

Joe, of course, went on to write other successful books. It seemed to be our destiny to have John Foster Dulles. After he had ascended to the Cabinet and was conducting his brinksmanship foreign policies, the inconstant public taste and the changing fortunes of *The Saturday Evening Post* would result in Ben's being squeezed out of the magazine in the first of many changes in format and fundamental conviction.

Joe Alex Morris's book on General Mark Clark was not the only military biography I was to represent. I enjoyed an enviable personal and professional relationship with the publishing house of Harper, first through Frank MacGregor, then Cass Canfield, who was to become chairman of the board. In time I was honored by being their selection to represent all of their non-agented books for subsequent sale of magazine, motion picture and other subsidiary rights. It did not prove to be an especially profitable participation, but it was a proud vote of confidence and a prestigious credit in the business.

I am sure it was because Cass Canfield found me reliable and tactful that he called one hot midsummer afternoon to ask if I could come immediately to his office—he wanted me to do him a favor. In fact, it was the other way around. By the time I reached his office, the gentleman he wanted to entrust me with had already arrived.

He was General of the Army Henry Harley "Hap" Arnold, Chief of the Army Air Forces. He was surrounded by an entourage befitting his rank. I didn't know whether they were from West Point, Annapolis or the Annapolis of the Air, the Air Force Academy at Colorado Springs, but all of them were dripping with brass and braid, fruit salad and scrambled eggs or tinsel, whatever it was called.

It was one of those occasions when instinct and reflex served me best. I went a bit limp. I may have fluttered ever so slightly as I whispered, "I'm *terribly* sorry if I seem a little confused, but I've *never* met a five-star general in my life." General Arnold's ribbons seemed to inflate. He smiled. His satellites relaxed and smiled too. Literally and figuratively, everyone was at ease.

I left that unscheduled meeting with the promise that I would shepherd the general through his commitment to deliver his book, *Calculated Risk*, to Harper. I did. He did.

Judge Jerome Frank was responsible for my meeting William O. Douglas, Associate Justice of the U.S. Supreme Court. But it was Abe Fortas, who was appointed to the Supreme Court himself many years later, who arranged the introduction. The Justice had written his first book, *Of Men and Mountains*. Judge Frank advised Mr. Fortas, a close friend of both, that the Justice should have professional advice and representation by a literary agent.

It was one of those protracted periods of intense heat and unmoving air that can encase Manhattan during August. I had escaped for a few days' vacation at Montauk on Long Island when I received a phone call from Mr. Fortas, asking me to return to the city to meet Justice Douglas. I was tired and badly needed that rest.

"Another time," I pleaded. I was told in swift and certain terms that that was no way to treat a Justice of the Supreme Court. It wasn't, but I imagined that I could see the wall of heat waves rising to distort the Manhattan skyline, ready to vaporize any fool attempting to penetrate it when it was not absolutely necessary.

Mr. Fortas added that the Justice, who was en route from Europe to Washington, would not be back in New York for about a month. Subsequently it was arranged that I would meet Douglas at the Hotel Pennsylvania, then located on Seventh Avenue, directly opposite Penn Station. The meeting was scheduled early in the morning. As I entered the Justice's suite, my knees shook a little. My tongue didn't tie, though it looped a bit. I counted down, wondering who'd start the conversation.

"Would you like breakfast?" said Bill Douglas warmly.

I often wonder if he knew how in awe I was of him in that moment. On reflection, I was never in awe of the man, whom I was meeting for the first time, but of his position and the courage with which he had voiced decisions wrought in conviction and out of an unquenchable thirst for that knowledge which yields truth. I'd been lucky so far, but I had met and seen enough men in government to know the arrogance of power. I was still a bit apprehensive about handling political figures, many of whom were prima donnas to shame the naughtiest diva. I had no such doubts about Justice Douglas, whom I greatly admired.

I got to know the man, realizing that beyond his warmth and friendliness was a figure of many moods, deeply concerned with the ills of the world and their solution. He could be remote and taciturn, perhaps never known whole by anyone.

We went for a walk that morning, a still, hot and humid September day in 1949. I can never forget that walk, which turned out to be a full-scale hike along the steaming streets of New York City. I knew little about him then, but through the years I would get to know him quite well, learning that the hiking, the mountain climbing, the exploration of strange foreign lands, the quest to seek out other peoples in their hidden corners and illuminate their needs as well as their strengths, all of this was a driving passion in his life, to know, to understand.

I began to understand when I read the manuscript of *Of Men and Mountains*, which was published the following year. As a child, Douglas nearly died of infantile paralysis. To rebuild the strength in his wasted legs, he began hiking through the sage-covered foothills near his home in Yakima, Washington. He regained his strength.

His continuing love for the mountains, extending across the ranges of the world, made him aware of man's senseless destruction of nature and made him want to help stop it. He has said of mountains, "Man can find deep solitude and conditions of grandeur that are startling, and he can come to know both himself and God."

I represented Bill Douglas from the time of the long hot hike in New York until I quit the agency business, and it was one of the exciting episodes in my career. Yet he was not an easy client. He was usually gracious, sometimes impatient and impetuous, but I was flattered that he did trust me implicitly.

I made many trips to Washington, and that first trip to the Supreme Court was a great thrill. I didn't realize the first time I made the journey to Washington that I didn't have to walk up that long flight of stairs from the street to the entrance of the Supreme Court, that there was an elevator at the side. Protocol was strictly observed in getting to the Justice's chambers—first to the Marshal's office and then, in the company of an escort, to the office.

There is a grandeur manifest in the Supreme Court, as there is in the White House. One is overcome by a sense of the prevailing power of the office and the heritage of the great men who have further dignified it.

These visits with the Justice always concerned his writing and his travels. It was my function to discuss his projects with him, and he relied on me to advise him which of his ideas seemed best for him to pursue for articles and books.

I believe Bill has always been cruelly misunderstood and often very much maligned. Even while his travels in the Orient and his need to understand the people's problems and to question our policies with them brought him attack from the right, Radio Moscow branded him a notorious spy brazen enough to pose as a mountain climber at an age when other men retreat to their armchairs.

His liberal decisions and painfully considered liberal views regarding China and civil rights, for example, made him the object of harsh and sometimes cruel criticism by some members of Congress. Years ago, returning from an extended tour of the Far East, he told an interviewer at the airport that we must recognize Communist China. Immediately someone in Washington grabbed a headline by accusing the Justice of being a Communist sympathizer. Had we been able to consider recognizing mainland China then, the course of history might have been changed.

Douglas did not consider Julius and Ethel Rosenberg innocent, but he strongly argued that there was a question about their having been tried under the proper law. Naturally, his point of law was neither understood nor respected by those whose inflamed passions drove them to attack his allegiance to informed justice as treasonous allegiance to some alien specter.

Douglas's greatest weakness was his naïveté with women and his almost fatal susceptibility to their flattery. How often I watched him being taken in by pretty speeches and the flutter of feathered eyelashes. Girls at parties were always making a fuss over him, as if he were some callow movie matinee idol rather than one of the pillars of the highest court in the land. At a few of these parties it became my duty to free him from the clutches of some panting Supreme Court groupie, breathily entreating him to share his tales of scaling the Himalayas or wrestling some landmark court decision. A contradiction of the black-robed and icily remote dignity of the judiciary, he was a vital, ageless and exciting man.

One night in Washington, between wives, he took me to dinner at a very popular restaurant, and I began to understand the kind of excitement he generated and the fascination it inspired among lady fans. Everyone treated him as if he were visiting royalty. Yet there was unconcealed affection and genuine respect for the man himself. Frankly, I enjoyed being a part of the reflected glory which illuminated our table, and suddenly knew what it was those women felt.

He had complete faith in me, was responsive to professional advice and scrupulously fair in his dealings. He was also anxious to direct others among his Washington colleagues to me.

When I had been his agent for only a short time, Douglas began to promote me to his friend Adlai Stevenson. He talked with him. He dropped him notes. He sent me memoranda of those nudgings, and finally a meeting was arranged between Stevenson and myself. Mr. Stevenson was, in the words of Archibald MacLeish, "One of the great articulators of his time," and although he had been defeated in his initial run for the presidency, his style and wit and substance had made him a very hot literary property. Every publication was anxious for him to make its pages his forum. Indecision happened to be another of his characteristics.

We spent nearly six weeks trying to arrive at some conclusion regarding what he wanted to do, what he was going to do and how he would do it. Stevenson couldn't decide which of the available offers stirred him. But something else was troubling him. Suddenly he grew coy, and I found myself dealing instead with Lloyd Garrison of the law firm of Paul, Weiss, Rifkind, Wharton and Garrison, the firm Stevenson joined after his defeat. Garrison would now call me, asking advice on a particular outlet and offer. Garrison relayed the decisions to me. Garrison asked my approval. Garrison discussed the details and directed the changes in terms. I got no direct answers from Stevenson, no explanation of the new proxy setup. Any clarification would also come by proxy, and the explanation was that Stevenson had decided he did not want to pay commissions, that he was so in demand as to preclude any need for an agent, that the legal firm could probably handle the technicalities. I did not embarrass Mr. Stevenson by accepting his news face to face.

In time, I was to deal with most of the Kennedys, but I started at the top, and it was through Bill Douglas that I met the patriarch, Joseph P. Kennedy. We had a lunch date in New York at "21," and Bill brought Kennedy along. I knew that he had been the first chairman of the Securities and Exchange Commission under Roosevelt and the last peacetime ambassador to the Court of St. James's, and that he had wrapped up the U.S. distribution of such prime United Kingdom liquors as Haig and Haig and King William IV the minute Prohibition was repealed.

I don't know what I expected of this powerful millionaire and alleged kingmaker. Something other than what I encountered, certainly. Bill explained that I had been his literary agent since he began writing professionally. Mr. Kennedy looked me over sharply, and said, "I've heard it called a lot of things, Bill, but *never* a literary agent!" Suddenly I could believe a lot of what I'd heard about him.

Kennedy had a special interest in William O. Douglas. He might have been a great President, with his bountiful compassion for people and causes combined with an uncompromising quality of toughness and an adherence to truth. He was an intimate of President Roosevelt and could have been the President's running mate for the fourth term, before the compromises which placed Harry Truman in line for succession to the presidency. But Douglas did what he wanted, stayed where he felt most valuable and rewarded, and was able to maintain some measure of privacy and freedom of movement.

There is a misconception that those gentlemen in exalted positions of state, such as the Supreme Court of the United States, make a great deal of money. Of course, they do not, considering that they are or should be our most accomplished men and women, considering that those employed in commerce who don't have the background, the knowledge or the all-encompassing responsibility frequently make (not *earn*) far more than those who dedicate their lives to public service. Understandably, for those in government who can write, a borrowed phrase like "publish or perish" has a different and special application. It costs money to stay informed and to maintain contact with the dynamic world that lies beyond the too often insular community in Washington. Additionally, those who have the ability to communicate bear a responsibility to inform, enlighten and stimulate thought and resulting opinion among the public.

Douglas realized much additional revenue in the form of awards and grants for his contributions to understanding in the fields of economics, foreign relations, sociology and civil rights. His lecture "The Black Silence of Fear," for example, was published in *The New York Times Magazine* and was cited for the $1,000 Lauterbach award for its substantial service to the cause of civil liberties.

In 1955 Justice Douglas planned to go to Russia, fulfilling a desire which he felt he had held too long without satisfying it. One of the factors that had delayed his decision threatened still to postpone the venture. It would be very expensive, not an undertaking the Justice himself could afford to finance. I would have to secure some commitments which would help to underwrite the project.

Look seemed an ideal outlet for the subjects the Justice had in mind and would be researching during his travels. Dan Mich, the magazine's managing director, agreed with me, as did Mike Cowles of the Cowles Syndicate and *Des Moines Register-Tribune*. I arranged for Bill Douglas to contribute a series of articles. *Look* would pay the expenses, arrange the trip and attach a top photographer to the traveling party.

Look's deal dictated that no one traveling with the Douglas contingent was to write about it and that no photographs could be released or printed until after the publication of his articles in the magazine.

As the date for departure neared, the Justice and his second wife, Mercedes, asked a few friends to join them on the tour. I was asked, and I have often had reason to wish that I had been able to see the U.S.S.R. in such distinguished company that summer of 1955.

The Justice, who had extended such invitations before and knew of the many more that I had turned down, kidded me: "I'm sure Helen would rather go to Central Park, and not much beyond."

I would probably have declined out of concern for my clients and deals pending, books incubating, confidence called upon. It would be a long trip, and there was much that required my personal attention and concern in the office during the period. Yet I was interested in that special trip to a powerful and largely feared country which was just beginning to submit to the curious eyes of outsiders.

There was an unspoken yet more painfully decisive reason for my not accepting the invitation. Both of my parents were on a decline toward the death which would soon claim them. I could not predict the turns their separate illnesses would take, though I anticipated it. I could not and would not leave them.

One of those who did make that journey with the Douglases was Robert Francis Kennedy, son of the man who had championed the Justice's presidential candidacy and chief counsel to the Senate Investigating Subcommittee, who had yet to gain his reputation as a ruthless inquisitor through the televised Senate Rackets Committee hearings. I remained in contact with the travelers as they made their way across Russia. Upon their return I sent Douglas's completed articles to *Look* and arranged with Doubleday for an expanded version to be published in book form. It seemed that our work was done, that my part in that specific project had ended.

I was returning from a meeting with another client one afternoon when I received a telephone call from Dan Mich. He sounded uncommonly annoyed. "Have you seen the new issue of *U.S. News and World Report?*" he asked. I answered that I had not.

"Robert Kennedy has written up the full Russian trip," he explained. "It's on the stands now. You'll also discover that he had his own photographs taken and that he has sold those to a photographic agency, which is already servicing them to other publications."

I immediately placed a call to Bill Douglas. When I finally reached him, I began, "Bill, did you know that—"

Before I could complete the question, he interrupted with a resigned sigh, "Oh, yes."

"Is there nothing that can be done to stop further distribution of the pictures or any further use of his articles," I asked, desperately grasping for some shred of hope to salvage the wreck of what seemed to me a conscious and most willful betrayal.

"No, Helen, there is nothing to be done. That's Bobby Kennedy."

Look printed the Douglas account of the Russian expedition, but they were upset about the whole deal, as the incident caused them a great deal of embarrassment both in publishing circles and among their readership. In 1956 Doubleday published Bill's full account of the trip in *Russian Journey.*

Several years ago, when I was living in Beverly Hills, my telephone rang. It was Bill Douglas. "I called to let you know," he said, "that the book you are responsible for is finished."

That book, which I had urged him to start writing nearly a decade earlier, eventually became his two-volume autobiography.

I represented Madam Pandit during the period when she served as President of the U.N. General Assembly. She was sent to me by another Indian client, Santha Rama Rau, and my representation of her was as sporadic as her infrequent writings dictated. These, in turn, were inspired by nothing more altruistic or ideologic than a dip in her bank balance. When Madam Pandit felt the pinch, she picked up the phone and summoned me to put her back in print until her kitty was purring again.

"Summoned" is an altogether accurate description of her dealings with me. I would suddenly receive a call in the morning, even in the late afternoon, bidding me to present myself at her offices that same day. It was like taking part in a command performance to be ushered before her to receive my latest field orders, and then just as ceremonially to be ushered out again.

Through Madam Pandit, I was privileged to have an especially thorough tour of the United Nations' facility. Too, a great deal of prestige accrued from our handling of the distinguished lady.

While Madam Pandit was presiding at the U.N., Eleanor Roosevelt gave a very small luncheon at her house in the East 60's. She invited me because the affair was in honor of an aspect of American writing. Abe Lastfogel, the head of the Morris office, happened to be in town, so we arranged to go to the luncheon together.

As we arrived at Mrs. Roosevelt's, another car drew up bearing Madam Pandit. She greeted me rather effusively, with her usual great charm. I introduced her to Mr. Lastfogel, who, as we entered Mrs. Roosevelt's house, said to me in a whisper, "How do you know her?" Lastfogel, who never interfered in my operation and granted me such autonomy that even he did not know my full client list, was as surprised as he was pleased upon learning that she, too, was a William Morris client.

Generally, only a few at the Morris Agency knew who my clients were, and because they occupied my own tight little island within the company, they had no reason to care. While I might move into television or the legitimate theater or the motion picture arena on behalf of these clients, or devise authorships for the agency's big-name performing talents, my clients carried a "hands off" to the other agents.

But there was a great deal of excitement throughout the company when Cass Canfield, the chairman of the board of Harper, sent me Chester Bowles, who had just returned from his post as our ambassador to India. The agency was doing a large volume of business with Benton and Bowles, the advertising giant which bore his name. It involved a number of lucrative television series and specials packaged for B&B sponsor clients.

Like a number of his political confreres, Mr. Bowles proved to be a prima donna the equal of any actor. He promptly laid out his terms. He told me what I could collect commissions on and what I could not. He further intended to arbitrate what percentage could be taken. Because the agency was looking on with held breath, I played along for a time.

As would be the case with a number of my liberal Democratic clients, my contact with Bowles became Theodore C. Sorensen, who appeared to play a greater role in their corporate literary pursuits than anyone was anxious to acknowledge or define.

I soon became aware that every time Bowles wished to speak with me, I would receive a call from Sorensen. After telling me where in the world Mr. Bowles was on that day, he would ask, "Will you call Mr. Bowles this afternoon at this number?" I was always speaking to Bowles by long-distance.

One day, after receiving my instructions for another transcontinental rendezvous, I asked Sorensen, "Hey, is Mr. Bowles trying to double his wealth by saving on toll calls?"

Finally I wearied of the honor of representing the ambassador and asked him to leave the agency. The office shook. Wally Jordan, the head of the television department, was livid. Mr. Bowles, who had left the advertising agency he founded when he entered public service, did not exact any retribution, but merely took his terms elsewhere.

Ted Sorensen was soon back in my life. One did not merely represent the Kennedys or their individual satellites. One inherited their massed armies, their appointed lieutenants and self-appointed generals. Nor did anyone ever have exclusive representation of any single Kennedy in a single endeavor. At best, a representative for a Kennedy promotion plan would be one of several simultaneous starters, unwittingly in competition not only with the others but with lieutenants who hoped they could swing a better deal first. I had to work at it to reach that conclusion. I was naïve as a babe when I responded to the first starting gun.

Actually, it was a bell, a phone call from Cass Canfield. Harper had published Senator John F. Kennedy's *Profiles in Courage*, and Jack Kennedy thought that now he should have an agent to explore the possibilities for keeping the book and his name in circulation through residual sales of theatrical rights. After my credentials had been thoroughly checked, the senator's book was turned over to me.

The year following the publication of the book, Kennedy was awarded the Pulitzer Prize for biography. I believed that his admission of gratitude to Ted Sorensen on that occasion confirmed a widespread feeling that Sorensen was responsible for authoring a major portion of the book, but the two men were prepared to do battle with the first major television network that suggested the possibility. They assembled a convincing case and vindicated the senator's literary standing.

Yet if Jack Kennedy was solely responsible for writing the book, it was Sorensen who shepherded it, as he did so many other interests of the Kennedy clan.

I had some initial talks with a television producer Robert Saudek, but it was not until a year after *President* Kennedy's assassination that a *Profiles in Courage* television series was realized. The program was drenched in praise and parched in the ratings. Long before, virtually every one of the book's true tales of heroism-under-fire had been reprinted in slick magazines. And long before that, I had summoned my own courage and put an end to this Kennedy chapter in my life.

It was not Ted Sorensen alone, though most of my contact was with him. That single book was soon calling upon more of my time than a majority of the other clients I handled and the many books in which they were involved. There were constant telephone calls from the various Kennedy headquarters.

Sorensen regularly called for progress reports. What was I doing about this outlet? What were the results to date? Had I been in touch with so-and-so? What did he say? Meanwhile, Kennedy and his representatives were often at work on the book themselves, in direct conflict with my own efforts. The duplicated and bureaucratic effort brought embarrassing collisions. That demonstration of committee overlap and overkill made me wonder how anything ever gets done in Washington.

Finally, when I received a particularly nervous call from Sorensen, informing me that he had to make a full report to Kennedy and immediately needed a full accounting of my efforts, I stopped him in midsentence.

We were working against each other. The senator's little beavers were driving me crazy. I had been recruited for a nonstop scrimmage on a team which flew only one banner, and I had many other loyalties. I wasn't even dealing directly with the quarterback himself.

"Mr. Sorensen, you would do well to cut out the middleman," I said firmly. "I think maybe you ought to take care of this yourself. I cannot work this way." And I didn't.

•   •   •

They used to kid me at the agency that every time I headed for the West Coast, I managed to pick up a client on the East Coast. It did happen frequently enough, and one of those trips toward the Pacific brought me brow to brow with the toughest-dealing Kennedy of them all, the former staff investigator for the McCarthy committee and the spy from Bill Douglas's Russian journey, Robert F. Kennedy.

He was soon to be the Attorney General in his brother's Cabinet and had written a potential bestseller, *The Enemy Within*, on his work as Chief Counsel with the Senate Rackets Committee.

No sooner had I checked in at the Beverly Wilshire than I received a pair of calls from Peter Lawford, the Kennedy brother-in law and a William Morris client, and Milt Ebbins, Lawford's personal manager. Ebbins was an old friend and had recommended me highly to Bobby Kennedy, who was anxious to see his book made into a film. Kennedy, in turn, had conducted a quick investigation to determine my stature among publishers and my suitability for a Kennedy team assignment. Peter Lawford told me to call Bobby in Washington at once.

I called Bobby, who skimmed over the preliminaries and commanded, "I'll see you tomorrow."

"Mr. Kennedy, I've just arrived in Los Angeles on business," I explained. "I simply can't see you tomorrow. My work here should be completed in a week to ten days. Is that soon enough?"

"No!"

"I'm very sorry, but I didn't start this whole thing. Your brother-in-law did."

"Then call me directly when you get back to New York."

We met as soon as I returned and he tried to make his deal. "I'll let you handle the book if you will do so on a five-percent commsission," he said.

I'd heard that before, usually from politicians. "I won't give you cut rates. I don't give Bill Douglas any bargains," I answered. "Or Michener or any of the rest. How can I cut a fair and standard commission and expect them not to feel betrayed and incensed?"

"Frankly," he countered, "I really don't know why I should have an agent."

"I didn't start this," I repeated.

"We'll put it on this basis, then. If you can get me a better deal than Harper has offered, we can work out some sort of arrangement."

I called a friend at Harper and learned the terms of his deal. Mr. Kennedy had gotten as much out of it as he possibly could, since they were very anxious to have the book. He was to spend all of the money on advertising and publicity, constantly fueling the talk of an imminent feature-film production.

After I called Harper, I phoned Mr. Kennedy.

"Mr. Kennedy, if *I* ever need an agent, I'll come to you."

I did not expect to hear from Bobby Kennedy again, but I had counted my blessings prematurely. Rose Kennedy, the mother of the clan, decided after the death of the President that she would occupy herself by writing her autobiography. Robert Coughlan, for many years on the staff of *Life*, was a client of mine and was selected to write the book for her.

My phone rang. It was Bobby Kennedy. "Miss Strauss, you may handle the book if you wish," he said. "But you may not collect any commission. The commission will have to be given to the Kennedy Foundation." I assumed he meant the full ten-percent commission, not the cut-rate five percent.

"As much as I would like to handle the book, I am merely an employee of this company and they are not in business for love. For their sake, I cannot accept your terms."

Late in 1963 I flew to Los Angeles on business. One evening Abe and Frances Lastfogel asked me to join them for dinner. As it happened, the dinner in question was one of those annual fund-raising affairs to which the Lastfogels lent their support, in this case the National Conference of Christians and Jews. One of the speakers taking his turn at the rostrum was Sander Vanocur, then the White House Correspondent for NBC television. I was impressed, turning to Frances Lastfogel to say, "If he wrote that speech, the man knows how to write."

The dinner ended and the Lastfogels got involved with a group of friends, while I ran into someone I knew from NBC and joined another group in the bar. I forgot my comment to Frances, enjoyed the evening and gave it no further thought.

However, Frances did not forget. She called me the first thing the following morning, saying, "I met that NBC fellow. I told him that you said he can write, and he was very pleased. He told me he didn't know you, but that he knew about you. He was delighted and would love to talk to you about it."

"About what?" I was about to say.

"I told him you'd call him."

He was staying at the Beverly Hills Hotel. I was at the Beverly Wilshire. I picked up the phone. "I'm really quite embarrassed," I began when I was connected to his room. "I don't conduct business like this normally."

"That's all right," he assured me. "I'm delighted that you called. And my wife is delighted. Let's make a date and talk about what you think we might do."

I wasn't sure whether I was delighted or not.

We made that date, but didn't keep it. The next time I heard from Sandy, it was a terse and painful message. President Kennedy had been assassinated in Dallas. Sandy had to take the first available flight East. He would contact me in New York after the days of madness and national mourning had passed.

By the time he came to my office in New York, he and Pierre Salinger had already arranged to compile *A Tribute to John Fitzgerald Kennedy*, a collection of international eulogies, published by the *Encyclopaedia Britannica* for the benefit of the JFK Memorial Library.

We went to "21" and I asked him what he wanted to write.

"A political novel, I think. Something on the order of *All the King's Men* or *The Last Hurrah*."

"I handle both of those writers," I said. "And it took them many years before they rose to that quality. Frankly, I have no assurance that you can write, only a faith, a hunch, that makes me think you can. Is there something you could work on soon so that I would have a sample to show?"

We decided that he would write an article drawn from the last trip he took with the slain President, a conservation trip. I was able to sell it to *Harper's*, and it was the sample that enabled me eventually to obtain a commitment for a book.

During that first luncheon he had boasted of his close friendship with Kenneth P. O'Donnell, David F. Powers and Lawrence F. O'Brien. I suggested that he get them all together and do a book on that group of close presidential friends and advisers whom the Washington press had labeled Kennedy's "Irish Mafia."

Enthused, Sandy arranged for us to have lunch with the survivors in Washington, D.C. They thought it a marvelous idea. Inevitably, there was talk of serving history and preserving perishable memories and reinstating the wit and humanity of the man who was being lost in posthumous deification. There was talk of a vanishing era in Massachusetts political life, but after all of that philosophical chatter, they sang in unison an Old World lullaby to which the Irish can make no exclusive claim: "How much money can you get us?"

I was able to auction off the idea alone on the basis of the men involved and Vanocur's *Harper's* article. The bid was almost $400,000 from Little, Brown, with a necessarily big advance to spread amongst the many Irish hands committed to the memoir. I then took the idea to Dan Mich at *Look* and sold him the serialization rights. I sold the British publication rights for what was then an astronomical guarantee.

I was not especially enchanted with the Massachusetts political cronies, but I found Larry O'Brien very interesting, bright and witty. One of my bonuses on the deal was receiving a tour of the White House with O'Brien. As we passed through rooms that the widowed First Lady had displayed on a television open house not too long before, I marveled, "What magnificent taste she has! Did she have any help?"

O'Brien simply looked at me as if I were some country cousin who believed everything she saw on television and thought models stitched their own dresses. "Are you kidding?" he chuckled.

Unfortunately, Larry O'Brien was eventually forced to absent himself from the project. Vanocur continued his television work, walking that tight-rope between an anti-Establishment adversary attitude and Brahmin foppishness.

The book wasn't being written. Deadlines passed. I was stuck with the Little, Brown contract, the *Look* commitment, the British deal—and no book. The project hibernated. Years passed. I had moved to London.

I returned to New York in 1967, remembering that my client Joe McCarthy had written one of the first Kennedy books, *The Remarkable Kennedys*, seven years earlier. He also had a commitment with Doubleday to do a book on the Boston Irish, a subject he knew well and had researched extensively.

I called Joe at his home in Blue Point, New York, and arranged a meeting at the Union Club in Boston with my old friend Arthur Thornhill, Sr., chairman of the board of Little, Brown; the editor Ned Bradford; O'Donnell and Powers. The project was revived and re-formed. It was still to suffer a lengthy incubation, but eventually it was born as *Johnny, We Hardly Knew Ye*.

Once more I flirted with a major presidential by-line. I had met Arthur Krim—then head of United Artists and a major fund-raiser and adviser to President Lyndon Baines Johnson—on the plane en route to Hollywood to make the deal for James Michener's *Hawaii*, and we had become friends. One day he called me on his return from Camp David.

"How would you like to be Lyndon Johnson's agent?" Arthur asked.

"Sure," I responded. "Why not?"

"The President wants to do a book on foreign policy. Will you go to Washington?"

I did not meet LBJ. I dealt with William White, the Texas newspaperman who was selected to work on the book with the President.

The most remarkable thing was that for the first time in years of dealing with liberal Democratic authors, I wasn't being asked to split or surrender the office commission. I wasn't being farmed out to cronies. I didn't have to feel that the book which would result was being written by a team of anonymous advisers tucked away behind the podium somewhere. In short, it was an uncommonly cordial and professional relationship. I began to like the Texas style.

I made a deal for a publisher, Doubleday, secured a large advance and breathed a sigh of relief. I'd come through. All the dealings with Washingtonian prima donnas lay behind me. I was finally handling a President and he was cooperating.

Unfortunately, despite Johnson's overwhelming reelection victory, his foreign policy was coming under fire. There was a particular rising cry against his involvement in Southeast Asia. It became expedient to back away from the subject of foreign policy. He canceled the book.

Sometime later I received a diamond pin from the President and Mr. White, a souvenir of the book that never was.

Washington has caught up with Art Buchwald. It may have passed him by. The plausible fancies he once carried to satirical extremes have become the numbing Washington headlines of the early seventies. Where does Buchwald go once his Swiftian imagination has been assimilated and reduced to humorless administration policy? Only Buchwald can guess. I knew him along the route toward the Watergate follies.

It was back in the late forties that he walked into my office one day and announced, "You don't remember me."

I looked him over and had to agree. "That's right."

"Well, I used to deliver manuscripts for you when you were associate story editor at Paramount Pictures."

He was interested in writing for magazines, having already developed a following in the pages of the Paris edition of the *Herald Tribune.* He had gone to Paris after the war and had also been a stringer for the trade paper *Variety.*

I agreed to make whatever inquiries I could and he scheduled his return to Paris. In the meantime, he had met Beatrice and Bruce Gould, who were then running *Ladies' Home Journal.* They requested an article, and I received a letter from Art requesting that I coordinate with them.

Instead of sending the submission to me first, he dispatched it directly to the Goulds, and Bruce Gould sent me an apologetic note, explaining that he could not use the piece. My next contribution to the international postal exchange was a facts-of-life memorandum to Art, chiding him that I could have saved everyone embarrassment and very likely have suggested changes in the article which could have maintained the commitment. I made the mistake of enumerating a number of things that were wrong and what might have been done to fix it.

He was wounded. He sent me a letter, saying that I didn't have enough respect for his writing ability because I had known him too long. That bit of rationale dumfounded me and I said so, and he was angrier still. I lost patience and he lost no time in severing our relationship.

With continuing success, he grew more mellow and our friendship resumed and endured.

My representation of politicians did not end at the Atlantic shore. There was one other, one of a bloc of British clients I was to inherit. Maurice Edelman was deposited at my desk as a result of a brief alliance entered into between the William Morris office and the respected London-based Curtis Brown Ltd., a literary agency that had been in business since 1904. Technically, the William Morris office predated the British company by six years, but I had not established the literary wing until the mid-forties.

Edelman, the author of such novels as *The Minister*, was a Labour member of Parliament. He proved to be a fiery number, whose tenure with my offices was ultimately neither lengthy nor memorable.

The collaboration with the Curtis Brown agency followed an earlier and possibly briefer hookup with Pearn, Pollinger and Higham, but it was that reciprocal arrangement which led to my becoming the representative of some of the most distinguished literary lions (and a lioness) of British letters.

Pearn, Pollinger and Higham was a very respected, highly conservative, properly stuffy and maddeningly penny-pinching outfit. On one occasion Dorothy Sayers had given permission to a nonprofit church publication to reprint a short piece she had written. I communicated the commitment to the London office as a point of information, and a feisty exchange of correspondence ensued. They insisted that we must charge something for the use of the story. I argued that since she wished them to have it and since it was both a nonprofit and a religious endeavor, it did not seem appropriate to require a fee. Then they demanded a token commission on her token fee. We were arguing a commission of from two to four dollars. It didn't seem worth what the bookkeeping would cost. We were spending more in time and postage just quibbling about it.

One of the first authors to arrive bearing the PPH brand was also the one who precipitated my final break with that office. Dylan Thomas—already afflicted by the weight of his legend, the momentum of a boastfully self-destructive course and the eroding currents of a short, swift torrent of a lifetime supply of booze—arrived already fatally weakened by his fourth tour of this country, his strength further tapped by readying *Under Milk Wood* for its first public performance.

He came to my office one afternoon, wildly incoherent. With him was the poet Karl Shapiro, who stood like a shell-shocked bystander watching the sudden irrational fury that erupted. Like a wounded and cornered animal, the enraged Welshman suddenly began grabbing furniture, throwing anything he could get his hands on and smashing it against the wall.

He cursed his poverty. He was always broke, certainly, but the reason for his present desperation, his orgy of recrimination and destruction, was still not clear. As the nightmare settled and his energies drained, bits of information surfaced.

Cyrilly Abels, the managing editor of *Mademoiselle*, had been to the reading at the Y.M.H.A. in New York of *Under Milk Wood* and determined to grab the first serial rights for her magazine. She was a shrewd and dispassionate bargainer. I was supposed to handle the negotiations for the work, but Dylan, desperate for cash, had personally signed the work away for $750, without telling me. Then came the self-recrimination, the rage.

Though it was a frightening and distasteful scene, I could only pity the wild and pathetic figure and the violent form his confession took.

Pearn, Pollinger and Higham, of course, clucked across the Atlantic that I should never have allowed Dylan to do what he should not have done and what I had not known he did. They quickly added, just as reasonably, where was the commission? It seemed ghoulish and crass to worry about half of a seventy-five-dollar commission; better simply to leave Dylan's pitiful fee intact.

I wrote back that if the seventy-five dollars was so important to them, I'd send them a check for the full amount. In their way, they were creating an uglier incident than that of a drunken poet who had just pawned his flesh. I wanted nothing more to do with them. Dylan, of course, was dead within a matter of months.

After the fallout I received a note from Edith Sitwell, another of the PPH clients I had been representing in this country. "My dear Helen," she wrote. "You can discharge everyone in the world, but you cannot discharge me."

Sure enough, I couldn't. She wouldn't allow it, and I was to represent her and her brother Osbert until she died.

I am certain that I would not have been entrusted with Dylan in the first place had it not been for Edith Sitwell. As one of the prime cultural arbiters of her era, she had used her considerable influence to sponsor Dylan Thomas. She had ensured his fame and currency—would that she had been able to ensure his solvency. But that she was not able to do. Nor could she ensure his sobriety.

Whenever I used to journey to London, she would host a luncheon for me at a ladies' club, the Sesame Club, on upper Grosvenor Street. She enthusiastically set about introducing me to that sector of the literary community she chose to recognize, all of whom I thought highly amusing, few of whom I could have helped commercially. She presided as the grande dame over these receptions and salons, and like some benighted court jester, Stephen Spender was usually circulating on the periphery.

Dame Edith, first-born of the towering literary troika, descendant of Elizabeth I, raised in the hothouse atmosphere of Renishaw Hall, which had been in the Sitwell family for six hundred years, decried our estrangement from grandeur in modern society and art. Extravagantly, often eccentrically, she created by her life, her personality and her works an outpost for those abandoned glories of nobler times.

Her pride in this creation that was her image, her façade, could be quite childlike. Her personal notes always ended with a signature wagging a trail of monograms indicating all of her titles and degrees—real, arcane or honorary. When she and Sir Osbert traveled, they did so in elegance and grand fashion and always with very little cash on hand. They were, therefore, more than somewhat at the mercy of that untitled bourgeois breed of modern patrons who threw open their homes and their checkbooks for a short-term lease on culture and legend. The Sitwells never forgot that they were only centerpieces on loan in the haunts of the super-rich and took perverse delight in making their benevolent reigns as memorable for themselves as for their benefactors.

Early in the 1950s, and largely through the interest and urgings of her friend and mine, director George Cukor, then working at Columbia, I sold Harry Cohn *Fanfare for Elizabeth,* Dame Edith's 1946 biography of the future queen's childhood in the court of Henry VIII. Cukor was very anxious to make the film and I secured a contract for Edith to write the screenplay, a new challenge which she accepted with about as much modesty and reticence as Genghis Khan felt on his tramp toward Russia. Hollywood would simply have to adjust.

New York was still in the process. She liked "21" and I remember many a memorable head-turning entrance there, particularly one bitterly cold Manhattan day when she swept in like the cold gust of wiser centuries into our own.

She always wore black, and her imposing height was further elongated by an imperiously erect posture and heavy floor-length dresses, whose lines were broken only by a half pound or so of crusty baroque brooches. She always wore a wimple, with scarcely a wisp of hair visible about a taut and polished forehead. As she moved, you might catch a glimpse of her flat outsized shoes.

But on this particular frosty day, those magnificent Michelangelo marble hands, with their buffed and enameled nails and clusters of aquamarines, were not to be seen erupting from that pillar of black. Instead, at the end of each full sleeve was a grizzly bouffant of fur mitten. It could not have been a more memorable luncheon hour at "21" had Alicia Markova shown up in snowshoes! When she spoke, it was like a Bach organ recital in Albert Hall.

Since Dame Edith and her brother would be staying in this country for an extended period for the film assignment, and since there was no presuming that it would be in any manner other than the style to which she was inclined to accustom herself, I thought it would be wise to ensure some additional income for her before she left for the West Coast.

I called one of the editors at *Life* and suggested that it would be a good time to bring a Sitwell by-line to the pages of the magazine. Eight editors promptly reported to her suite at the St. Regis to determine what spectacular event would occasion her debut in the weekly. She enjoyed the formidable audience, but the size of the conference inevitably involved too many mouths to produce speedy decision.

Finally, Tom Prideaux, associate editor specializing in theater and entertainment arts, leaned toward me and said, "Why don't we have her do a profile on Marilyn Monroe?"

I repeated the suggestion to Dame Edith, who responded, "Who is she?" After a spirited briefing, we all agreed that she would set out to answer her own question.

The Sitwells continued on to Hollywood. Edith checked in at the Sunset Towers and promptly pulled up the drawbridge. She never reported to the studio and she seemed prepared to spend as much time learning the film craft and reworking her material as she had originally spent in researching the book, a matter of many years. Her pace and her aristocratic eccentricities were alien and unnegotiable with a man of Harry Cohn's impatience and facility for counting minutes in precise dollars and cents. *Fanfare for Elizabeth* was silenced, though Dame Edith continued her research and completed the Elizabethan epic with *The Queens and the Hive* nearly a decade later and in her seventy-fifth year.

She did manage to hold an audience with Marilyn Monroe, who immediately appealed to her protective instincts and impressed her with her intelligence. She repeatedly referred to Marilyn as a "poor misunderstood child" and "a beautiful ghost." She then announced that as much as she would enjoy the fat fee from *Life*, she could not do the article because she would not write anything critical that might injure the homeless sparrow she had decided to take under her wing. It proved to be one of her least profitable sojourns in the States.

Much later, when Marilyn Monroe and Arthur Miller were married and went to London to film *The Prince and the Showgirl*, it was Edith Sitwell who served as sponsor and mentor for their introduction to the community of artists there.

The last book that I represented for Edith Sitwell was her autobiography, *Taken Care Of,* which was published after her death in 1964.

My last vivid memory of the Sitwells is a departure from New York after one of their last visits. While he was younger than she and would outlive her, Osbert Sitwell did not have her extraordinary energy, the oracular tones or the tireless flamboyance. He was by then already made frail by the progressive illness that slowed him down. He was frequently vague, and in those moments the more endearing.

We met for dinner before their return to England. It was one of those times when one is made aware that cherished friends may not be seen again, and the moment is savored even as any hint of sentimentality or undue reflection is avoided. But there was another touch, both comic and pathetic, which made the night indelible.

When they arrived, Osbert was carrying a crudely wrapped bundle. Inside were two items that had apparently been part of a joke presentation, the significance of which I have either forgotten or was never meant to understand. He could neither pack nor manipulate his booty and was entrusting it to me for eventual crating and shipment to Great Britain.

They embarked, and my misty attention came to rest upon the bundle. It contained a stuffed duck of indeterminate species and a mounted rhinoceros horn—I learned what it was only after extensive research. The duck was molting. The horn was flaking and curiously aromatic. As I set about shipping these mementos, I imagined some crumbling Sitwell castle, its many rooms heaped with similar taxidermy and artifacts and fur mittens and Newport ashtrays and antiquities, the set dressing in a laboratory in which a magical epoch of English literary history was blended and fired.

John Masters, who was already living here, was another of the writers who arrived on the Pearn, Pollinger and Higham conveyor and stayed. He volunteers the following reminiscences:

I remember that when we first knew you, you had a summer place on Long Island, which we thought was very nice, but that you would fit in much better with the people and have more fun if you moved out to Rockland County (N.Y.). Trying to persuade you to get a summer place in Rockland was a recurring theme in my memory.

You should say as much as you can about your mother and father, as their influence over you, as though you were still a young virgin at school, was quite amazing when we first met you and for some years afterwards, until they were both gone. For the rest, everything seemed to go smoothly, and we all got on so well together, that I have nothing in my memory except pleasant dinners in the Oak Room at the Plaza in New York or your apartment, occasional weekends in the country—and good contracts!

On the business side, I think you could give the inside story of the film sale of *Bhowani Junction* to MGM. You will recall that when I was passing through Santiago some time in March 1954, you said there was interest at about $25,000, and what were we to do. I cabled or wrote to the effect that you were much more competent than I to decide what we would get and I left it to your discretion. Then about three weeks later, when I was fishing in Villarrica, Chile, you cabled that you had sold it for $155,000. The story of how the first figure grew to the second would be interesting.

The truth of the *Bhowani Junction* matter is not as dramatic as John might imagine. I had learned very early never to oversell the client on the potential income of his work, never quoting more than I was absolutely sure a property could command even as I was aiming for the highest figures and guarantees that I could secure for him.

What seemed to John Masters an astronomical leap in the price of his book on the film market was due primarily to a dropped digit at the receiving cable station in Chile. I had told John that we could get $125,000. A hundred thousand dollars got lost in telegraphic translation. I only squeezed an additional $30,000 out of MGM.

In my dip through the literature of the Empire, I was to handle three Indian authors, in addition to sometimes authoress Madam Pandit. The second, N. K. Nayaran, was recommended by the first, Santha Rama Rau. Nayaran, in turn, recommended his astrologer in India, who promptly forwarded a bill for one hundred and fifty American dollars, to be paid before he would release my chart. He's still holding it and I'm still charting my own course.

My third Indian—Anglo-Indian, to be precise—was introduced to me in the form of a packet of manuscripts which arrived in the mail on the referral of another already successful writer, forgotten by both of us now. Aubrey Menen, a writers' writer, had already established himself with *Prevalence of Witches*, but had yet to translate his critical acclaim into financial stability.

Born of an Irish mother, he was the cousin of Krishna Menon. When the two boys were growing up in India, they decided to differentiate the spelling of their common name, Aubrey dropping the "o" in favor of a second "e."

I did not know who he was as I read that initial submission of stories. I did not know that these were the work of the author of *Prevalence of Witches*, which I'd greatly admired. I might not have read them at all, but they were short and I had the free time. I didn't even note the name of the author, only that of his sponsor. What an exciting discovery I had that evening.

We did fairly well with his later books—*The Abode of Love, The Fig Tree, Dead Man in the Silver Market* and *The Ramayana*—but it was the continuing series of assignments I secured for him with *Holiday* which helped to ensure his immediate economic security, allowing him to maintain residence in Italy.

Like Edith Sitwell, Aubrey converted to Catholicism. As a convert, he seemed to be granted extra stars in his crown and most-favored status at the Vatican. That open sesame and the encouragement of the magazine subsidy eventually led him to produce a number of exceptional volumes concerning the Holy City, its history and its treasures.

Unlike John Masters, who was always very stubborn about what he wanted to write and just retreated and did it, whether anyone thought it was a practical idea or not, Aubrey liked to go over every future project in fullest detail. It was not unusual, therefore, for me to stop over in Rome after a trip to London or Paris to meet with Aubrey and my other client there, the expatriate Gore Vidal.

On one such trip, Aubrey met me at the plane in Rome, a broad grin stretched across his face. "I've arranged something very special for you tomorrow morning," he blurted. "It's something I think will amuse you."

"What?"

"You're having an audience with the Pope!"

Aubrey arrived early the next morning to dress me for my tour of the Vatican and the audience with Pope John XXIII. When he had approved of the suit and the bag that I selected, he opened the box he was carrying and presented me with a black mantilla to complete my outfit.

"You'll be the only non-Catholic there today," he explained. "Come on. We'll be late."

Our guide was an ancient and eccentric Irish priest, and thanks to Aubrey's premium stock at the Vatican, I saw everything, with the exception of Pope John's private chambers. I was fascinated by the ritual and riches of the Catholic Church and thrilled to have so thorough a tour under such special auspices. Aubrey, who knew so well the rooms we wandered and the stories they held, supplemented the commentary. He had even managed an additional dispensation for that long day—I was allowed to smoke.

Pope John did not speak English and Aubrey served as our interpreter. The Pope asked what I did. Aubrey explained that I was a great help to writers, and the Pope commented that that was a very worthwhile endeavor. After we had had our photographs taken, the Pope blessed the mantilla, which I carried home as a present to Joe McCarthy's wife, a very devout Catholic.

Aubrey Menen lives in Bombay today and I may never see him again, but that day in the Vatican remains vividly in my memory as one of the treasured moments in my life.

My personal and inscribed copies of the books that I have represented or caused to be published, together with those books I never worked with but simply cherish, have been gently crated and insulated to follow me across the Atlantic and back again and thence to the western shore. They are children, trophies, footprints, the only record of my journey, and the associations I have diligently maintained, other than the living record of memory and personal contact.

Many times during the preparation for this book I have rooted through my bookshelves, selecting old volumes and spreading them before me to bring some sequence and order to the events I have attempted to reconstruct. I find now that I have very few books written by that group of British authors.

I know, for example, that I entered into a brief and bumpy representation of Wolf Mankowitz. The only book that I can find that resulted from that dead-ended transatlantic dance is one that fascinating and frustrating author presented to me on Wedgwood, a subject of mutual interest. He did not write that volume and I don't remember any of his that I did represent during that mid-fifties period.

I have a copy of David Divine's *Atom at Spithead*, which I sold to Hollywood, inscribed "To Helen Strauss, whose part in this explosion has been enormous." Yet I can't find my copy of *The Golden Fool* or other works that I sold for him.

There are too few of the works of novelist, essayist and critic Anthony West, who joined the staff of *The New Yorker* after his arrival in this country. That is in part owing to the fact that so much of his excellent critical work in that magazine, in *The Nation, The New Statesman* and his articles on theater for *Show* did not find their way into hardcover or paperback anthologies.

Anyone who loves books and authors would be fascinated to meet the son of H. G. Wells and Rebecca West. That initial curiosity would be amply satisfied by the fabulous stories he could tell about his mother and father, but beyond those choice eyewitness footnotes to literary history, I was to discover a most fascinating and talented man in his own right, a fine writer, a man with a richly sardonic sense of humor and a good friend.

The British authors who gravitated to my office at the William Morris Agency were always gracious hosts whenever I came to London on business, sharing friendships which were to last, introducing me to sites and insights which colored my love for that city and contributed to the decision I later made to move there.

They were generally less troublesome and more reliable than some of the political clients and only sometimes less flamboyant than the celebrity pen dabblers who became another subgroup on my roster through equally chance circumstance.

During a reorganization at the Morris Agency a number of shifts in personnel were discussed, and I was given the option of taking charge of the theater and motion picture department—which meant that I would be representing actors and actresses who were Morris clients. It was a satisfying vote of confidence in my ability; it also would have involved a change of scene and focus which might well have been refreshing, had my interest needed refreshing.

In one sense, it would have been no more than a shift from one department to another, but it was probably considered a major advancement. Working autonomously with my own literary department, I had accomplished, I had proven, a good portion of what I had set out to prove. Certainly I considered the change. It was a new challenge. Perhaps it was time to move on.

For about twenty-four hours I convinced myself that it was the greatest opportunity of my career. For that one day the prospect excited me. Then I gave serious thought to the people the job would require my dealing with. The agency represented Rita Hayworth, Judy Garland and Lana Turner, lovely presences all, but tigresses who had learned to attack first. And it represented some tough old cookies who had survived the abuses of booking wars and substandard accommodations during the era of vaudeville, had earned their star and learned to use it as a defensive weapon. In the marketplace, they submitted not the proxy of a written proclamation from their souls, but their own flesh.

I had always argued that writers were no less neurotic than actors, but that they were considerably more interesting and worthier of the effort required. I would rather deal with the most prickly egocentric writer than any actor or actress whose narcissistic qualities combined with sometimes understandable insecurities can make a representative's life a living hell. There are many exceptions, of course; the ones for whom I have affection include Glenda Jackson, Katharine Hepburn, Angela Lansbury and Anthony Newley.

I let the honor pass and remained with my writers. But I did serve Morris "personalities" in other ways. Perhaps my greatest contribution as a literary agent was that of catalyst, the bringing together of talented collaborators and the providing of ideas which initiated books. Often this process would provide supplementary income and reveal another facet of personality and talent for performers who were just coincidentally Morris clients.

Throughout her career on the stage, Tallulah Bankhead had never had an agent, preferring to command her terms in the first person. Probably no one could have dealt so well in her behalf as she did herself. Yet there were juicy guest star fees to be made in radio, and when she determined to cut herself in for a share, she admitted being alien to the angles of the airwaves. She signed with the William Morris Agency on her own specifically prescribed terms. The office was to represent her in all bonus fields but could not intrude upon her lucrative home base in the theater.

It occurred to me that Tallulah's story would make an unusual and lively theatrical biography. From the moment the notion struck me, through the four and a half years it took before the book erupted on the nation's best-seller lists, it was a colossal production.

I telephoned Miss Bankhead on a day her beloved New York Giants were idle, sure that she would not be in residence at the Polo Grounds or glued to her radio speaker. I dangled the idea of an autobiography. She was not unusually cordial, nor did she greet the proposal with a banshee cry of contempt. Yet she was uncommonly cautious, a trait quite foreign to her personality.

Encouraged, since my idea was not readily dismissed, I tentatively and tactfully suggested the services of a collaborator. Vesuvius awoke. I was showered with a blast befitting the Bankhead reputation. "And what makes you think that I couldn't write it *myself?*" she snapped. And, Miss Bankhead added, why did she need a literary agent, anyway?

Not one to labor a point and alerted by instinct that a successful pursuit required an immediate retreat, I retired to plot another assault. It seemed wisest to approach the fiery bearer of legend through someone in whom she had complete confidence.

My first client, Bob Sylvester, proprietor of "Dream Street" in the *New York Daily News*, knew about everyone, and everyone had a great affection for him. I took my idea and my problem to his corner.

Bob chided me for my naïveté in not realizing that all of Tallulah's pithy public utterances were penned by her great friend and public relations representative Richard Maney, an overstuffed, sapphire-eyed Irish Catholic who outdrank and insulted her as only the dearest ally would be allowed.

Irving Hoffman was also a friend of Tallulah and Dick Maney. I asked Bob to call Dick for me. Then I asked Irving, who had done so many favors for me throughout the years, to submit a recommendation to Tallulah. Thus primed, Miss Bankhead agreed to entertain discussion about the possibility of a memoir.

Maney did not initially take the project seriously, but in his fondness for Tallulah, agreed to consider it, though he had little faith that Tallulah would sit still long enough to tell all. All parties concerned were agreed to the meeting. Getting them together was another matter entirely.

Tallulah was rehearsing for a revival of *Private Lives*. There were endless phone calls and a trail of broken appointments. At long last we met for lunch at a then-famous restaurant, Robert, which was situated on 55th Street between Fifth and Sixth avenues. Even in those days it was one of the most expensive restaurants in New York. It was Tallulah's choice. She insisted upon a very private and quiet summit. As the liquid lunch progressed, it was anything but quiet. It was raucous and it was memorable, though not fully printable at that time.

Both Tallulah and Maney were renowned for their wit, but with the added stimulus of martinis and memory, they could not have been funnier. I wish we might have recorded the dialogue that day. Captivated, I kept thinking that if these two devoted and outrageous collaborators could get it written, it would become one of the most amusing theatrical biographies published. They did and it was, but it was neither easy nor swift.

It was a cold and bleak winter day. By four o'clock, when the luncheon finally gurgled to its close, a downpour of icy rain had begun. I thought I had made sure before I left my office that I had enough cash to pay the check. This was, of course, before the era of "fly now, pay later" and "eat now and get indigestion when the credit-card bills come due."

When the headwaiter presented me with the bill for the bonded luncheon, I calculated quickly. If I had two dollars more than I was carrying in my purse, I would be able to leave without having the headwaiter, the captain and the waiter glaring at me. What to do? I whispered to Dick Maney that a small loan of two dollars would save me from an embarrassing situation. He obliged and I survived.

When we emerged from the restaurant Tallulah and friend swooped into her waiting chauffeured limousine to keep an appointment for a dress fitting at Hattie Carnegie's. Dick asked me if I wanted a taxi. I admitted that I did, but I had no money. Maney came to my rescue for the second time in minutes. He took me back to my office. In the taxi he told me that Morris Ernst had advised him that if the collaboration came about, I should not be able to represent both of them.

The next day I sent Dick a letter which said:

Dear Mr. Maney:
   Thank you for your help.
   Enclosed please find two dollars, an odd amount for a lady to pay a gentleman.

Immediately after receipt of the letter, Dick telephoned. He had decided, regardless of counsel, that I would have to be his agent as well as Tallulah's.

An article bearing Tallulah's by-line, prepared as part of the pre-publication promotion for the book, appeared in the Sunday *Chicago Tribune* on December 7, 1952. It had some nice things to say about the book and me:

Prodded by Helen Strauss, a young woman with the patience of Job and the courage of a lion, in the spring of '51 I typed some seven pages under the heading "Mutterings of a Memoir."

For two years Miss Strauss had badgered and heckled me. It was her contention that could I pull myself together long enough to write my confessions, I might wind up as the modern Marie Bashkir-tseff, or a distaff Jean Jacques Rousseau.

Periodically, I agreed with her, usually at three in the morning after my fourth snifter. The next day my temperature receded, I shuddered at the prospect, pondered the possibility of having Miss Strauss jugged on a charge of contributing to the delinquency of an adult.

Cornered, flight cut off, "Mutterings of a Memoir" was a gesture to appease my opponent. Miss Strauss snatched it from my hands as if she had suddenly come on the original manuscript of *Beowulf*, and raced to a mimeograph machine. Soon copies of my threat were speeding to every publisher with a roof over his head.

The newspaper article, also ghosted by Maney, continued for another column and a half, increasingly amusing. It made delightful reading, but that is not the way it was.

After that first luncheon, I had to get Miss Bankhead and Mr. Maney to agree on terms for their collaboration, the apportionment of shares in the book royalties and other monies to be realized from the publication of the book. Though Tallulah was generous and frequently even careless about her money, she began to play games with Dick and me about the financial aspects of the project.

Actually, Maney was the only one who could have written the "autobiography." While neither Tallulah nor Dick had much respect for most people, they did have mutual respect for each other and were devoted and long-time friends. Dick was the dean of theatrical press agents and Tallulah never appeared in a production on Broadway unless the producer agreed to having Dick handle the show.

Tallulah, of course, contributed much of the inspiration as well as the distinctive delivery to her Tallulahisms, but it was Maney who embroidered them and made them quotable. Once she had delivered them or seen them immortalized in print, Tallulah embraced them as her own. Where Tallulah left off and Maney took over, none could say, least of all the legend herself.

After a great deal af haggling between the pair, with me as referee, Tallulah finally agreed to share the proceeds of the book on a fifty-fifty split with Maney. Neither of them would start to work until I secured a sizable guaranteed advance. In those days of book publishing the package deal did not exist. Authors received an advance against royalties for the North American (United States and Canada) publishing rights only and the agent had to hustle all other rights, magazine serialization, reprints, foreign rights, and the like.

I decided again to follow a procedure which was my trademark in the business, that of auctioning off a property by simultaneously submitting it to a number of publishers. I asked Dick to write a statement or synopsis describing what the book would be like. He delivered a seven-page outline unlike any presentation I had ever seen. It was a "selling" outline, hilariously funny. It made my job a lot easier.

I selected ten very strong publishing houses and submitted the outline, with a letter requesting bids within two weeks. Each publisher on the list was interested, but it was Cass Canfield at Harper and Brothers who came through with the best offer, a $27,500 advance.

Tallulah and Dick got to work. Tape recorders were not yet in general use, so Dick conducted lengthy interviews with Tallulah, making notes in longhand and lubricating her memory with martinis. The book that slowly evolved from those sessions was as authentic as any of these recitals can be, but as each of them got progressively juiced, they co-piloted quite a few flights of fancy. Tallulah, accredited by her advance, was not only convinced by this time that she was indeed the author, but I believe she came to accept the fancy and the fact with equal weight in her history.

Briefly, she considered such titles as *Hew and Cry, Ah, My Foes* and *Oh, My Friends,* but no title was so apt and appropriately unique as *Tallulah.* I did not sit through the lengthy sessions between Maney and Tallulah. Professional tours and personal detours protracted their creation and the delivery was delayed for more than four years.

During that time I got to know Tallulah quite well. She was still attractive, with her good figure and lovely hair, but too much of everything in a life pursued with desperation and excess had begun to show in her face, which now parodied and mocked a once-great beauty. It strikes me as a shade patronizing for one woman to say of another, but she was tragically lonely. She could enter a room and create a party, but sooner or later the nights and the parties ended and the audience went home. I developed a great affection for her, but there was always mingled with that feeling a deep pity.

I saw her scream and attack Dick and carry on like a banshee, but no one ever doubted the intense loyalty that held them together. When she got drunk, she could get sloppy and outrageous. She could be infuriating, particularly as she impulsively turned hot and cold on the book, stopping and starting, walking away from it, having to be lured back. She was time-consuming, and often the time invested—the time demanded—had nothing to do with the book and produced nothing, but only betrayed her loneliness. Any meeting threatened to expand into a marathon.

But she was never boring and she was wholly original and inimitable. She was also, in her own special fashion, kind. I remember taking my mother to her opening in *Dear Charles*. We went backstage after the play. It was a mob scene of the famous and the celebrated, but the only one Tallulah wanted to talk to was my mother. She had a great deal of respect for family. She adored her father, Speaker of the House William B. Bankhead. Her book bore the dedication "For Daddy." In the copy she autographed for me, she added to that line, "and Helen. I don't know whether he would have approved of the book, but I know he would have approved of you. I do, too. Love, Tallulah."

I also auctioned off the magazine serialization of the book prior to its publication. *Woman's Home Companion* won that bid, but when the book was finished, they insisted upon certain changes. Tallulah, now enraptured with "her" deathless prose, refused to permit the slightest change and turned down the generous bonus those rights would have brought her.

Once she had made that decision, she telephoned me. "Helen, does that make a great deal of difference to you, about the commission?" she asked.

I told her that it was all right, that I'd get along just fine.

"Well, if it does make the slightest difference, we can arrive at some compromise." She was a very nice human being, and I appreciated her concern.

In the original manuscript, she and Dick wrote a full chapter about me and my efforts in getting her to write the book and shepherding her through its delivery. The one change I demanded in the final text was the excision of that chapter, which seemed too "inside" and too far removed from the personal story readers would expect. They reduced it to a one-paragraph reference.

The book was launched at the Pen and Pencil Club with a party that disbanded, drunken and disorderly, at dawn. At various moments during the long night Tallulah tried to convert Cass Canfield to the support of her beloved Adlai Stevenson, sang "I'll Be Seeing You" and "May the Good Lord Bless and Keep You" and applauded when Fritzi Scheff reprised her famed "Kiss Me Again."

Forty thousand of the first printing of 100,000 books were sold prior to publication. The book, awash in critical cheers, rode the best-seller lists for six months and had an initial Dell paperback printing of 400,000 copies.

In the wake of that success, I set about trying to convince Maney that it was time to write his own memoirs. His ornate and aromatic prose, his fabulous tales, the contacts and insights he had gleaned from a quarter century as Tallulah's press agent and the greatest of all theatrical press agents, and his surly and sardonic outlook on it all promised an even more valuable piece of literature. But the self-educated man from Montana was less aroused by the prospect of blowing his own horn.

Compared to *Tallulah*, Maney's *Fanfare*, finally published by Harper in 1957, was an even more painful extraction. It took five full years of dogged pursuit, surpassing Tallulah's record. And it was well worth it.

After I had managed to get *Tallulah* between hard covers, the lady's good but nonetheless highly competitive friend Ethel Barrymore decided that it was time to commit her own "autobiography" to print. The distinguished actress, like Tallulah, was a client of the William Morris office and may well have been miffed that Tallulah had taken the first literary bows.

She expressed her aspirations to authorship and whatever annoyance she might have felt to Abe Lastfogel, who followed through by requesting me to place a call to Miss Barrymore on the West Coast.

Ethel Barrymore was, of course, theater royalty, descendant of a noble bloodline, and one upon whom supporting players were not encouraged to look too directly or address without proper appointment and recognition. She was a star, a great star from a theater tradition which held the line against familiarities and backstage democratization. She was fused to the pedestal which held her aloof from the spear carriers and court attendants. I approached with caution, but unfortunately retained that basic flaw in my professional character, which was, and is, candor.

We discussed her interest in an autobiography, the potential outlets and possible financial terms. We discussed suitable assistance she would need to put the memoir in publishable form. For my part, I committed myself enthusiastically to the project. She was pleased. We were approaching the conclusion of the conversation. I would then set about putting the book on the market and in the works. It had gone well.

"One other thing," Miss Barrymore added. "Tell me, Miss Strauss, will my book sell better than the Bankhead?"

"Well, Miss Barrymore," I began, directing my immediate attention to a professional consideration of her question, rather than to the psychology of great ladies. "No, I honestly don't think it will."

Click!

She had slammed the telephone down. I waited for the call I knew Lastfogel would soon place to me, and it came.

"You certainly don't know how to handle lady actresses," said Lastfogel from his hot seat in Beverly Hills.

"But an Ethel Barrymore biography *won't* sell as well as the Tallulah Bankhead," I argued. "Tallulah has always made headlines, been quotable and is simply more earthy and naughty in the public mind. Barrymore is cooler and more austere from their viewpoint."

"That may be the truth, but that is not the point," said Lastfogel. "You can't deal with actresses."

"Did I ever suggest otherwise?"

Ethel Barrymore found someone else to represent her memoir. I did not handle it. It took several years, but she got her book. It did not challenge the sales of *Tallulah*. It did not sell well at all. I wonder if her publisher had the effrontery to tell her so.

One night in 1960 Gerold Frank and I had a date with Zsa Zsa Gabor at the Plaza Hotel. I think the appointed hour was 5:30 P.M. Gerry was playing Gertrude Stein to Zsa Zsa's Alice B. Toklas at the time. We had made a deal with World Publishing for a $20,000 advance against royalties on Zsa Zsa's as-told-to "autobiography." Herbert R. Mayes, who was then president of *McCall's*, had given us a sensational $100,000 for the first American serialization rights. The book, still in the writing, had already been bought for paperback reprinting for another $67,000.

Those were great prices then. Today they are "chicken feed." But Zsa Zsa—never a genuine star, but a freak public personality thanks to television—was worth every bit of it . . . so long as she had Gerold Frank to nurse her through it.

I forget whether we were meeting for drinks or for dinner—but at that time it became an academic consideration as we approached the after-dinner and midnight-snack hours.

A stream of messages and telephone calls were directed to our table, while my blood pressure rose. She was at the hairdresser's, delayed by a reluctant toner, or whatever. She was en route to her hotel in heavy traffic. Her zipper was stuck, her lashes wouldn't stick, one delaying catastrophe after another befell her, each SOS relayed through the Plaza's central control.

I'm a bitch for punctuality. The biggest, shrewdest, most honest and intelligent people I have dealt with in business have coincidentally proven to be most reliably punctual. I personally maintain a very tight schedule, but have found that I can always conclude my business and make it across town or across the country to be at my next scheduled appointment with time to spare. I have a ration of tolerance, to be sure, but ultimately I tend to expect from others the same courtesy I would show them, since I know it has involved no miracles on my part.

I remember a night in my early teens when I had a date with a young man who had promised without fail to call for me at seven. At a few minutes after seven I insisted that all of the lights in the house be extinguished and bullied my entire family into sitting in silence in the dark until the suitor arrived and finally gave up his entreaties at our front door.

When William Dozier, one of my old Paramount colleagues, was in charge of programming at CBS-TV in the fifties, he pulled the fairly common Hollywood technique of putting the agent at a disadvantage and emphasizing his self-importance by keeping me waiting in his office while he caught up on his telephone calls for the day. Quite apart from the feeling that such a person was simply discourteous and disorganized, I have always believed that the client works I represented were worthy of the interest of the studios or I wouldn't be there, that no one should ever kid himself that he was doing me or the client a favor. In effect, he insulted my client, and I wouldn't allow that. I took my deals elsewhere.

Jerry Wald, the hypertensive producer who rather unfairly took the rap for the composite character Budd Schulberg created in Sammy Glick, tried the same trick when he was producing at Twentieth.

I waited for a while, then announced that I didn't have time to waste while behind his closed door he did warm-up exercises for the dealing. I had barely cleared his bungalow's landscaping when Jerry promptly burst out the door and came huffing after me.

Gerold Frank and I were receiving yet another preview of the coming attraction at our table in the Plaza. I started to stand up. "Gerry, you stay. I've no intention of waiting for Miss Gabor, not a minute longer!"

"Sit down," he said firmly. "You don't understand these women."

It was true enough, and I didn't care to. Then, to a degree, I did. Every entrance, every appearance is another test of legend and longevity, a threat of unmasking, the occasion upon which a fickle following may turn away to another and more novel attraction. Behind the glamorous image there is always the gawky adolescent convinced that she is not beautiful, the friendless child now adored for the most superficial reasons, rightly suspecting the jealousy behind the easy praises, the circus audience which has come to witness the tightrope fall.

"Well, that's your role in life, not mine." I said with obvious annoyance.

And it was his job and his very special gift. He was able to win the confidence of that special breed of lady, and he had the patience to persist through the bedeviling manifestations of their fears, to be finally entrusted with the panicked little girls closeted within the glamorous guest stars.

If, too often, Gerry's as-told-to chronicles emerged as peasant Cinderellas, Doll Tearsheets and Little Match Girls, I think that is ultimately in the nature of many of those fragile and wounded creatures who are pushed into or lust after celebrity and try to live it, self-dramatizing, self-destructive and often as banal as the plots of a movie magazine.

Certainly Gerry found himself typecast as well as enormously successful, and he tried and soon succeeded in breaking away from his charting of shooting and falling stars.

Gerry is an excellent reporter, uncommonly well organized and disciplined. The patience which won the confidence of actresses in the confessional now leads him around the world in the course of documenting a story, to examine each testimony from all angles to test its weight and its worth.

I did not leave the Plaza that night. When Zsa Zsa descended at last from her suite in the hotel, the entrance was almost worth the wait, and in time I rather came to like her. Though she doesn't do anything with uncommon skill other than manage her own singular personality for profit, she is an original and never boring. Her act is her life, and the book was a well-received program to accompany one of its peak seasons.

Gerry was already successful when, in the early sixties, he was sent to me by Bartley C. Crum, an FDR crony and the famous San Francisco attorney who published the valiant but ill-starred New York daily *PM*. Gerold had salvaged a rambling and vulgar 180,000-word collaboration by the late Hollywood columnist Mike Connolly and Lillian Roth, a once-bright Broadway star who had begun to repeat her success in Hollywood—when she went on a binge which lasted through five marriages and every rung of horror en route to the bottom before Alcoholics Anonymous briefly granted her a way back and a comeback. At 95,000 words, *I'll Cry Tomorrow* was an enormous success and became a hit movie.

Ironically, Connolly, though bitter over the shared credit on the rewritten Roth book, later sent Zsa Zsa to Gerry.

When another Hollywood gossipist, Sheilah Graham, was ready to confess giving her cockney heart to F. Scott Fitzgerald during the last four years of his life in Hollywood, she entrusted that contribution to American literary history to Gerold Frank. And that's the point where I came in.

When Gerry and I met in 1957 to discuss the first book I would handle for him, I made another of those goofs which at best add a note of human fallibility to my text. He announced that he would like to do the Diana Barrymore story.

"Who?" I gasped. "Who in the world is going to care about Diana Barrymore? No one will ever buy her story, however sordid." I did not yet fully respect Gerry's keen reporter's sense for a good story, nor did I let up soon. His wife, Lillian, and I were in agreement that it was a *very* bad idea and we sang many a duet of derision. Fortunately, he wrote *Too Much, Too Soon* anyway, and he never let either of us forget that we had been too skeptical too quickly.

Gerry then turned away completely from the confessional biographies and we worked together on *The Boston Strangler*. His book on Martin Luther King's assassin was a marvel of research and organization, though it did less well

Gerry again wrote a Hollywood biography, but the subject this time was dead, done in at least in part by a life that was overtaken very early by its legend. For the first time Gerry approached a female personality, in the perspective of her time and the phenomenon of Hollywood, with the same reportorial skills that served him on *The Deed*, *The Boston Strangler* and *An American Death*. Her name was Judy Garland. The book, *Judy*, was published in 1975 and was a huge success.

Fred Allen, whom I'd met years before in the corridors of the writers' wing at Paramount, used to chide me for having waited too long to become an agent. Fred, who seeded what was perhaps the richest vein of original satire in the golden age of radio broadcasting, numbered among his writers such talented men as Nat Hiken, Larry Marks, Arnold Auerbach, Harry Tugend—and a frustrated novelist named Herman Wouk, who joined Fred in 1936, upon his graduation from Columbia.

Wouk's experiences as a naval officer in the Pacific during World War II provided the ore for *The Caine Mutiny*, but before that walloping success, when Herman was beginning his off-duty writing and seeking an agent to represent him, he had sought Fred's counsel in the quest. Fred knew writers and publishers, and had been wooed years before by the legendary editor Harold Ross to try his own hand at writing in the pages of *The New Yorker*, but he knew few literary agents. Finally he sent Herman to the one he had any reason to respect, Harold Matson. I acquired my agent's credentials after that decision was made, otherwise Fred would have placed Herman in my hands and I might have represented *Aurora Dawn* and the giant volumes which followed.

I did have the pleasure of representing three books of Fred Allen's writings. Sadly, the second and third were published posthumously. I don't know precisely how the first one, *Treadmill to Oblivion*, came into being. I think I just asked Fred one day if he would write a book and if I might secure a contract and an advance to speed him into print. I do know that H. Allen Smith and other friends of Fred's had long encouraged him to commit to the printed page what he had so freely circulated in his generous correspondence and over the weekly radio ethers. Herman Wouk claims that Fred was responsible for the writing on ninety percent of what was heard on his weekly radio shows, and he was on the air continuously for seventeen years.

Years of weekly broadcast deadlines made Fred a facile writer, and *Treadmill*, which was to stand as a battlefield chronicle and an epitaph for the prime era of radio broadcasting, had a reasonably swift delivery. It brought Fred great praise—at all brow levels— from those who had too long underrated one of America's great satiric humorists simply because he had occupied himself so long in that most ephemeral and popular medium.

As a pillar of the Boston Irish Brotherhood, Fred did not have to face his primary literary outing alone. Edwin O'Connor worked with him on *Treadmill* and on *Much Ado About Me*. The latter book, which covered Allen's days in vaudeville and musical comedy, was not yet completed when Fred was stricken by a fatal heart attack as he walked along West 57th Street on the night of Saint Patrick's Day in 1956. I attended his funeral even though I was still recoiling from the death of my mother some days earlier.

Though I knew him for many years, Fred wasn't the sort of person you really got close to. You just liked him enormously and cherished his recognition. He was a sensible man and a practical one, unaffected by his celebrity and downright stingy—New England frugal—with his wife, Portland, and himself. Yet he was one of the most notorious easy touches, as generous with those who were merely thirsty as he was with those who were unlucky, unemployed, needy or infirm.

Treadmill to Oblivion was released toward the end of 1954 and enjoyed the hearty endorsement of friends like Herman Wouk and the unsolicited hosannas of book critics, but Fred was disappointed that Little, Brown did not capitalize on the excitement with a larger advertising budget and personally assumed the cost of ads in *The New York Times* and *Tribune* throughout the Christmas holiday season.

He agreed to address an author and bookdealer function in Virginia and was presented with a plump Virginia ham. Upon his return, he arrived unexpectedly at my office, bearing a platter on which rested a glazed and lavishly decorated "ten-percent" slice of his Virginia trophy. With it came an autographed copy of *Treadmill to Oblivion*, inscribed, "For Helen, to whom I owe ten percent of my success as an author."

Among the many letters I should have kept but did not were those memorable lower-case typed missives which flowed from Fred Allen's desk. Fortunately, I was one of the few to let them go through my hands. Others who received letters from Allen passed them around, to be sure, then tucked them away with other cherished mementos. After Fred's death, his widow, Portland Hoffa, began recalling those letters, and in 1965 Joe McCarthy edited a forty-five-year representative compilation, published by Doubleday.

It is interesting to compare the Allen correspondence with the published letters of Groucho Marx. Allen's observations and wit could be tart and he certainly saw most of the men-in-charge as fools and their bureaucratic cat's cradles as an intricate tangle of nonsense weaving little but their own perpetuation. But you will search in vain for any hint of mean-spiritedness or self-serving or patronizing. One does find abundant affection which rigidly resists sentimentality, and a tolerant shrug of understanding for what James Thurber described as the "human gargoyles."

I knew Groucho and his brothers, and it is not an experience one easily survives. To read the Groucho letters is to discover, despite the facile volume of gags and gibes, an exploitive and mean-tempered comic elevated from "Take my wife—please!" jokes only by a sophistication of the most callous sort, a master of put-down responses far less sensitive to the inherent human comedy of situations and character.

Jimmy Durante, whom Walter Wanger had lured to Paramount's Astoria, Long Island, studios long before Broadway learned that it would have to do without him, had for years enjoyed Abe Lastfogel's most personalized star treatment at the William Morris Agency. It was Lastfogel who foresaw that television would be the best medium to capture and exploit Durante's warmth and the fullest scope of his bountiful talents, and he had moved quickly to see that Durante's television debut coincided with the prime explosion of the medium in the early fifties.

I had represented Durante for one of the early photo caption humor books, an election-year exploitation titled *The Candidate*, which had capitalized on that most famous physiognomy. Then, shortly before Durante made his assault upon the infant television medium, his devoted partner and manager Lou Clayton decided that it was time to commit Jimmy's era and life to print.

The alliance that we initiated to reconstruct the trail which led from speakeasies and Broadway through radio and films to the conquest of the newest entertainment Everest involved a veteran author and journalist whom the Durante camp referred to as "The Monsignor." The title had been bestowed upon the writer by one-time sports editor Mark Kelly in honor of the hard-living gentleman's not-too-surprising retreat to the simple life in his sixtieth year.

He was yet another Irish Catholic writer, Edward McSorley, best known for his novel *Their Own Kind*. McSorley set out to interview all of the available survivors of Durante's Broadway years, catching many before they expired, taping lengthy interviews. I secured a contract with Doubleday for the book.

While not that many years separated Durante and McSorley, the former was still a dynamo while the latter had resigned himself to the leisurely pace of old age. Inevitably, Durante got away from his Boswell. McSorley simply couldn't keep up with him, and Durante couldn't sit still long enough in his race to Hollywood for films and around the country for live appearances. McSorley flew after him whenever he could, but it was not an advisable pace for him to sustain. While Durante and his friends were very close to McSorley and shared with him the impending tragedy of Clayton's losing battle with cancer, that concern and the heavy schedule of club dates and the preparations for the television debut torpedoed the projected biography.

That was not the end of the project, though it was the end of my role in it. Spurred by Jimmy's success in television, the biography was reactivated by Gene Fowler, was published serially in *Collier's* and emerged in hardcover through the Viking Press as *Schnozzola*. Fowler's style and understanding were right for the assignment and the book was successful, but Fowler acknowledged his debt to the extensive research materials made available to him from McSorley's lengthy preparation for the earlier biography.

One of the legendary stars of early vaudeville, films and radio, whose later literary efforts I represented, lavished some rather expensive gifts upon me. There was not the slightest romantic involvement between us and I seldom saw him face to face. What was remarkable was not his apparent generosity—I had in fact been offered many expensive gifts during my years as an agent, and before. But for a woman made queasy by a compliment and fiercely proud of the independence with which she satisfied her own needs and indulgences, gifts had no place in an efficient business relationship. What was unusual was that I found it easy to accept Eddie Cantor's glittery gestures of appreciation, could not easily reject them and came to discover that I would earn each and every bauble.

When I was still a novice in the movie business, Walter Wanger had called me into his office, complimented me on my work and told me to go over to Jaeckel's and charge whatever I wanted. Jaeckel at the time was the finest furrier in New York and had been the agent for warming many a young girl's heart.

I could not accept Wanger's offer. I had furs already, but more important, I was determined never to relinquish the professional "distance" which ensured my claim to his continuing respect and friendship.

When I sold John Masters' *Bhowani Junction* to MGM for that sum he thought was such a jump from the first bid, he decided to express his appreciation by buying me a new car. He called my mother to determine what make and model of auto I would fancy. "Save yourself the trouble," my mother informed him. "She wouldn't accept it."

When Frank Yerby decided to move to Europe, he had acquired one of those monuments to his early success which he could not comfortably ship ahead with the household goods. It was his yacht, a cozy floating *palacio* for getting away from it all. Thinking that I might like to do the same, he offered to turn over the papers to me. It wasn't the landlubber in me that prompted my declining the offer.

But I accepted the jewelry which arrived by registered mail from the fanciest jeweler in Beverly Hills, the conspicuous excess of my author-client Eddie Cantor.

Eddie, of course, had prematurely penned his autobiography, *My Life Is in Your Hands*, in 1928, when he was already one of the few entertainers to become a millionaire several times over, though he had conquered only half of the fields in which he was later to reign. Radio and films were yet to be added to his stage and recording conquests, and television would not be ready to afford his song and dance for decades.

The writing he did later, the by-lines that I represented for him, came only when that extravagant ego and the talent it carried had seen his power and influence shrink. This writing was less a demonstration of his versatility than it was an essential tactic in keeping in the limelight a name so long illuminated in a million mazdas.

The Eddie Cantor of the teens, twenties and thirties had commanded record fees and audiences, immortalized a dozen songs, launched countless new talents on the strength of his endorsement and the penetration of his weekly radio broadcasts. His movies added to his luster and drew upon it. They brought Busby Berkeley to Hollywood, but they were disappointing and he was not the giant in films that he had been on Broadway, records and radio. He made no new song hits, but began to cue applause by reliving the old ones, by merchandising his yesterdays and the nostalgic memories of an aging audience. His radio show had high ratings through the forties, but was no longer among the top leaders. A man whose popularity, as well as his income, once eclipsed that of Presidents, a man whose greatest legacy may have been his aid in the defeat of polio through his public efforts in behalf of the March of Dimes, commanded respect for what he had been, a somewhat dated old-timer whose place in the judgment of the past as well as the present was not Number One.

The energy and the ego were still there. He entered television and he did well initially, but Uncle Miltie was Number One. Then, in 1953, he suffered a heart attack which was to slow him down, though he did do more television and make more recordings. The old-timers were dying, others seemed driven away by that ego so essential to any performer's success, an ego which never subsides from its peak performance, or perhaps audiences were attracted to the younger and more popular talents of the moment. He had more time and he was lonely and he made use of those hours by seeking his audience in print whenever he could. He was a William Morris client, so I inherited his writing efforts.

Only one book resulted from the association, a memoir, *As I Remember Them*, published the year before his death in 1964. But over the years there were reams of slick magazine articles. One I remember was "Taxi Drivers I've Met," a 1958 article capitalizing on his Maxie the Taxi Driver television character, which I sold to the national Sunday supplement *This Week*. With the appearance of each such article, Cantor would write at least a hundred times more copy in the form of personal letters to cronies and columnists, with advance copies of the publication attached, together with a few old jokes and none-too-subtle bids for publicity plugs.

Eddie had someone who was helping him with the writing of the pieces and of course he also drew upon the humorous material written for him by an army of comedy writers over the decades. As is customary, he naturally believed the authenticity of his sole by-line credit, and though editors polished it to his credit, he believed that they were tampering with deathless prose.

One day when I received one of Eddie's first little packages from Beverly Hills, Louann and the other girls in the office kidded me about the apparent lapse in my general rule against accepting gifts.

"Don't worry," I said. "He's going to take it out in blood." And he did.

Though he was always nice to me, extravagantly generous, often amusing, frequently kind, he was the world's worst pest. Every light filler piece was wrought with the anguish of the Magna Carta. They were born only after endless long-distance telephone calls and desperate letters, and committee conferences. There were agonizing post-mortems.

Cameron Shipp was a Hollywood press agent out of the classic mold. He had served at Warner Brothers and then had been in charge of publicity for David O. Selznick's company. But the letters I received from him did not bear the Hollywood postmark, nor did they come in envelopes from those famous entertainment factories. His correspondence with me arrived in specially printed envelopes with a return address legend almost five inches across. It read:

HELEN STRAUSS TORCHLIGHT & CHOWDER CLUB
PLUMBERS' AND LADY WRESTLERS' DIVISION
Glamorous Glendale, California

They did in fact come from Glendale, the home of Cameron Shipp and Forest Lawn Cemetery. The return address was not the primary eye-catcher on those missives, however. In the lower left-hand corner, in block letters twice as tall, appeared the message:

STRAUSS CLIENTS OFTEN EAT THREE TIMES A DAY!

He called me in 1948. A graduate of the University of North Carolina, he had taken special courses in drama, literature and criticism at Columbia University, had written plays, been a motion picture editor for the *Charlotte News*, a news editor for the *Cleveland Star*, and had been published in magazines prior to his Hollywood move. He remained first a writer and was frustrated and anxious to be in print again.

He told me that he would like to do a magazine article about Billie Burke, covering her early stage stardom, her marriage to the legendary Florenz Ziegfeld and her later character work as the perennial scatterbrained matron in films.

We hit it off immediately, and I suggested that he should really be thinking of approaching his research in terms of doing a book. I asked him to let me check the interest in selling the serial rights to one of the magazines to guarantee financing the book. I called Walter Davenport, then one of the editors at *Collier's*.

"What would you think of Billie Burke's autobiography, Walter?" I asked, already having convinced Cam that the wisest course would be a collaborative autobiography.

"I love Billie Burke," said Walter, who remembered when she had been one of the most breathtakingly beautiful stars of the Broadway stage. With *Collier's* committed to serialize the lady's story, Cam set to work. Appleton-Century-Crofts also published the book, *With a Feather on My Nose*.

When it came out, Cam sent me a copy autographed by Miss Burke, who wrote, "To Helen Strauss, the lovely lady who waved her magic wand over my life and brought so much joy and happiness. I send my most affectionate thoughts. Billie Burke." Beneath her inscription, Cam added, "With admiration for that minor force of nature, the great and good Helen Strauss." It was at this time that my letters from Cam began arriving in the special Helen Strauss envelopes. I kept Cam busy with magazine articles, usually on film personalities, in between as-told-to book assignments.

I had flunked my opportunity to represent an Ethel Barrymore biography, but was to handle another viewpoint from within that famous theatrical family. At one of our periodic meetings to discuss salable ideas, Cam asked me if I thought brother Lionel Barrymore's story of the family would be interesting. I thought it would be very much so.

I sold the six-part biography of Lionel Barrymore by Cameron Shipp to *The Saturday Evening Post* for $50,000 in 1950. The following spring Appleton-Century-Crofts published the long form, *We Barrymores.*

Shipp's style was ideally suited to the popular magazines of the day, though the hardcover biographies he left behind are less valuable and more superficial than the diligently researched writings of Gerold Frank, with their attention to documented motivation, causes and effects. He would not have survived the style of more recent biographies, with their exposed warts, their flagellant and confessional tone and more aggressive assault upon the fringes of libel. That is unfortunate because he often revealed in our preliminary discussions an acute understanding of what really made his collaborators tick and where the stretch marks on their psyches were.

One of his happiest alliances was with the veteran creator of Hollywood film comedies Mack Sennett. We had many meetings with Sennett prior to the publication of that Doubleday book *Mack Sennett, King of Comedy.* Though he didn't have a dime and had lost more than money over the years, Sennett was an astonishingly jolly figure, one of the most serene men I have met, one of the few to have ridden the peak and managed to coast down the other side with grace. One of the chapters in that book, "How to Throw a Pie," has been reprinted in many subsequent anthologies on film history.

The Sennett book was initiated upon Shipp's suggestion. The next "autobiography" was my suggestion and it burned our colleagues at the rival MCA agency.

I suggested that Cam do a book with Fred Astaire, and together they wrote Fred's "autobiography" *Steps in Time,* published by Harper. Astaire was a Music Corporation of America client, so they were greatly embarrassed that our agency was responsible for getting his story into print simply because they had never thought of initiating it for him themselves.

I secured a contract for Cam with *Woman's Home Companion* to do a serialized profile on Lana Turner. Unfortunately, the series emerged when Miss Turner was between headlines, but provoked a great deal of reader interest nonetheless, though it was never brought together in book form.

When Cam arrived in New York after researching the piece, he happened to be in my office one day, talking about Judy Garland, who was a Morris client. I asked him to compare Lana and Judy.

"The difference between Lana Turner and Judy Garland," he said, "is that Garland could commit suicide and Lana Turner never would."

From the time of my first meeting with him at the Waldorf in the early fifties, Frank Sinatra had been uncommonly gracious with me. Once, his courtesy caused me a great deal of discomfort and embarrassment. Once, my courtesy elicited my only encounter with the famous Sinatra rage.

I was on one of my regular trips to Hollywood and stopped off at MGM. Sinatra was filming *Some Came Running* on the lot at the time. As I entered the soundstage where he was shooting, he promptly stopped working to greet me. It was a lovely and considerate gesture on his part, except that the company also stopped working while he entertained me—and I very quickly became aware that it was a very costly delay for the production, the crew cooling its heels on golden time.

Then I ran into him at the party Harold Mirisch threw to announce the purchase of Jim Michener's *Hawaii*. Sinatra had put away a few drinks by then, and greeted me by saying, "Helen, I didn't know that you were in town."

I told him that I had been to the studio, but that I hadn't wanted to bother him while he was working. I had remembered that earlier production stop. But I used the wrong word.

"Bother!" he screamed, and he proceeded to berate me for not knowing that I couldn't bother him and he had hoped that I wasn't one of those who kowtowed to him, and so on, for minutes that seemed hours.

Broadway columnist Leonard Lyons reported that he introduced Justice William O. Douglas to Sinatra at Toots Shor's, where I was dining with him and Hubert Humphrey, and that Sinatra looked at Douglas and said, "I see you're a William Morris boy too."

I had always wanted to work with Frank. He is an extraordinary talent. We almost made it once. I had convinced him that he should stop worrying about the garbled press reports that infuriated him so by getting his own story into print. He finally agreed to have his autobiography written and we decided upon Jimmy Cannon, the *New York Post* columnist and former *Yank* staffer, to work with him. I made a deal with *Look* magazine for the serial rights. Sinatra didn't do it, after all. He backed out and the details get a bit muddy after that, with lawsuits and threats of lawsuits and hard feelings.

In my continuing job of trying to match ideas with the people who could realize them in print, I went to visit another of Hollywood's great producers, a man who never takes the producer credit he rightly deserves, preferring to settle for esteem as one of the world's foremost motion picture directors.

My meeting was arranged by a publicity man who had worked with Alfred Hitchcock since the time of his earliest international successes with Gaumont-British in England. Hitchcock was then still a relatively new invader in the U.S. film industry, though his very first film here, *Rebecca*, had earned the Academy Award as best film of the year and his reputation as the master of suspense was already secure.

Al Margolies, who was a publicist, took me to meet Hitchcock at the St. Regis, where he was staying during one New York visit. It was my idea to encourage Mr. Hitchcock to exploit the hallmark of suspense conveyed by his name by writing a mystery novel, if that were possible, or serving as presenter or editor for a series of mystery anthologies.

He gave me a wry greeting: "What's a nice girl like you doing as an agent?" I was still a freshman in my job, and I'm afraid he took what I had to say with no more seriousness than his opening remark suggested. He listened, he smiled, he shook his head and returned to his assignments in Hollywood.

It was my turn to smile, many years later, when the first of a never-ending series of Alfred Hitchcock anthologies began their parade through the book market.

•　　•　　•

Another attempt to initiate projects very early in my career brought me face to face with the reality of one of the most fascinating images of our time. We will probably never have such a one again. Our country and our world have grown too sophisticated in the least complimentary meaning of that word. The *paparazzi* of the daily tabloids and slicks expose every fallible pore, leaving little mystery to feed the illusions of glamour.

Never again will the glamorous shadow creatures of the movie screen be shielded from a sharp public eye and their own reality as they were in the youthful years of the film industry. The now-dead studio system manufactured, like some immaculate conception, dream childhoods and backgrounds for its stars, so successfully that the bearers of those bogus passports usually came to believe them.

That same studio system enveloped its stars behind impenetrable studio walls, manufactured the only stories that appeared about them and serviced those stories to allies in the press. The studio carefully tailored film stories to enhance the image of the mortals who emerged on the screen. Series of writers took turns adjusting the fit. The stars were wise and noble, had no facial hair, no sweat glands and no alimentary canals. They were taught how to walk and sit and talk. They were owned, which was not good, and prevented from indulging many of their independently foolish notions in public, which was often very good.

When the star system collapsed, the survivors were cut loose, but remembered how to walk, talk and act like stars, and carried the residue of mystery that had been invested in them. The increasingly critical film stock and perfected camera lenses exposed the paunches and pores, but we very often kept the filter of nostalgia in place. But the studio no longer kept them from being discovered in the unemployment line or from making public utterances that had not been carefully scripted.

Certainly many of the stars of that era, probably the best of them, were not so readily and blindly shepherded—I don't mean to imply that they were. But all were insulated from too direct gaze by the public they fascinated. You met your idols at your own peril.

It happened at a party at the home of John Gunther, whose agent I might have been had I accepted his terms or had he accepted mine. He had been sent to me by Elizabeth Janeway. We liked each other well enough and he was looking for a new agent and was agreeable to signing with the Morris Agency. But he saw no reason why a writer of his stature should be required to pay any more than half of the standard ten-percent commission on the sales of his work. He did want to come with me, but only on terms of five percent.

"Sorry, no bargains," said I, though signing Gunther would have been a major coup for my new department.

One evening I was invited to dinner at his home. The gathering was small enough so that his friend Greta Garbo consented to attend. I knew she was a very good friend of Santha Rama Rau, who was a client of mine, and Santha had told me a bit about her. And I knew that Walter Wanger would have succeeded in luring her from retirement in 1949 to star in Balzac's *La Duchesse de Langeais* had he not poured his own money into the disaster of *Joan of Arc*. Frankly, I set out to corner the elusive fugitive from MGM to hear if she had anything meaningful to say. She didn't!

I discovered the living Garbo to be as passive as that other pair of famous ladies—the Mona Lisa and the Sphinx. Such genius as she might ever be able to claim lay in her decision to hide away and perpetuate that phenomenon of mystery. Generations of enchanted fans and critics would define and interpret the meaning of that image the better for her silence and her absence.

Later I represented the first biography of Greta Garbo, the achievement of John Bainbridge, the veteran profile writer for *The New Yorker*. Originally published by Doubleday in 1955, it was revised and reborn seventeen years later through Holt, Rinehart and Winston. Bainbridge is still with *The New Yorker*, though he now lives in England. When the original book was ready for publication, I was able to sell an extract to *Life*. The strength of Bainbridge's book probably lies in the fact that he did not interview Garbo, but filled in the factual details of the legend through interviews with some who knew her.

I also represented John's book, *The Super Americans*, and was able to summon my knowledge of restaurateur Toots Shor to salvage a threatened biography of that Broadway character. John had already written three or four parts of a *New Yorker* profile on Toots, and because of them, I was able to interest Houghton Mifflin in publishing the full biography. Toots suddenly grew coy and refused to cooperate or approve the book.

Things were at a standstill when I suggested to John that we meet for lunch at Toots Shor's. I insisted that we not seek Toots out, but wait until his curiosity drove him to join us at our table. When finally he did, we exchanged cordial regrets, carefully shuffled between general topics of the day. When his ego was exposed, I casually mentioned a number of authors who were published by Houghton Mifflin.

Toots happened to be a Churchillphile. Virtually ignoring our host, I recounted the extensive volumes of Churchill memoirs which were committed to Houghton Mifflin in this country. Toots listened and was hooked.

"If you and John were to proceed with your biography," I mused, "then you would be in the same company with Winston Churchill." Toots read that to mean that he would be in the same league as well as on the same release schedule. Work resumed immediately on the Toots Shor biography.

If Greta Garbo kept legend alive by keeping her mouth shut, Marlene Dietrich threatened hers by maintaining a nonstop patter.

Dietrich actually maintained two mutually supportive images, which helped to broaden her appeal. On screen she was the husky-voiced eternal glamour puss, *The Blue Angel, The Scarlet Empress,* the *Blonde Venus.* Whatever eroticism director Josef von Sternberg was able to pump into those early classics eventually met with Marlene's longevity to earn her the respect of women as well as men.

While she set fashion trends, her off-screen role as the hausfrau Queen of Ajax, getting down on her hands and knees to scrub the floors of her dressing rooms before making her nightly entrance in diaphanous gowns, was well known and served as a great equalizer. She combined elegance with a capacity for the common touch. It was a natural setup. Women wanted to know how she did it, how they, too, could do it.

Here was the figure of a woman of the world who maintained a pair of the most gorgeous knees even though she made it known that she used them to share the labors of every housewife movie patron. That deep, accented voice indicated worldly wisdom, the confidentiality of a fortuneteller who had the answers to eternal youth. Naturally, Marlene set out on a profitable mission to save womankind.

Marlene ran through the ABCs of pleasing a man, compiled lists of the qualities which distinguished the ten most exciting men she knew—Noel and "Papa" and others in that rarefied international set. She answered the intimate questions of a few for a readership of millions. Like some bejeweled latter-day evangelist, she accepted the inevitability that her missionary work would just coincidentally add to her riches. She delivered her sermonettes, had them polished by anonymous deacons of the writing profession and indulgent editors, and saw them illuminated in the pages of national women's magazines, confident that every word and punctuation mark had fallen divinely from her lips.

I was the agent for this vanity fair, and she was generous and friendly to me throughout our association. With many others, she could be bitchy and nice in the same phrase.

One night Marlene Dietrich ran into James Michener in London, author to author. "I get twelve thousand five hundred dollars an article," she announced. "In the *Journal*." She was referring to one of her articles about love. "Do you get that kind of money? Does Helen get that kind of money for you?" she prodded.

In those days Michener was indeed not making that kind of money. "Oh no, Miss Dietrich," he responded, pausing for effect, "But then, my name is not Marlene Dietrich."

Like Tallulah, Marlene often seemed conspicuously lonely, but for Tallulah, an audience required and received an original and entertaining performance, however eccentric, however outrageous it could become under the influence of bonded spirits. Tallulah was never a bore. She may have resisted her exit cue, but she knew how to exit spectacularly. Marlene couldn't stop talking, and all of her topics were ultimately the same one—herself, her health tips, her beauty tips, her art and others' opinions of her art, and her authoritative views on any subject.

Marlene could be extravagantly generous if she liked you, and it could be embarrassing. If you admired anything she had, she wanted you to have the same thing. I was having lunch with her one day and happened to comment on the very handsome Gucci wallet she was carrying. Gucci had just become chic. The next day she came to the office and left the same-style wallet at the desk for me, leaving without saying a word.

She could also be embarrassingly persistent. I happened to be in Los Angeles when Marlene was there, filming *Witness for the Prosecution*, but had made no attempt to contact her. One evening I returned from the office to my hotel, and finding a number of messages for me at the desk, went up to my room with the intention of getting right on the phone to answer some of them. As I was trying to rouse the operator, I suddenly heard the unmistakable voice of Marlene Dietrich on the other end of the line.

"I heard that you were in town," she said. "When am I going to see you?"

"Well, you must be very busy with the picture, and I wouldn't want to . . . I really don't know what my schedule is, but why don't I give you a ring when I get to the office tomorrow morning?"

"No, what are you going to do *tonight*?" she pressed.

"I'm having dinner with some friends. They're taking me to Romanoff's." Without thinking, I added, "Would you like to join us?"

"Yes!"

"You're at the Beverly Hills Hotel. I'll have someone pick you up."

"That's not necessary. What time?"

She arrived promptly at eight o'clock, looking absolutely smashing. She sat down, the object of every stare, the event of the evening. Then she began to talk. It was a guest appearance, a town-hall-lecture event. She seemed oblivious of her audience, whose eyes slowly glazed. Finally, as the evening dragged on, one of the men at the table seized the initiative. "You have to be on the set early tomorrow morning, don't you? Well, I'll drive you back to your hotel."

She drove her editors at *McCall's* and *Look* batty. They complained finally that circulation increases be damned, it was not worth the monologues.

When my mother was ill, the gracious Marlene emerged again. She visited the hospital. And when my mother died, she sent the most lavish floral arrangement I have ever seen. The following day she called me. It was a very revealing call, though not exactly what I needed the day after burying my mother.

She said, "You've lost the most important person in your life. Men can't compare with the relationship you have with your mother." She meant it, of course, though I don't for a moment believe that what I came to recognize as her obvious disrespect for men indicates any sort of aberration. She just seems so totally, narcissistically wrapped up in her own image that she cannot recognize anything but its reflection in the matriarchal line—mother, daughter, granddaughter.

Another writer who reported upon the entertainment scene was Maurice Zolotow. He wrote for *The Saturday Evening Post, Cosmopolitan, Look* and *Life*—the best commercial markets, to be sure, catering to the general readership and the popular taste. He also wrote for the movie fan magazines. In some quarters that carries a penalty, even though that outlet was once less disreputable and he brought stature to it then.

Zolotow did massive research and often penetrating analysis, then tried not to show it. The facts slid in inconspicuously, the specifics submerged to support the easy generalizations in a breezy, unpretentious style. I mean neither to overrate nor underrate his writing. It was workmanlike and entertaining, suitable to subjects and the readers.

Maurice Zolotow spent six years researching his unauthorized *Marilyn Monroe: An Uncensored Biography,* published by Harcourt Brace less than a year before her death. So thorough was his work, and in many ways so prophetic, that it was to become the easy source for many a cheapjack patchwork volume on the actress by those with no better excuse for further Marilyn books than a publisher's advance and access to a folio of old publicity stills.

There are other celebrities, of course, beyond the few square blocks which happen to co-join the Broadway theater and the handy resources of national publishing, beyond the names on movie marquees and the television credit crawl. Arguably their celebrity is greater than that of the steady turnover of performers and entrepreneurs in the entertainment business. Linus Pauling and Ray Bradbury, Arthur C. Clarke and J.R.R. Tolkien have their devout campus covens. The public will always be as interested in their stories, and those of Channel swimmers and astronauts, quintuplets and tell-all croupiers.

Their stories were told and will probably continue to be told by a legion of veteran reporters. One such man was Bill Heinz. His byline was always W. C. Heinz and it appeared alongside those of Frank Graham and Grantland Rice on the sports pages of the old *New York Sun*, long ago absorbed and subsequently deceased. When he came to me he had never written for magazines or considered doing a book. He was proudly a newspaperman. I kept trying for years to get him to write a book. He seemed too strong and flavorful a writer to limit himself to the readership of the sports pages alone.

When the *New York Sun* folded in January of 1950, Bill called me and told me the whole story of its final days, the great shock, the emotions which surfaced among hardened professional newspapermen for whom the paper was a very real and living personality. I was deeply moved by his vivid account and suggested that it should be shared, that it would be a great piece for *Life*. I called them and obtained an immediate go-ahead. Bill wrote the story overnight and "The Day the Sun Went Down" appeared in the next issue of the magazine.

Through Bill, I met the Derby winners and jockeys and touts and prize fighters and ballplayers and coaches who peopled his world. I got to know Rocky Graziano and I met another champ, Sugar Ray Robinson. Sugar Ray wanted to have Bill write his autobiography, and that first meeting in my office was memorable. Sugar Ray arrived in a purple Cadillac. I remember also that he was married to a schoolteacher. What I remember best is that he insisted upon climbing the twenty flights of stairs to my office because he was claustrophobic and couldn't stand elevators. Fortunately for him, under the circumstances, the book didn't progress beyond that first hike.

Bill used to recall the anxious days when he was awaiting a

report from me on his first novel, *The Professional*, the story of a prize fighter. He would describe each painful countdown as he waited for the morning mail and dashed to the mailbox for the news that it had been accepted. The copy I have bears a dedication: "To Helen Strauss, who never conned me. My thanks."

Surgeon grew out of a series he wrote for *Life*, and he would have been content that it end there, but I insisted that we work to sell it as a book. It became a Literary Guild selection. For *Look*, he wrote the first penetrating series on coach Vince Lombardi. *Look* was so pleased with Bill's work that he was assigned for many subsequent multi-part profiles of sports figures. They never resulted in as many books as I might have wished, but they were among the most colorful features ever written in the mass-readership publications on the giants of the sports world.

If I seemed to gravitate to or attract the Boston Irish, political figures, the British and the celebrity biographies, the French generally eluded me. I did represent Pierre La Mure, the author of *Moulin Rouge*, and that assignment ultimately cast me as a referee when I had to physically separate the temperamental La Mure and the testy José Ferrer in the middle of Madison Avenue during the stormy months preceding the production of the *Moulin Rouge* film. What began as a difference of opinion regarding interpretation ended with La Mure trying to cut Ferrer down to size for his role as Toulouse-Lautrec.

In my first years as an agent Glenway Wescott recommended me to Jean Cocteau. In fact, we never met, but I am a fool for having failed to save the increasingly comic correspondence that passed between us during those months we tried to establish a coherent working relationship. Cocteau couldn't write in English. I couldn't write in French. He would have needed an American publisher specially versed in the French language and the French character. Cocteau's French business manager was also involved in the exchanges and he spoke only in dollars and francs. Had Cocteau and I been meeting face to face, we might have overcome the impasse in pantomime or through an omnipresent interpreter. As it was, we were never certain the transmitted answers matched the questions.

Had I involved the same publisher with Cocteau that I later enlisted with Jean Renoir, the relationship might not have gotten lost in and at the post. But had Cocteau taken as long to deliver a manuscript as Renoir did, he would have been dead before anything could have been published. It took thirteen years to get Renoir in print.

I love Jean Renoir's films. I knew that he collaborated on all of his screenplays and that the writing was superb. I became determined that Renoir could and should write the definitive biography of his father, the Impressionist painter Auguste Renoir. I secured his address and quickly sent off a letter to him in Paris. I received a very gracious reply—and I wish I had kept that letter too!

In effect, the director responded: "What makes you think that I can write a book, and thank you very much." That was that.

A short while later I was scheduled to go to Paris on business. I wrote again, asking to meet him there. When I arrived I took Jean and his wife, Dido, screenwriter Alberto Cavalcanti's niece, to dinner.

I talked, pursuing my interest in the biography. He found it an interesting idea, but wasn't terribly excited by it. The book was getting nowhere, though a lengthy friendship with the Renoirs was taking root. When they came to New York we dined again.

Inevitably, the subject of the book arose again. "I'll just say this," I said. "If you should be interested, it is really worth a great deal of money."

Dido, having the instincts of a French merchant, turned sharply. "How much do you think it is worth?"

"I would think a minimum of about two hundred thousand dollars." The figure came out of my head.

"You *really* think so?"

"Yes."

Before I received the subsequent bill for the dinner, the Renoirs and I set out to meet with publishers. All were intrigued by the idea. We finally settled with Little, Brown, because the editor there, Ned Bradford, spoke French. And his wife spoke French. Jean's English, even then, was superior to my conversational French, but he was more comfortable with an editor with whom he could revert to the French in any situation in which the subtleties did not quickly translate to English.

We signed the deal only when I was sure that Jean was committed to attack and complete the assignment. From the time I first forwarded the suggestion until the book was completed, my faith was unfaltering, but there were days, oh, there were many days, when I might have hedged my bets. It took a dozen more years before *Renoir, My Father* was published. Jean did earn the wild figure I had volunteered that evening in the restaurant, if not more, but it was spread sheer by the divisible years.

There were good reasons. Jean was then already advanced in years. Despite his many screenplay credits, writing a book, with no prior experience, was an altogether new trick. Though he is one of the few truly great film directors of the world, the time, the financing and freedom necessary for him to work, were not as frequent as his talents should have dictated. He pursued every opportunity, many of which aborted, and when the chances came, he naturally dropped the book to seize them securely. He finally pioneered the making of films for television when no other sources of backing arose.

I wrote gently nudging letters, and whenever I saw Jean and Dido, on the Continent or at their home in the canyons of Beverly Hills, Dido would produce a sheaf of manuscript, tightly measured between her fingers. She used to call me the "midwife" of that lengthy delivery. I drove up to their place whenever I went to Los Angeles.

Another problem facing Jean in the preparation of the book was that the years had grown over the sources of his research—eyewitnesses who could spur or confirm his memory had died and he had to return to the locales when he could take the time to trace the courses Auguste had walked before and without him.

Finally, at the end of one of my drives up Benedict Canyon, I was greeted by Dido, holding the final section of the book. The prose was sensual and compassionate, reminding me of something Jean had expressed once: "The only thing that I can bring into this illogical and cruel world is my love."

The book had been written in French, but I was determined to break precedent and sell serial rights to *Look*. I had someone do an

English synopsis, a long synopsis to capture the fullness and flavor of the book. It was on the strength of this synopsis that the editors of the magazine bought it.

In any career, one hopes to attain one's accomplishments with dignity. I have tried through hard work and a good measure of luck and have some reason to be proud of my service. But there are always those few peaks, those special achievements which merit special pride and satisfaction. *Renoir, My Father,* an idea set in motion and finally realized beyond expectations, is one of those few special moments which enriched my career and my life.

The next book from Renoir was easier and took only four more years. It was his first novel, the fictionalized autobiography *The Notebooks of Captain George.*

PART
SIX

B ECAUSE I was still new to the business and lacked the confidence necessary to inspire confidence in a client, I lost the opportunity to represent, for instance, Arthur Miller when Frances Pindyck recommended me to him.

The mystery diffused, my confidence grew—but I still did not move to make Broadway my beat. I learned the value of specializing, granted the latitude to make those exceptions I could dictate. Though I turned Gore Vidal over to the Morris television department for his golden age teleplays and to the theater department for his playscripts, it was advisable for me to personally handle Jim Michener's *Adventures in Paradise* TV series and Archibald Mac-Leish's play *J.B.*

I represented Robert Penn Warren's volumes of poetry, but that was little more than expediting the continued traffic between Warren the poet and his publishing sources. I became involved when his novel *All the King's Men*, which had been written initially as a verse play, was produced as a drama by the New School's dramatic workshop in New York City early in 1948, but that was to satisfy Warren the frustrated dramatist. And it wasn't exactly Broadway.

I learned that, temperamentally, I couldn't handle plays. If you sold a book, it was delivered by the author, subjected to some mutually agreeable alterations and published in hardcover, immutable, reasonably permanent, if not precisely immortal.

Excepting the butchery of short-form afternoon television screenings, even a movie, once made, is frozen in its final form. But a play is hustled into alien territory, into the panic of out-of-town shakedowns and breakdowns, mauled and molested upon the whim of one night's audience, caught in a downpour as they entered the theater, or curdled with bits of undigested pork loin and hinterland resentment by an auditioning Boston or Los Angeles critic.

A play is the victim of every 4 A.M. expert, second-guessing to justify his weekend summons. It is disfigured in the crossfire of instant diagnosis by roving bands of quack play doctors, its limbs hurriedly stitched back by an exhausted author, pressured by pre-dawn and pre-rehearsal deadlines and denied the perspective of time to reflect upon the irreparable damage that can be inflicted in minutes upon a work that had been nursed through months of careful considerations. After one of those disastrous sessions on the road, a play too often limps back to Broadway with the teams of interns merely applying first aid to the wounds they have inflicted upon what was once the healthiest tissue. The corrective surgery too often leaves the ugliest scars.

Strong characters can be scuttled to accommodate the replacement for a defecting actor. The author's reason gives way to delirium. The more I saw of it, the less I wanted to go through it with an author. It was like any roadside accident, I preferred to turn my head away. Through my own business associations and those of office clients and friends, I saw too many scripts brutalized and drained of life by choruses of out-of-tune committees and desperate egos pointing the faulting finger at any other vulnerable spot rather than sacrifice their small contribution to the whole.

Despite my preference to avoid that strain, I did, of course, ride many a train to Philadelphia and Washington, D.C., and Boston and New Haven, and I sat in on many a nightly after-theater post-mortem, returning to New York to share the special torture of the nightwatch for the morning papers which would tell the playwright or the producer whether or not the effort would bring everlasting glory or instant oblivion.

A flop novel can still be picked up, held in the hands and read, and it reaches some audience through the remainder tables along Sixth Avenue and a thousand Main Streets. A flop movie will finally be seen by millions on television. There isn't that much solace in a vacated theater and a defaced marquee. The quickie review and the closing ads are swept up with the week's trash. The playwright may feel that he has been, too.

Occasionally those opening nights take their place in history and the play takes its place in the world repertoire. Fortunately, I have shared in those evenings, as well, and the continuing pride they bring.

Bobby Fryer is one of my volunteer press agents, always quick and generous in crediting me with launching him in both his theater and film production roles. His loyalty is a rare quality in either of our country's coastal entertainment centers.

Certainly he would have gone on to produce with or without Helen Strauss. We met almost by accident, certainly as an afterthought. He was my client throughout his enviable chain of Broadway successes, though the office collected no commissions from him until he made his move to Hollywood. In truth, my eventual involvement in the legitimate theater owes its true beginning to my association with him. While the stage hit of which I am most proud, and the one whose inception I can take credit for, did not happen to be one of his productions, it did result directly out of our negotiations. It is I who owe him the credit.

Bobby had studied production under George Abbott and had been his assistant, operating a summer theater for him at Ogunquit, Maine. He was ready to produce and was sent to see Bill Morris, Jr. He had the promise of some backing and a few tentative commitments with creative talent. He didn't have a property. I met Bobby just as the century was approaching its centerfold.

My interoffice telephone buzzed. It was Bill Morris. "Have you got any ideas for a musical?" he asked.

"You mean, just like that?" I responded.

Bill Morris then led Bobby into my office and we started going down my list of clients and properties. We were both getting pretty discouraged as we approached the S's. Betty Smith. *A Tree Grows in Brooklyn.*

"That's it!" Bobby exclaimed, raking a hand through that vermilion shock of hair. "It suits all of the requirements: nostalgia, turn-of-the-century period, sentiment and a strong story. Do you think that she'll consent to it?"

"No question about it," I responded, knowing that she had wanted it done on Broadway even before the best seller had been sold to Twentieth Century-Fox for the film version, and knowing that the book actually had its roots in a play she had written in

1930 while a student at the University of Michigan. It was about a poor family living in Brooklyn and it was titled *Francie Nolan*. The play had won the Avery Hopwood Award in Drama, but was never produced.

Francie Nolan reemerged more than a decade later as the pivotal character of *A Tree Grows in Brooklyn*. Betty had never written a novel, but had written some seventy-five one-act plays by then, so she drafted *Tree* as a play—all stage directions and dialogue. Then she rewrote the playscript as a novel. Her admitted intention in writing it in the first place was to provide herself with a ticket of admission to the Hollywood screenwriting fraternity. Instead, the book became a runaway hit, selling four million copies, and she promptly got to work on another novel, *Tomorrow Will Be Better*, the fourth best-selling novel of 1948.

Still, she had had one previous and bitter experience on Broadway. She had rewritten a play seventeen times for Mike Todd and it hadn't even seen a first rehearsal, owing to one of Todd's not infrequent regressions into financial instability.

Fryer was already putting on his coat to keep a luncheon date. By midday Saturday he called me, saying, "George Abbott is interested. Now, what about Betty Smith? Will you arrange a meeting?"

She had been a client only a matter of weeks. Her professional affairs previously had been handled by her agent, Leland Hayward, and her attorney, naughty old Morris Ernst. In time, she had become dissatisfied, and my friend at Harper, Frank MacGregor, had sent her to me. We met for dinner at the Savoy-Plaza, and as we were seated she looked me over critically and announced, testily, "You know, I can't stand women." Then, over the final cup of coffee, she added, "Well, *you're* not like the rest of them. I like you. I can't stand women, but I like *you*." We became close friends and I represented her until I departed the business.

I reached her at her home in Chapel Hill, North Carolina, where she was teaching at the university. On the fifth day following Fryer's entrance into the Morris Agency and my life, we were all assembled in George Abbott's office. Mr. Abbott agreed to direct the show and produce it in association with Bobby. He agreed, as well, to collaborate with Betty on the book for the show, and they set to work immediately on the outline.

With Abbott set to collaborate with Betty, I decided that it would be tidier if I represented them both. Abbott had no agent for the co-authoring efforts which were an integral part of all of the shows he created, and had little need for one. Audaciously, I placed a call to Abbott, one of the towering talents and great personalities of the theater.

"Mr. Abbott," I blurted. "May I be your agent?" I felt like a schoolgirl on Sadie Hawkins Day.

"Why?" said George, quite logically.

"Frankly, I can't justify it, but it would be very good for me."

"Okay, Helen. Will that be all? I'll ask my lawyer to take care of it."

During all the years I knew Mr. Abbott, I had reason to parody that call on other occasions. Later, when the Morris Agency was wooing him to do television specials, I was dispatched to resume the courtship.

"Mr. Abbott, may we sign you for television?"

Again he asked, "Why?"

"You really don't need us, but it would be very good for me."

"In that case, okay."

Honesty, it seems, is the best policy.

When Mr. Abbott wrote his autobiography, his lawyer, Eddie Colton, asked me to read the manuscript to assess its worth as a corporate asset. The purpose of my judgment had something to do with the highly creative business of tax projections.

I read the book, and while I did so with great interest, knowing Mr. Abbott and his remarkable record in the theater, it did not capture the extraordinary personality of the man or the impact of his shows. Perhaps it never could capture and confine that bright light.

While he has directed films and worked in television and has done some memorable turns on stage as an actor, the general public knows the shows the man created, but not the name and man who made them.

"Nobody's going to buy it," I reported to Eddie, with regrets. Random House published it, and I was right.

Throughout the years I dealt with George Abbott, I was constantly impressed not only by his knowledge, imagination and acute perception, but by his organization and reliability. He wastes no time or words and seems never to be guessing. If I had a play that I thought was good, I could call him at four o'clock in the afternoon, and he would say, "Get it over to my hotel by five, and I'll call you at ten in the morning." Promptly at ten he'd call with a detailed appraisal.

When I last saw Mr. Abbott he was well into his eighties, looking several decades younger, still dancing and showering an aura of sparklers.

George and Betty completed the first draft of the musical in a little more than three months, at which time Arthur Schwartz came in to do the music and Dorothy Fields signed on to do the lyrics. Irene Sharaff began costume sketches. Herbert Ross was committed to create the dances and Jo Mielziner joined up to design the sets.

The delivery of a working script brought the book's total gestation period to ten months. As Shirley Booth was to be the star, the role of Aunt Cissy grew to accommodate her, while those of Johnny and Katie Nolan fell into partial eclipse. Francie Nolan was held offstage until the second act.

Once the show took to the stage out of town, the long days and nights of paring and rewriting began as nerves unraveled. The call went out for the "experts." There are always aspects of a show that are clearly sound, but that have not yet had the time to grow in the flow of a production. Though it is clear they will work, too often, on the road, they can be snipped before they have a chance to bloom.

Leland Hayward, who was one of the backers of the show, was among those offering suggestions from the back of the darkened theater. Josh Logan wandered in with some off-the-cuff remarks. Blind Hindus swarmed the theater, groping about the elephant's hoofs and tail and trunk to diagnose its ills.

The show was, in fact, working well, though moving a bit shakily. It might have danced on to Broadway had everyone stopped changing and refitting its shoes after every step. The show opened in New York on April 19, 1951. It ran for a year, but it was not the hit it might have been with a little less doctoring. If you call any man who simply deals in opinions a "doctor," he immediately starts performing surgery, amputations primarily.

I continued to represent Betty, who enthusiastically sent me writer friends of hers, including Richard Milton McKenna, the author of *The Sand Pebbles,* whose untimely death intruded before his next book was completed. I handled Betty's *Maggie Now* and her last and largely autobiographical book, *Joy in the Morning,* in 1963. I sold that one to Bill Douglas's SEC friend at MGM, Bob O'Brien. The public was not quite ready for the romantic relief of a *Love Story,* and that sentimental picture, starring Richard Chamberlain, was a major flop in an era of switched-on relevance and violence.

Prior to the Broadway premiere of *A Tree Grows in Brooklyn,* another musical opened. Exclusive of a number of subsequent major revivals, it ran continuously for 1,246 performances, and it is being performed somewhere, many places, tonight. It was at one of those first *Tree* meetings in George Abbott's office that the impetus for *The King and I* arose.

At some point in the discussion, someone suggested Gertrude Lawrence for one of the roles in the Betty Smith musical. The suggestion was very quickly dropped, since it was obvious that neither of the two principal female roles was to her order. But that started me thinking about her.

There were other roles for which she would be perfect, and there was one in particular that would fit her like a merry widow and a hoop skirt.

When I sold the film rights for Margaret Landon's *Anna and the King of Siam* to Twentieth Century-Fox, I had promised her that one day we would finally get a deal to bring the novel to the legitimate stage. Gertrude Lawrence would be perfect as the British governess Anna Leonowens! She could sing and dance. Why not a musical version of *Anna and the King of Siam* with Gertrude Lawrence?

Despite the immediate involvement in *A Tree Grows in Brooklyn* and the other business of the office, that idea persisted and excited me. I called Fanny Holtzman, Miss Lawrence's attorney, and asked her to pass the idea along to her client, who was filming *The Glass Menagerie* in Hollywood. I counted to ten, then wired Miss Lawrence, who expressed immediate interest.

Everyone with whom I discussed my idea spontaneously agreed that it was the sort of show Richard Rodgers and Oscar Hammerstein II ought to write. One day I happened to be discussing some business matters on the telephone with Bennett Cerf. I mentioned my idea to him and my feeling that Rodgers and Hammerstein were the team to do it.

Bennett enthusiastically agreed, adding that Richard Rodgers was going to be his dinner guest that night. He offered to test the idea on Rodgers, and I quickly agreed, since I felt it would be better form and more politic if the suggestion arose in private conversation than if I, as the author's agent, prematurely opened it in formal discussion with an obbligato from a chorus of lawyers.

Dick Rodgers liked the idea, all right, but he and Oscar Hammerstein did not move immediately. They were in the midst of plans to produce a dramatization of Graham Greene's *The Heart of the Matter*.

While Rodgers and Hammerstein talked with Miss Lawrence and courted Rex Harrison, who had played the king in the film, Cheryl Crawford still hoped to produce the property as a musical with Mary Martin. She communicated with Rodgers that if his interest should wane, she would like to commission Alan Jay Lerner and Frederick "Fritz" Loewe to do the musical transformation. Lerner, Loewe and Harrison went on to do *My Fair Lady* instead.

While Rodgers and Hammerstein weren't saying yes and weren't saying no, even their attorney, Howard Reinheimer, got confused. He signed Gertrude Lawrence to a two-year contract to star in the show, though the deal for the material was not yet closed. That was fine for the William Morris Agency, since I secured her representation as part of the deal.

They finally signed, and Margaret Landon's *Anna and the King of Siam* became Rodgers and Hammerstein's *The King and I*. Mrs. Landon's name managed to be submerged rather efficiently in the news about and advertising for *The King and I* in favor of the famous R&H possessive prefix. Disappointing but not surprising. For Mrs. Landon, there was the promise of sweeter solace. Part of the deal I made for her included a provision that she could invest in the show. Additionally, I had made a request that I be allowed to invest, a reasonable enough one to my thinking, just reward for an idea that might make millions for its investors.

Two weeks later I received a letter, gushing with regrets, stating that the closed circle of original investors would not permit any new participation. Meanwhile the daily papers carried stories attributing the idea for the musical to everyone from Gertrude Lawrence to the wives of the songwriting team. Consistent with the contract agreement, Mrs. Landon was permitted to purchase one share in the production for five thousand dollars. She called me to say that she did not have that much money. Would I care to split the share with her by putting up twenty-five hundred?

My pride took precedent over the profit motive. I wouldn't do it. We were in for more disappointments. The show, starring Gertrude Lawrence and Yul Brynner, opened at the St. James Theater on March 29, 1951. Mrs. Landon noted with pleasure that the theater stood just five and one-half blocks from the site where Anna Leonowens had lived when she came to the United States in the latter half of the nineteenth century, the site on which her daughter Avis had run a kindergarten. But the Broadway opening night held greater significance for Margaret. It was her daughter's birthday. She made plans to attend with her husband, Dr. Kenneth Perry Landon, and her daughter.

Tickets were doled out as if they were passports to heaven. The wife of Prime Minister Nehru arranged through diplomatic circles for tickets accommodating a party of six. She got clipped down to two. Margaret Landon requested three, only to learn that Rodgers and Hammerstein would allow her only two, and she would have to pay for those! She did not make the trip from Washington for the opening night.

Walter Winchell, in his syndicated column, and Abel Green in his weekly edition of *Variety*, that bible of show-business fact, managed to sort out the many claims to credit for the idea behind the musical and to mention my rightful involvement, but the whole experience with the incredible Rodgers and Hammerstein machine left hard feelings all around.

Understand, then, that one of the more amusing lunches I ever had came several years later, when I received a call from Richard Rodgers. I accepted his unexpected invitation to join him for lunch and sat patiently while the conversation drifted aimlessly from the state of the weather to the state of the modern theater, waiting for the moment when the real purpose would surface in this sea of synthetic social patter.

"Now, Helen," said Richard Rodgers, returning his napkin to the table, "why don't you dream up another idea like *Anna and the King of Siam* for us?"

Anyone who doesn't want my opinion had better not solicit it. Bobby Fryer was constantly threatening to have me barred from theaters. I wasn't involved directly in his production of *Hot Spot*, but visited the show on the road as I did all of the shows Bobby did. I went backstage in Washington, D.C., and the star, Judy Holliday, turned to me and said, "Whadya think?" Bobby held his breath and I tried for a moment to bite my tongue. "You've been better," I said. Bobby swore he'd kill me.

Bobby had an uncommon string of hits: the New York Drama Critics Award-winning *Wonderful Town*, *The Desk Set*, *Auntie Mame* and *Mame*; the Pulitzer Prize-winning *Advise and Consent*, *Redhead* and *Sweet Charity*.

I worked with him on two of his bigger busts. I was there when Peter Larkin's setting of massive lucite Himalayas fell through the floor of the Winter Garden during *Shangri-La*, Fryer's ill-fated musical production of *Lost Horizon*. But that thud was not nearly as disheartening as the failure of the Harold Arlen and Johnny Mercer musical adaptation of Edna Ferber's *Saratoga Trunk*. When that dream sank into the Hudson River during the 1959-60 season, five and a half years of my life and hopes went down the drain. An idea that should have been equal to that which brought *The King and I* into being only brought forth *Saratoga*, a mediocre musical whose passing drew few mourners.

It began when Douglas Black, then chairman of the board of directors of Doubleday, gave a dinner party for William O. Douglas. I was Douglas's date for the evening. He picked me up, and we arrived at Doug Black's house just as Edna Ferber was stepping out of her taxi. I found out later that she had asked to come to the party specifically to meet the Justice, whom she greatly admired.

We stepped into the elevator at the same time. I did not know her, but recognized her, so I introduced her to my escort. It was a small gathering, but when dinner was over, Edna retreated to a quiet corner, alone. In an effort to be polite and include her in the gatherings, and grasping for conversation, I said, "Have you ever thought of *Saratoga Trunk* as a Broadway musical? It could be wonderful."

She looked at me and said, "That's very bright of you. I conceived it originally as a musical play."

That was that. It was a night off for me and I wasn't about to act like an agent at a party. My feeling was that one didn't discuss business at parties, though I find it standard operating procedure in Hollywood today. There were some words about the meal and the elections and the current extreme of New York weather, and then, goodnights.

I thought about the idea all night. The first thing the following morning I called Miss Ferber's attorney, Harriet Pilpel, at the firm of Greenbaum, Wolf and Ernst. I told her about my meeting Edna Ferber and the conversation. While I had thought I was just making polite party conversation, the more I thought about it, the more I became convinced that it could and should become a smashing musical.

"May we meet to discuss it?" I asked.

Harriet arranged for us to meet for lunch at "21." As we started lunch, Miss Ferber immediately got down to business.

"So you think that *Saratoga Trunk* can be a great musical. Well, what do you intend to *do* and how long will it take you to get a producer?"

"Two weeks!" I had set my deadline and made a promise. That concluded the business of that luncheon.

I immediately called Bobby Fryer and his partner, Jimmy Carr. They, too, were excited, and I beat my two-week deadline for producing a producer.

Edna Ferber wrote me a note, saying: "Have you ever considered running for mayor?"

Now Miss Ferber wanted to know who was going to do the music. My first choices for composer and lyricist were Alan Jay

Lerner and Frederick Loewe, and they agreed to do it. They were then working on *My Fair Lady* and should have been wrapping it up, but there were successive delays. Patience prove to be no reward and our waiting game led eventually to bitterness.

I went to Moss Hart to ask him to direct, and plans materialized for him to do the book and direct as well. Briefly, it seemed that the creative team was complete: Lerner and Loewe doing the music, Moss Hart directing and doing the adaptation. But Lerner and Loewe dropped out.

We had a dream and it seemed to be coming together, then very quickly it began to diffuse and move toward what were to be years of compromise. At a memorial tribute to the late Moss Hart, Frederick Loewe, who let us down so scandalously, spoke of another dream, the one that he and Lerner had. Their dream, according to Loewe, was to interest the great Moss Hart in their own *My Fair Lady*. Loewe admitted that after some considerable time they had only completed half—six or seven—of the songs for the Shaw adaptation when they finally got Hart to agree to listen and talk.

Loewe said that before Hart agreed to hear their partial score and talk to them, he made it absolutely clear that he would not be able to direct their show, because "he was in the middle of writing a musical show that he was going to produce and write himself." But then Hart listened, got hooked and stayed.

Edna Ferber and Moss Hart had been friends for many, many years. Together they had ridden the trains to New Haven to minister to the sick plays of mutual friends, the formidable Edna and the flamboyant Moss sharing a love of the theater and a special understanding of one another. What other director would she have chosen to entrust with her novel? Which one could she have hoped to bring her a success as great as the one she had known with *Show Boat*?

Moss reneged on his agreement to do *Saratoga Trunk*. That is a legal or ethical footnote, but Edna must have seen it as a cruel abandonment and betrayal by a trusted friend. They had a terrible fight and their friendship lay in ruins as Moss sprinted off to cut himself in for a share of one of the most spectacular Broadway successes of all time, while we were left to salvage an already tarnished dream.

Earlier, everyone's confidence in the venture had been so strong that Harriet Pilpel, in securing dramatic rights from Warner Brothers, who had made the film of the novel, had leased back the film rights to preclude any competition from remakes or sequels and, thus, to facilitate the possibility of a film musical version. Producing the musical took so long that the foresight rapidly looked like hindsight.

After five years Edna Ferber stood backstage at a theater in Philadelphia. There were nerves and depression and blind hopes and panic circulating there, but Edna's response was much closer to anger, blessedly couched in angry wit.

Outside the theater, the billboards announced "The MORTON Da COSTA Production *SARATOGA*." Above that legend and the equally large billing for the stars Howard Keel and Carol Lawrence, but in minute type, half as tall and one-tenth as noticeable, there was a modest prefix: "Robert Fryer presents."

Below Edna's legal credit and the mention of Harold Arlen's music and Johnny Mercer's lyrics, Cecil Beaton's settings and costumes, Jean Rosenthal's lighting and Ralph Beaumont's choreography, the lawyers engaged in slide-rule credit apportionment had reserved the final words for Mr. Da Costa. Cozily encased in a box frame was a humble footnote: "Dramatized and Directed by MR. Da COSTA."

Edna gave Morton that famous Ferber whammy and snapped, "Why didn't you try directing the orchestra in the pit?" Then she walked away and the curtain went up. *Saratoga* opened on Broadway on Pearl Harbor Day, 1959. Audiences had only eighty chances to see it.

"Tec" Da Costa had come to us festooned with the laurels of *Auntie Mame* and *The Music Man*. At that moment he could do no wrong. Yet among the mistakes he made, in addition to the presumption that his rather decorative talent was too thick to ever be spread too thin, was that he had selected for the leading lady a highly promoted prima donna who was briefly judged a major Broadway star due to her participation in *West Side Story*, a show which in fact did not have its star personalities on stage.

I liked Edna Ferber and respected her, and she liked and respected me. I cannot say that we were close friends, because she was not the sort of person one gets close to. You remained at a respectful distance.

Sometime before *Saratoga* passed into oblivion she came to my office. We discussed some current detail of the production, but it was clearly not her purpose in having arranged this meeting. My office was on the twentieth floor, offering a spectacular full view of Central Park, and she stood at the window for several minutes, lost in the view, and did not turn from it when she spoke.

"Would you like to be my agent?" she asked, offhand, suspiciously playful, as if I did not have to take it seriously if I optioned not to. I am not sure if I even said yes. I may have nodded, but she wouldn't have seen that. No, I think I said, "Oh? That would be a nice idea."

She turned slightly, a tiny wicked smile lifting her features. "In that case, you will have to chop off that building blocking the lower right corner there. When the view is completely unobstructed, perhaps you can be my agent."

"Yes?"

"And I won't pay you ten-percent commissions. Five!"

I was smiling now. "That's not the way I work. I think you've set the price too high." We went to lunch and forgot the whole matter.

During the years that I represented Robert Fryer in his Broadway productions, the Morris Agency made no claims upon him for commissions. Legally, they could not, though it was an association which brought as much profit as prestige. It was not until I sold Bobby to Twentieth that the agency directly benefited from his income.

According to the rules of Actors Equity, that union watchdog of the theater, an agent could not collect commissions from a producer. Reasonably enough, though it is slightly different in Hollywood, the producer was considered management, the enemy. What I did, then, was to work with Bobby and other producers I represented in putting together the package. This process frequently allowed the agency to bring together with the producer talented writers, directors and actors in its camp. The producer had no real obligation to use them in preference to his own coterie or talents in the street, but they did get the opportunity to be considered; and if the producer felt some family tie, some sense of moral obligation or indebtedness, so much the better. On *Saratoga*, for example, the agency earned commissions from Morton Da Costa's work as writer and director and from several performers in the cast. That was a couple months' worth of commissions anyway.

Had I had more sense and daring and been the opportunist I might have been, I would have negotiated my better ideas and my talent as a catalyst in bringing together sympathetic creative talents and set myself up as a producer or cut myself in for production shares. But I did not envy Bobby Fryer or the others their hard and often unrewarded labors and I still preferred my own job.

Among the many special moments added to a lifetime by that job I preferred was an ill-fated but noble venture which would eventually also involve Bobby Fryer. It was the dream project of my client Santha Rama Rau, and during its short and none-too-happy life it would involve the enthusiasms and far-sighted plans of nearly as many people as those who finally witnessed its meteoric burnout.

Santha was established as a fine writer and reporter when she was sent to me by Jim Michener and Harry Sions at *Holiday*. She was then married to Faubion Bowers, the great expert on the art of Kabuki, and he, too, was to become a client, until that unstable alliance was dissolved.

Though she is one of the best writers I handled in terms of quality, having earned the respect of some of the giants of the scene, she has never had a spectacular best seller. Ironically, she is probably known to the greatest readership through a monthly column on astrology she writes for *Family Circle* magazine.

She is a delightful storyteller and a popular raconteur. When Dylan Thomas made his disastrous final tour of the United States, some of his happier moments in Manhattan were spent at small dinners in the company of Santha and Faubion, in spirited political debate and in challenging exchange of dramatically enacted and chillingly effective ghost stories.

It was Santha's dream to adapt E. M. Forster's *A Passage to India* for the stage. To facilitate that dream, I journeyed to England to coax the rights from Forster.

I went to Cambridge, where he was a professor. It was one of those rare, beautifully clear English spring days, made more memorable by that gentle and ancient gentleman, who generously gave me a personal tour of Cambridge with a running commentary on the investment of history in every stone.

In turn, Forster was fascinated and encouraging at the suggestion of having his novel dramatized. Certainly it was a promising venture, a drama of two cultures which cannot meet, written by the scholarly representative and critic of colonial British culture and interpreted out of her own Indian heritage by Santha, two points of view synthesized in a study of cultural conflict.

I left England with Forster's permission for Santha to begin her adaptation. I did not see the first production of the play, which was performed at Oxford, but it was so enthusiastically received that it was then restaged on London's West End. I attended that premiere.

Lawrence Langner of the Theatre Guild originally committed himself to produce the play on Broadway, but he ran into difficulties securing the necessary financing and eventually agreed to coproduce with Robert Fryer and James Carr.

The West End reviews also alerted the interest of Irene Mayer Selznick, who began pressuring me to turn the project over to her. *A Passage to India* precipitated a brief and bitter feud between us. At one point I hung up on her.

She argued that since I had no signed contracts with the Theatre Guild and Langner, merely an understanding, I was free to switch the production to her offices, and obviously she was convinced that she could do it best. She is a lady who pursues her convictions with zeal.

I was leaving for London. I had to catch an eight-o'clock plane when Irene caught me at home at six. Two strong wills met on deadline. I had not finished packing. She wanted one more minute to convince me. I had no intention of defaulting on my unnotarized promise to the gentlemen in question. She didn't understand that my decisions were as final as hers. As she started one final pitch, I said, simply, "I'm sorry, Mrs. Selznick." Then I hung up.

The reason for my trip was that the ecstasy of the London reviews had excited interest in a film version of *Passage*. Director

Fred Zinnemann, whom my office represented, wanted me to package the film sale.

I went again to Cambridge, but Forster made it quickly clear that he would never agree to release film rights. "They will never get it right as a film, but the film would persist to haunt me. I shall leave it to the executors of my estate whether or not the motion picture rights will *ever* be sold. When I am dead, I shall cease to care," he said. A television version of *A Passage to India* was eventually permitted, but to date no film has been produced.

While the critical acclaim—no doubt inspired by the esteem for Forster in his homeland—had been clamorous, the run of the play was only mildly successful. As an outsider, I had greater doubts about its worth, but hoped for the best.

The Theatre Guild–Fryer presentation of the play opened out of town in Boston. It was an encouraging period. Santha was a Wellesley graduate and found herself embraced with a hometown chauvinism that was surprising for that staid citadel. The critics were tolerant, encouraging. Surely the play would get better, and it seemed in that friendly climate that it might even get very good indeed.

The cast was exceptional: Anne Meacham, Eric Portman, Gladys Cooper and Zia Mohyeddin. Santha had reduced the complex themes and content of the novel into a well-made play that inspired slick performances. The intelligence with which she considered the problem of Anglo-Indian and race relations gave the play a weight and consequence that livelier, more entertaining and original Broadway vehicles lacked. It commanded respect as the workmanlike fulfillment of an ambitious task, as the evidence of an intelligent writer at work, but it brought the intellectual considerations of the text to the stage without engaging the involvement of the emotions.

The play opened on Broadway late in January of 1962. The critics were not tolerant or gentle. It ran less than three months. *Gifts of Passage*, a book of Santha's reminiscences of her years in India, South Africa, Europe and America, written a year earlier, will probably be valued and read for many years. I doubt anyone even remembers the play. Another writer had had her fling with the Broadway dream, learning that novelists aren't the best dramatists. The novelist can expand material, embroidering and examining it from every vantage. The dramatist must condense and clarify. Few who master one art well can manage the other, and fewer still should try.

I involved Bobby Fryer in one other aborted theatrical venture. The playwright was Irene Kamp, whom I had met during my first year as an agent. She had sold two short fiction pieces to *Collier's*, and when a third was rejected, someone suggested that she should find an agent to open up other outlets for her work. She sent me the story and I liked it. I liked it well enough to resubmit it to *Collier's*, for which it was well suited. To her surprise, they accepted it this time and she received substantially more money than she had for the first two stories.

She had grown up in that rarefied world of the New York fashion magazines, and remarked that I was totally unlike the career women she had known in that business. It soon became clear that she had a particular talent as a dramatist, and we worked toward that time when she could move from writing stories for the slicks to creating flesh and wit for the stage.

I was very excited when I read her first play. It was titled *The Young Strangers* and in many ways anticipated the later plays of Neil Simon. I made a production deal with Robert Fryer and Bertram Bloch, then a story editor for Twentieth Century-Fox.

While the strength of the script was apparent, it was also raw and demanded revisions and polishing. Irene, who was still young and growing in her craft, would learn a great deal in the process of reworking her script. And it would have been worth it. But craft was not the only lesson she had to learn. She was simultaneously reworking her personal scenario in search of maturity, and trial and error was her course.

Faced with the opportunity and the responsibility that the possible success of her play might impose, she panicked, defaulted on the prescribed revisions and finally ran. She fled to the West Coast. Eventually she put her life in order, but it required that her talents lie dormant for a time and it meant that one of the best plays I had ever read by a new playwright simply never was.

The talent and the friendship remained intact through the years which followed. She did finally have a play, *The Great Indoors*, produced on Broadway.

Odd, what is remembered and what is forgotten. I cannot remember just when or where I met Edward Albee, and I'm reluctant to ask him. Edward is not noted for committing himself to any single answer or answering a question when he can raise a better one.

Yet I remember at this moment, most vividly of all, the night between Christmas and New Year's in 1964, when I attended the opening of *Tiny Alice* at the Billy Rose Theatre.

I remember it not for the powerful and disturbing opacity of the play or Edward's moody and characteristically enigmatic vigil at its trial by strangers. I remember it because I attended the opening with Gore Vidal, who carried into the theater a fat bag of hard candy and proceeded to assault it throughout the play's most puzzlingly elegiac moments. In the sensors of my memory, *Tiny Alice* is registered as a long-playing record of storm and thunder sound effects and the march of mice over crunching autumn leaves.

Just as George Abbott is always respectfully addressed by all who know him as "Mr. Abbott," Edward Albee is always "Edward." He was not officially my client, though I took a more than casual interest in his career and played a very active role in one of the important decisions he made.

Edward Parone, who is now the Director of the New Theater for Now program at the Mark Taper Forum of the Los Angeles Music Center, which regularly presents the works of new playwrights, was Edward's agent. He was also the director for all of the West Coast premieres of Albee plays and the first managing director of the Playwrights Unit which Albee, Clinton Wilder and Richard Barr sponsored.

When I met Eddie Parone he had published some poetry in *The New Yorker*, written some book reviews and had attended Trinity College with Edward Albee. He was working as an editor for a publishing house. He was reputable and bright and I respected him. I knew about his intensive training and continuing passion for the theater. When the Morris Agency had an opening in its play department, I urged them to bring Eddie into the office.

They did, and he became a valuable asset as an agent, until he moved to devote his full time to active creative participation in the theater.

It was Eddie who brought his friend Edward Albee into the office as a client. It was he who sold Edward's first one-act play, *Zoo Story*, to producer Richard Barr and subsequent works to the team of Barr and Clinton Wilder.

Albee erupted on the theater scene and made as much news losing an occasional award as he did winning the others. John Gassner and John Mason Brown resigned from the Pulitzer Prize drama jury when Edward was denied that award for *Who's Afraid of Virginia Woolf?* He was so popular on college campuses that courses were conducted to decipher the meanings of his plays, and at an after-performance seminar at the American Conservatory Theater in San Francisco, psychiatrists, theologians and theater people devoted serious discussion to whether the title of his play *Tiny Alice* was in fact a discreet pun or homonym for an intended "tiny phallus."

Those same moonlighting "experts" and many more were picking up honorariums nightly on the lecture circuit with even wilder interpretations. Seizing upon that public interest and its lunatic fringe, and to offer the plays as the best answer to the riddles circulated, I moved to get all of Edward's plays in print, with particular emphasis on popularly priced editions for Albee's vast campus following.

In most respects, Edward took his success well, but like many another artist boosted to the top of a pedestal, he became wary of counsel and subject to intimations of omnipotence. All too often so much bad and unsolicited advice is heaped upon the successful that they may suspect the opposite course is always best, and at very least, may want the luxury of making their own mistakes.

Suddenly, with every Hollywood studio expressing keen interest in filming *Who's Afraid of Virginia Woolf?* and with Edward in a position to demand some extraordinary rights of approval and control, the playwright decided he might like to try his hand at producing and writing a motion picture. Mr. Albee, Mr. Barr and Mr. Wilder, who had been having an almost unhealthy succession of successes and had achieved them by breaking many of the established Broadway rules, decided it would be interesting to form their own little do-it-yourself film production company and then tackle *Who's Afraid of Virginia Woolf?* as their first on-the-job-training venture.

It was a deliciously starry-eyed notion, the hardest sort to give up when one can afford the luxury of committing artistic and financial suicide—at least once. Once would have been enough, of course. Everyone wanted to buy the play. Most were willing to arbitrate the attachment of strings to placate the author, but the author was responding like the virgin about to be thrown on the casting couch by the nightmare prototypes in every trashy Hollywood novel. He wasn't going to sell, or as the popular Broadway oath goes, he wasn't going to *sell out*. If he waited long enough, he might not get the chance, and he most assuredly would not get it on his terms.

Male-pattern baldness threatened to become epidemic at the Morris offices for days of hair-tearing and molar-grinding. Worse, studios that were fearful that the play could not be transferred to the screen without serious censorship battles were being given time to reconsider whether their initial excitement was justified.

The play was about to open in London, and the author, still refusing to trade with the whores of the western Babylon, had left for England. It was decided that I would follow him to London and try to convince him of the wisdom of making the swiftest and best deal with full-time filmmakers.

When I arrived in London, I called Edward and made a date to meet him the following afternoon at five at Claridge's, where I was staying. That night I attended the opening of the play, and throughout the following day I prayed that the reviews would be good, both for the sake of his humor and the continued enthusiasm of the Hollywood bidders. One by one the papers arrived, and the reviews were great.

But Edward surely knew my purpose in being there. Might he not be convinced that there was nothing to discuss, that his answer, clearly stated already, was final? He was notorious at that time for not showing up on time, not showing up at all or canceling out at the last minute. Many people at the office had been willing to bet that he wouldn't show. This obvious setup to reopen what he may well have considered old business suddenly seemed the likeliest candidate for the last-minute scratch.

Edward was staying at the Savoy. At a quarter to five my telephone rang. Here it goes, I thought. He's going to cancel. I picked up the receiver and waited for the announcement.

"I'm going to be fifteen minutes late" came the pleasant voice of Edward Albee on the other end of the line.

Once he arrived, we talked for three hours. There were just the two of us, but the results of that conversation owed a great deal to a third person—absent, though her presence was strongly felt and very influential. Tallulah Bankhead played a role in the denouement.

Tallulah was a mutual friend and Tallulah could be a strong bond between those who knew her. He told me how she respected me and how often she had spoken of me. That endorsement provided me with a special transfer on that ride. We settled down to discuss what was wisest and surest for Edward and his play. I told him what was offered, what he should expect and what he ought to accept, as well as suggesting that a major studio would be in the best position to apply the muscle necessary to bend the industry's self-imposed regulations to ensure that the play could come to the screen without drastic compromise of its content and style.

After I left that meeting I cabled Abe Lastfogel that Edward had agreed to the sale of the motion picture rights for *Who's Afraid of Virginia Woolf?* That was not the end of it.

Who's Afraid of Virginia Woolf? was the film on which Ernest Lehman added the producer credit to his familiar role of screenwriter. It was a trailblazing film, one that opened the gates for many of the better and lesser excursions into screen candor which followed. But no trail is blazed without some fairly rough going. Throughout the filming, Ernie called me to recount the wounds he had suffered along the frontier, how his stars—the volatile Burton and Taylor—and the director Mike Nichols and Edward Albee himself had been mean to him or fought dirty in the clinches. By his accounts, the location site at Smith College in Northampton was splattered with the blood of the producer, who underwent his initiation there.

Edward, receiving his own initiation in the filmmaking process, became absolutely beatific. When he was quoted upon the release of the film as saying that Lehman's applauded screen adaptation involved no more than a change of twenty-seven words from the original text, it was not clear whether the remark was made with bitter or merely bemused irony. It can never be determined to what degree Albee's remarks cost Ernie Lehman the Academy Award for the best screen adaptation of that year.

The snob hit that *A Passage to India* might have been, *J.B.*, Archibald MacLeish's twentieth-century poetic drama from ancient Hebrew parable, was—and it was a great surprise to me. A snob hit, according to William Goldman, is a play seen by more people than really want to see it, a play of limited appeal to the mass audience, suddenly promoted to an obligatory mass *must see*, like it or not.

I received a telephone call from Boston from MacLeish's publisher at Houghton Mifflin, Hardwick Moseley, asking me if I would be interested in handling MacLeish and the play, which Curtis Canfield was staging at the Yale School of Drama. Brooks Atkinson had gone up for the tryout and had written a rapturous review for both the daily and Sunday *New York Times*.

An appointment was made, and MacLeish came to see me. He seemed somewhat taken aback by my first question: "Mr. MacLeish, which producer and which director would you want?" He looked at me as if I were quite daft, probably not expecting such a direct approach.

After a very brief discussion, we settled on Alfred de Liagre, Jr., whom we both knew and who was several rungs above the usual Broadway producer.

"Fine," I said. "We'll get de Liagre to produce. Now, for a director?"

Still incredulous, he said, rather tentatively, "Do you happen to know Elia Kazan?"

"Yes, quite well."

"Do you think he might possibly be interested?"

"I'll call him."

I called Kazan, who had graduated from Yale Drama School, and asked him if he had been up to see the production of *J.B.* He had not, but he had read the Atkinson review and was anxious to read it. I promptly rushed the script over to him by messenger.

The following day "Gadg" called to say that he and Molly, his wife at that time, loved the play, but asked for time to read it again.

"If it is what we think it is, I'll want to meet Mr. MacLeish," he said. The next day he called again, his interest reinforced, and an appointment was set between the author and his new director.

Despite some strong reservations which those of us involved in the production had regarding Kazan's choice for a leading lady, the play earned MacLeish his third Pulitzer Prize and was one of those occasions when confidence and luck meet and all of the components fall into place as ordered. The taste of de Liagre and the magic generated by Kazan's name and talent set the stage for success. We didn't have to start by compromising our first choices. MacLeish's revisitation of Job was a charmed event for many and deceptively easy to bear.

"I'd like to do a film biography of Eleanor Roosevelt and I want Archibald MacLeish to write it," said the tightly wound and expansive young man who had hustled himself an appointment and now stood before my desk at the Morris Agency. He was handsome, with dark, wavy hair, neatly silvered at the temples. He was the image of the promoter. His confidence was infectious. But I was prepared not to believe a thing he said.

"Do you mind telling me," I asked, "what you have done?"

"Nothing." He then explained that he could get the cooperation of the Roosevelt family. I grew more skeptical, even as I admired his nerve. I was still very much in awe of Archibald MacLeish, impressed by his dignity and his uncompromised stature in the artistic community. I was not about to foist a well-tanned speculator with a yen to dabble in films upon him. But this apparent road-company Sammy Glick obviously had taste and the confidence to bluff his way from wild claims to even more unlikely accomplishment. It was a quality common to some of the very best producers. If nothing else, I was ready to buy a used car from him.

He was from Philadelphia originally, and told me that he had spent his earliest years in an orphanage. He had worked as a movie usher and eventually managed theaters. He had been an Air Force captain, returning home as a fund-raiser for Israel Bonds, later becoming an executive for a Miami bank, and finally working with Eleanor Roosevelt as a director of her cancer foundation.

He could no longer postpone his film ambitions and had determined to produce a memorial to the life of the internationally admired late First Lady. Okay, he had captivated me. Now it was my turn. I asked him to substantiate his claims of cooperation from the Roosevelt family and the promises of films and archival materials for the projected documentary feature.

I'll be damned, but he did! A meeting with MacLeish was arranged. MacLeish, very sympathetic to the idea of the film and to its subject, agreed to write the narration. Thus Sidney Glazier made an auspicious debut as a film producer, winning the Academy Award for best documentary feature. MacLeish reworked his narration and realized a successful book as a bonus. Sidney next produced the hilarious *The Producers*, which won a screenwriting Oscar for Mel Brooks. As president of his own company, Sidney overextended with a reckless schedule of twelve films in eight months—all of them interesting—but he bounced back.

Shortly before Christmas, 1965, as I sat reading reports in the morning newspaper of the death of W. Somerset Maugham the day before, my telephone rang. It was Garson Kanin, breathless with the effusiveness of a man who was already making "friend of the famous" a career category. As Kanin relates it, Thornton Wilder had advised him as a pup out of school to keep journals, to write down everything that happened to him. He maintains them as the frugal maintain their bankbooks.

"Helen," the voice on the other end of the line announced. "I have it. Willie's biography. I have the biography of Willie Maugham!"

"You couldn't have!" I responded. There hadn't even been time for the survivors to make, let alone announce, funeral plans.

"Oh, yes I do," said Kanin confidently. "I've been keeping copious notes all these years." Suddenly it seemed almost rude of Mr. Maugham to have delayed Garson's book so long.

"I'll read it in a hurry," said I.

"Good. I need the money in a hurry," said he.

It was Garson Kanin, all right. *Remembering Mr. Maugham* turned out to be something more of an installment of Kanin's biography. I read it—and sold it several days later to Atheneum for the sort of advance that keeps Mr. Kanin in fashion. Fortunately, I was out of the business by the time he did the *Tracy and Hepburn* installment of his journals, because I would not have represented him on it. Katharine Hepburn, the great lady she is, never dignified the book by acknowledging its publication.

Whatever else I may say and feel about Garson Kanin and his more talented wife, Ruth Gordon, whatever scars I bear from having been one of their private servants rather than one of their public enthusiasms, I will always admit that Garson Kanin was unwittingly reponsible for having changed the course of my life. For that, he has my sincere thanks.

My representation of the Kanins was limited, by mutual agreement. Typically, they did not come to me until I had become fashionable, until I had established a reputation as a first-class literary agent.

Kanin had left Hollywood for the Armed Services after directing an inconsequential Ginger Rogers comedy, *Tom, Dick and Harry*, at RKO in 1941. Thanks to Johnny Hyde at the Morris Agency, Kanin established a record by selling his postwar political comedy, *Born Yesterday*, to Columbia for a million dollars.

Thereafter, he had written a successful series of films for Tracy and Hepburn and Judy Holliday, usually with his wife as co-author and George Cukor as director. His solo efforts for the Broadway stage fared poorly, among them *The Rat Race* and *The Smile of the World*, which collapsed after five performances. Ruth, on the other hand, did very well on her own, whether performing or writing for the stage.

Multi-talented is a phrase quite overworked in the trade and it means that the person so dubbed has more than one way to make a buck, whether or not any one of those negotiable talents might be subject to question. The co-star of a long-running television western may in time be kept happy by being permitted to write a new and mediocre theme song and have his none-too-original teleplay accepted and then direct it with plenty of help from the producer and the director of photography. That makes him a Renaissance man only in the judgment of the fan magazines.

Ruth and Gar had been personally watched over for years by Abe Lastfogel, but as I began to accumulate some reputation among their Broadway and publishing friends, they agreed to have me represent them for their printed works in magazines and books.

Ruth approached me first. She had written a short story. I read it, was pleased and placed a call to her, telling her that I was confident I could sell it to *Ladies' Home Journal,* which I did. She promptly submitted another story. This time I called her to say that I did not think it was publishable and suggested a possible rewrite. She was furious. The story did prove to be unpublishable, but regardless, she reported me to Abe Lastfogel for my audacity.

I had been handling Garson's magazine pieces and books with success and profit and a minimum of hurt feelings, when I happened to read the first-draft screenplay he and Ruth wrote for *Pat and Mike,* the film they were to do with Tracy, Hepburn and Cukor several years later. I did not represent the couple for motion pictures, but I read scripts for everyone in the office, so it was not unusual when Lastfogel called me into the office and said, oh-so-typically, "Don't be in a hurry about this. We can discuss it tomorrow morning." And he handed me the script of *Pat and Mike,* which was a long way from the one that was finally filmed.

The next morning, bleary-eyed and early, I hotfooted into Lastfogel's office with the bad news. "I think it's pretty bad, but it *is* a first draft. I suppose with revisions it will be okay. The idea is certainly good."

Lastfogel had to return to the West Coast, so he told me to call the Kanins and arrange a luncheon meeting with them. The date was set and we decided upon the old and ultra-chic Pavillon. When the appointed day arrived and revealed itself to be one of those miserably dreary, icy cold and rainy winter days that give Manhattan the blues, I did not immediately take it to be an omen. I should have.

We arrived, and I sat cautiously and consciously tactful, waiting for the opening—that question which would beg a candid response—and hoping that they wanted what they asked for and would get.

"Considering that it is a first draft, I'm sure that when you get to the revisions . . ."

There was dead silence. Then I seemed to hear the echo of a thousand doors slamming down the length of an endless corridor. Those were the last words I was allowed to utter. I was effectively excluded from their company. I had proven myself unworthy to discuss their handicrafts. Shut up and eat your sole!

We moved wordlessly out of the restaurant and toward the curb. Their chauffeur drove up with their car. They rushed in, out of the rain, slamming the door in my face, leaving me standing, wet and chilled, to wait for a taxi. It was a very long wait indeed.

When I got back to the office and had thawed, I wrote a note to Lastfogel in California. I told him that he would probably be receiving in the same post a letter from the Kanins, protesting that I was a pretentious snip, that I didn't know my business and that I should be fired. I don't know which letter he opened first, but both arrived on schedule.

I continued to do my usual job for them, while *Pat and Mike* moved through many revisions on its way toward a shooting script. But several months after that luncheon Kanin called a meeting of all available executives at the agency. He accused me of not being as enthusiastic about his writing as I was about other clients', of not having the proper appreciation for his work or Ruth's.

I listened to the charges, then responded, "Apparently you don't want to hear any criticism, so why should I offer any? You won't permit me to do the best job in your behalf."

Kanin turned to Nat Lefkowitz, who ran the New York office in his capacity as treasurer of the company, and declared, "I've been a client longer than she has been an employee. *Either she leaves or I do!*"

Several days later I called Kanin. "What would you like me to do with these manuscripts that I have of yours? Shall I file them or would you like me to send them to you?"

After a moment he uttered what sounded like an embarrassed laugh. "Don't be ridiculous! I have to have the best agent in the business, and that's you!" And so we continued together.

Like many other novelists, Edwin O'Connor had wanted to do a play. When the urge became irresistible, he wrote *I Was Dancing*. I had read it and was successful in encouraging him to put it aside and rewrite it as a novel. Kanin, somehow or other, heard about O'Connor's dramaturgical urge and practically demanded to read the play. He asked several times, and I kept being evasive. He finally became very annoyed that I would not surrender O'Connor's folly and began kicking up a fuss in the office again.

Unfortunately, O'Connor heard of Kanin's interest. I could no longer contain him. O'Connor, the sober novelist, now a star-struck playwright, knew only that Garson Kanin of Broadway wanted to read his play. So Garson and Ruth read it, and a bubbling Garson called to report, "Ruth agrees with me that this is a *great* play. It's the greatest one we've read in a long time."

They forwarded the script to producer David Merrick, who must have been looking for something to do that season. And Merrick agreed that it was a great play. And O'Connor became convinced that it really must be a great play, and great plays must be produced, so David Merrick produced it and Garson Kanin directed it—and they all went to Boston to try it out.

It opened in Boston and it was a bomb. Ed O'Connor and I walked around the Boston Common again and again.

"Why don't we just forget it?" I said, not wanting him to spend more weeks agonizing over it only to be wounded again in New York City.

But the stars were still in his eyes. The play was a trip to Broadway, where magic could still happen, at least that was the way it was always depicted in plays and movies. "No." he said. "It'll be all right once we get to Washington."

We moved on to Washington. I was standing backstage with David Merrick, whom I came to like a great deal. The audience, such as it was, sat motionless, absorbent as soundproofing, draining the sounds from the stage and returning a soft rustle of unison coughs and throat clearings.

"Okay," said a discouraged Merrick. "You're so smart, what would you do if you were the producer?"

"Close it!"

"You give up too easily," he replied, walking away.

"Only when it's the only wise course," I said, but he was already gone, seeking the backstage reassurances that can be had for the asking, despite all the messages on the wall.

Opening night at the Lyceum Theatre in New York, November 8, 1964, I developed a terrible cough. I couldn't sit still. I made it only through the first act, watching Burgess Meredith, Orson Bean and Pert Kelton give their best, even when it seemed more like an extended one-act monologue than drama. It was deadly. I stood outside the theater until it was over. The reviews were an anticlimax, not unjust, but each a cruel assault on Ed's open wounds. It was over in two weeks. The closing notice was posted with the reviews.

Some time later, when I returned from my stay in London, Ed and his wife, Veniette, came down from Boston to see me. I decided to give a small cocktail party for them and asked whom I should invite. David Merrick headed the list.

Merrick arrived with a group of people and during the party he turned to Ed O'Connor and said, "Did I ever tell you what your agent said to me when the show opened in Washington?"

"No. What?" Ed asked.

"She told me to close it."

Ed laughed. "Well, you should have!"

Garson Kanin was in the habit of finishing a manuscript on a Friday, then calling at the last minute to have me read it over the weekend, so I could get to work on the sale first thing Monday morning. One lovely spring Friday in 1962, after a telephone call from Mr. Kanin, Mr. Kanin's assistant and Mr. Kanin's secretary, it was established that at precisely five o'clock that afternoon I could have a messenger pick up Mr. Kanin's precisely typed manuscript of a story and would have the pleasure of reading it over the weekend, and at precisely ten o'clock Monday morning, report on how much money I could get him.

I had made plans for that weekend, had looked forward to going to the country, where I could garden, look at the sea, talk to people who were just real people, not inflated names. I decided not to sacrifice that sweet escape. I had the manuscript delivered to my apartment on Sutton Place, planning to read it Sunday night upon my return.

I savored my weekend, returned to the apartment and fulfilled my assigned chore. Actually, I came back a bit early, specifically to give the Kanin text its due. After I read the manuscript I felt peculiar, and it struck me that a dish of ice cream would put everything right. I walked to the kitchen and tried to open the refrigerator.

I never got that ice cream. I passed out and awoke in a pool of blood. I had hit my head and bitten my lip. I looked up at the clock. It was eleven something. I lay there for a moment more, trying to reorient myself and figure out what I was going to do. I wouldn't call the doctor, it was too late. I let the Harriet Craig in me take over, and scrubbed up the blood, and then she sent me to bed.

Monday morning I called the doctor and rushed to his office for x-rays and tests. Finally he asked me, "When was the last time you had a vacation?"

I had to think for a moment. "I haven't taken one since . . . 1953. But I'm planning to go to Europe."

"A business trip?"

"Yes."

"You simply can't go. You'll have to wait a few weeks. And if you go, you'll have to go by ship. Maybe you'll get a rest at sea for five days."

Still remembering the terror of waking up in a pool of my own blood, I dutifully followed his orders, and as soon as he approved the trip, booked passage on the second voyage of the *France*. Meanwhile, Nat Lefkowitz had informed Kanin of my condition and my plans. The Kanins had recently returned from Europe on the *France*. He called me immediately on learning my plan. "Don't take the *France*," he insisted. "You'll hate it! They're not organized yet. The service is awful. Why don't you take the *Queen Mary*? You like the *Queen Mary* and it sails at the same time."

I knew that the Kanins were a barometer to all that was in and out, chic and unchic. Maybe he was right. At the last minute, I switched to the *Queen Mary* and sailed for England.

Kanin had piloted me on a course toward the most romantic period of my life. Barely out of port on this voyage dictated by informed snob appeal, I surrendered to the lyrics of a Rodgers and Hammerstein hit. An enchanted evening, a crowded room—and across it, Bill. And a shipboard romance headed toward a love affair of four years.

PART
SEVEN

H ELEN Gurley Brown was one of the few friends I asked to tell me what was amusing in our relationship which could be included in the book. Here's part of what she wrote me.

Bel-Air Hotel   November 27, 1970

Years ago, before I married David, I had to go to Long Beach, California, to work on the Miss Universe pageant for several days. David wasn't mad for the idea.

On the Friday night when Miss U.S.A. was chosen and I was busy as a croupier, he informed me from Los Angeles that he was taking Helen Strauss to dinner. Her I'd never met, but her I'd heard about—brilliant, witty, totally remarkable in her field. David's friend, Ernest Lehman, a client of Helen's William Morris office, had once said, "Oh, Helen's one of the boys." I consoled myself that maybe she was a lesbian, during the long night I was flapping around interviewing Miss Iowas and Miss Nebraskas and trying to make them sound irreverent and dear—which was impossible.

I still wasn't what you could call *happy* that David was with his other Helen and that they were dining at *Perino's*—a sign of respect in David's case. I sweated out the evening.

Four years later, after David and I were married, I finally met Helen, and one of the boys she was *not*. Ernest Lehman had obviously been referring to her brain. It was considered a compliment in those days to say a woman thought like a man.

What Helen *was* was a voluptuous, womanly, not-full-of-crap lady who *indeed* was singularly accomplished in literary agenting, but who loved men and even tolerated women. I was always thrilled she tolerated me *fairly* nicely from the beginning. And after I wrote a book, she tolerated me even better, because I had now spoken in her language.

My most memorable impression of them all, Helen, is the night we had dinner at 21, upstairs, and you told me about Bill.

My whole credo is that one combines loving men with loving work, and the idea that man-love was a very big deal for you at that moment charmed me completely. I kept thinking this is the woman who guides the literary careers of James Michener and Robert Penn Warren and some other tigers and she's *got* to be over forty and some man, apparently loaded and eligible, wants her just as much, maybe more, than she wants him. I followed the romance while it raged, with complete fascination in every detail.

You and I never had a telephone conversation that lasted longer than 2 minutes and 20 seconds. We are both busy. We figure we can visit when we *visit* and do business when we do business and nobody has time to lollygag on the phone. Would that I had such a nifty agreement with my other girl friends!

The first night I met you was at Henry Ginsberg's apartment on 57th Street. We went to dinner and then on to a revue with Dudley Moore and the Beyond the Fringe group over the old El Morocco. You wore a low-cut black crepe dress, pearls, and a long, straight, opulent mink stole, and I thought you looked just sensational. That lady has enough brains to make something of the bosom that God has already made something of, I thought.

At your house one summer, the people who came for cocktails were all being taken on to dinner. In the parking lot, the zipper in the back of your print silk dress came unconnected from nape to fanny. Two of the men flanked you in the back and I slithered in front. I thought, "It really is something when a lady doesn't dither and carry on and keep reminding everybody that she is in this fix." All you gave a damn about was getting seated, and you probably even forgot the zipper was gone once we got there.

Nothing ever seems like a "big deal" with you—having guests, moving to another continent, making one of those dear six or seven figure deals, selling a house you've just finished decorating, moving to a new profession or life style. You seem to assimilate whatever is new like the sun sinking into a daisy patch.

Helen

After my parents died, I decided to purchase a home on Long Island, a secluded weekend retreat as close to the water as I could get. As close to the water as I could get proved to be too far to every place else I had to get, so I chose a home in the Three

Village section, on Abandoned Bridge Road in Strong's Neck. I had fallen in love with the area years before on a drive to Setauket.

In 1964, when the Strong's Neck house no longer seemed secluded enough, I purchased four and a half acres near the tip of Crane Neck at Old Field. There I built a similar house, but one incorporating all the changes I had desired in the first one. The house had broad kitchen windows, along which I hung bird feeders to attract the many and multicolored birds that passed that way. Pheasant and quail roamed the grounds, which were covered with enough trees to provide a constantly changing palette of seasonal colors. I delighted in that expanse of earth, in planting it and watching things grow and flourish.

I entertained more frequently. Helen and David Brown were among those spending many weekends.

I've known David long enough to remember when he wrote horoscopes. During the sixties his grasp of the industry and the properties it feeds upon made him the valued strong right hand to Twentieth Century-Fox's young production chief Richard D. Zanuck. His title, vice-president in charge of story operations, didn't begin to cover the scope of the trust invested in him. Much later, when the inflated economics of the old studio system and a series of unsuccessful but overpriced films caught up with them, Dick and David were thrown to the wolves, but the two remained in partnership to enjoy more of the rewards and fewer headaches as an independent film production team, and produced films such as *The Sting* and *Jaws*.

Helen Gurley Brown is an extraordinary woman, one of the hardest-working I have ever known. She relishes what she is doing and embraces her work with wonderment and a joyous innocence. Consistent with the sort of candid and perceptive advice she offers to the contemporary woman in the pages of *Cosmopolitan* and the level-headedness she retains in the face of success, Helen remains a surprisingly practical lady. I was amazed when she told me that she still rides the bus to her office, rather than take cabs.

There were others with whom I shared my non-working hours, though not a great many, always a select assortment of good, long-time friends. With rare exceptions, I have always been uncomfortable in other people's homes and felt unduly restricted. Better, then, to take pleasure in making my home comfortable for them.

For those weekends on the Island, I either hired help or had food prepared in New York and brought it in. If any compliments on my meals were forthcoming, they were a credit to my planning and my shopping. I am as alien in the kitchen as Tallulah was in the subway, if you remember that famous sketch she used to do on *The Big Show.* I can fight an egg to a draw, free style. I make a good pot of coffee, but it is a production, as is opening and heating a can of soup. I can prepare chicken in just about any form prescribed, without bruising it, but I am apt to take as much as five hours getting it dressed up to look like the retouched photography in the cookbook. By that time I'd prefer to look better than the chicken.

There were many more weekends during those years preceding my move to London that I did not spend on the Island. Those were the ones that I spent with my Englishman, Bill. There were weekends in Paris and in London, wholly romantic transcontinental idylls, completely removed from the realities we would one day have to face. It was an ideal love affair, and those hurried times together limited it solely to the ideal parts. In time, of course, Bill and I felt compelled to move beyond these idylls toward what is presumed to be the logical progression—to link our lovely weekends with the other days of the week. Perhaps I was ready to settle down and marry, and Bill seemed to be the best reason to do so. We do persist in the belief that a certificate will make a fine romance a better one.

We talked of marriage and I talked of living in London. To accommodate me and to keep me in the Morris family, Abe Lastfogel arranged for me to move to the agency's London office to expand the company's literary interests in Europe. I would still commute frequently to New York and Hollywood, personally attending to the affairs of my key clients and overseeing the rest.

The last major deal I handled before bundling off to Britain extended Robert Fryer's production activities to include Hollywood filmmaking. This diversification was overdue, but the timing could not have been better. He and his partners were enjoying their most successful season on Broadway. With the opening of

Mame, starring Angela Lansbury, and the continuing sellout of Gwen Verdon as "Sweet Charity," Bobby had two of the biggest smash hits in the theater.

I introduced Bobby to David Brown, who was impressed not only with his gentle manner and his golden touch, but with his tantrum-free ability to bring in a show with quality on a reasonably managed budget. David was excited, but said that he would have to discuss the proposal with Richard and Darryl Zanuck at Twentieth. The Zanucks, who were wheeling and dealing on all fronts, backed by the confidence and the cash that their *Sound of Music* had won them, were looking for dynamic new producers in whom to invest to guide their expanded production program. They were running daily full-page advertisements in the Hollywood trade papers, announcing each new talent they had attracted to their revitalized studio. The Zanucks thought that Bobby would look mighty good in their ads and on their lot. There was a small catch. What would Bobby do? Did he have a bankable property?

On one of my weekend trips to London I had seen Jay Presson Allen's play based on the Muriel Spark short novel *The Prime of Miss Jean Brodie.* I thought it would be a perfect film-debut vehicle for Bobby, and I suggested it enthusiastically.

"Are you sure, Helen?" Bobby asked.

"Absolutely," I assured him.

We quickly made the deal with Twentieth. It was immediately clear that Bobby's ability for bringing together the best complementary talents to produce a play readily transferred to his new role as a film producer. He understood film and knew his filmmakers. He knew the differences and the similarities involved in working in the two forms. Fox was pleased. The Zanucks were delighted and ready to discuss the second project even as the first was gestating. What next?

His second commitment for Fox brought two of my clients— Bobby and Gerold Frank—together. *The Boston Strangler* was a coup for Bobby and a juicy windfall for Gerry.

Bobby has been a good friend, and at any opportunity, continues to lavish praise on me for facilitating his start as a film and stage producer. While we will always be close, our present mutual admiration society gives no clue to the really terrific, inconsequential fights we've had in the heat of production. How many times did Bobby drag me backstage at some out-of-town tryout, only to swear he would never do so again when his star or some panicky member of the company asked me my honest opinion and got it? Director George Cukor, who values my opinion on scripts, sent me the first draft of *Travels with My Aunt*, which Bobby produced. Bobby cried "Sabotage!" when I went over that early script with George, telling him everything I thought was wrong with it.

In turn, I have snorted fire when Bobby has taken a month to return a call or arrived several hours late for a meeting he initiated. Those on-the-job irritations remain gnats in an otherwise placid ointment. In a town in which most finger-snapping producers try to dress like rock-star groupies, Bobby still sticks to ties and conservative eastern suits, but wardrobe is not all that sets him apart. Like Walter Wanger, Bobby has dignity and class.

For some reason, when my old friend Arthur Thornhill, Sr., who was then the chairman of the board of Little, Brown & Company, heard that I was planning to move to London, he interpreted it to mean that I was retiring from the agency business. He called me from Boston and asked me to come up for lunch.

I quickly agreed to the date, for Arthur was a dear friend and one of the men I most admired in publishing. He was also one of the few men I knew who could always be reached at his office at eight-thirty in the morning.

Arthur's rise had been in the best traditions of Horatio Alger-styled American success stories. His father had held a menial post at Little, Brown, and Arthur had secured a job with them when he was only fourteen. He had risen step by step, through devotion and tireless effort, to the very top of the company, which he sold to Time-Life shortly before his death.

The luncheon was a backdrop for a running monologue, at once naïve and sweetly concerned. "You can't retire," he admonished.

"But I'm *not*—"

"No one like you can retire. Publishing needs the concern of—"

"But I'm only *moving* to—"

"You must stay in the business. If you are determined to go to London, at least stay on the job. We've never had a European representative. I'll make you our European representative."

He was convinced that I was abandoning not just New York, but writers and the agency business. While I was a bit amused, I was also deeply touched by his tribute and his paternal concern. Yet I still could not help wondering just how tangible was his offer of a post for which Little, Brown had no imminent need. I let him continue. Then, as if wholly in fun, I shrugged, and said, "Well, I couldn't take it, of course, but what sort of salary might such a job pay?"

"Twenty-five thousand dollars." It was a rather large sum for the time, but obviously it was an investment in the anticipated potential of opening a new territory and a vote of confidence in the person selected to do it. Eventually, of course, I was able to explain to Arthur the reasons for following my heart to London and the concurrent change of scene which would refresh me in my job even as I sustained essentially the same functions. But it was a lovely and unforgettable gesture from one of the gentlemen of the profession.

No, I'm underrating Arthur. He was a wise and perceptive man and a close enough friend to have sensed my growing disaffection for the agency business, even though we never discussed it. The greatest challenges had been met. The excitement was waning. I was growing tired of playing Florence Nightingale, tired of springing authors from jail and knowing the intimate details of their marriages, weary of worrying about authors' rent payments and checking people into hospitals and holding vigils over them. Still, I could have tolerated playing mother, sister and psychiatrist, doing the handholding and the chiding, if only I weren't tilling the same old ground, doing again what I'd already done before. More than anything else, it was getting boring.

When I started the literary department at the Morris Agency, in 1944, movie rights for novels and plays were selling for as much as a quarter of a million dollars, but the most spectacular deals were yet to be made. I would make some of those deals, and through bidding and on terms that had not been attempted before.

By 1947 five billion magazines were sold, thirty-five for every person in the country, nearly doubling the figures for the previous decade. Nearly ninety percent of those magazines were sold on newsstands.

Fewer than 8,000 new book titles were published annually when I started in the business. By 1960 there were 14,876, and that included almost 2,000 novels. That was the record figure for the twentieth century and it was still rising, doubling in the next five years. But the sales of general-interest books were increasing as the ratio for fiction declined. That same year newspapers reached their all-time high circulation marks, but ad revenue and profits were beginning to fall as advertisers moved in increasing numbers to television. The Sunday supplements, always a good market for features and short fiction, suffered a thirteen percent loss of ads and were failing rapidly.

Also in 1960 Broadway was having one of its most disappointing seasons, and that one would look pretty good in a couple more years. Hollywood paid more money for a few pre-sold hits, but production was down and they weren't buying magazine stories or good novels that failed to make the best-seller lists.

Coronet, where Gerold Frank had worked as an editor, folded. *The Saturday Evening Post* dropped twenty percent of its advertising income in 1961, the worst year for magazines since 1956, when *American, Collier's* and *Woman's Home Companion* had shuttered. Production costs were up, cut-rate subscriptions and declining advertiser interest were demolishing a shrinking profit margin. Nervous publishers imposed reckless editorial changes, which failed to attract new readers while offending loyal ones. If the giants were in trouble, the smaller, marginal magazines, which offered a break-in market to young writers, withered away without notice. Strikes dealt some newspapers a blow from which they never awakened, or perhaps they only provided the excuse to give up. Suburban throwaway shopping weeklies were multiplying, but they weren't likely to provide a training ground for a generation of sharp new reporters and novelists

In 1965, 28,595 titles were published, but only 20,234 were new titles. The rest were new editions from existing catalogues, reissues, while the number of new titles dropped over 300 from the previous year.

Of course, I knew that in the future—at least I hoped so—there would still be runaway best sellers and million-dollar sales for film rights. New authors would still find fame and fortune. Great novels would still rise above the shelves of call-house madam and pimp memoirs and secretarial confessions and fad-diet books and guess-who titillations. A generation of newpapermen, too long lazily re-writing PR handouts, would be stirred by events of the seventies into an exciting new phase of investigative reporting. But there wouldn't be many places left for any of them to hone their craft. Where were the assignments like those which allowed Michener and O'Connor to travel and support themselves?

By the seventies, more and more publishing houses were swallowed up by ravenous conglomerates, traded from one to the other for paper profits and paper losses, the instincts of gifted publishers and editors often overwhelmed by an invasion of Univac cost accountants, packaging and marketing specialists with the figures to prove that how-to books on building your own backyard cesspool or barbecue had a more profitable right to exist than an introductory volume of short stories by a promising future novelist.

The highly questionable science of demographics rode in on the tail of the conglomerates, arbitrarily decreeing that this magazine with a million subscribers had too many of the wrong kind of readers, freeloaders who didn't buy enough of the products they didn't need. One season their slide rules told them that cars and other high-cost items were bought by eighteen- to thirty-year-olds, so scrap the ad budget for the magazine with the well-heeled over-forties. Better yet, scrap the large-circulation magazine or the highly rated television show. Make TV movies only for that demographic profile of the eternal adolescent. The next season the statistician who had argued that women make the buying decisions, and can be reached in women's magazines, will decide that the women make the decision only after the interest of their men has been piqued. Switch the ads to men's magazines. And if the magazines and movies and television programs fall victim during these mystic rites of hypothesis, too bad.

Television, they said, was selling more books than ever. I don't really believe that. Television creates personalities who may often coincidentally have their name on books. For every Jacqueline Susann, who relished her celebrity and collected her publishing royalties, there is a Gore Vidal, who talks when he should be writing, and a hundred authors who tour the talk shows coast to coast, being dragged on camera to tell the best anecdotes from their books in the final six-minute segment of the show before sermonette and sign-off. That program slot lends itself to the gimmick book, the quack-diet doctors, the flying-saucer experts, the transsexuals and the model posing as a secretary who wrote a staff-written book on making out in Manhattan. Television sells non-books. It talks some books out of sales, and I don't believe it can sell a good novel.

It wasn't simply the influx of meddlers who lacked the knowledge, instincts and integrity of the great editors. It wasn't simply the cheapening of the book business or the decline of magazines in which to build a young author while keeping him alive. It was the era itself, the sixties.

For all of the chasing after new life styles, for all of the mass assimilation of the vogues and vagaries of "the kids," for all of the swinging, switch-on films, psychedelic magazine covers, all the pros and cons regarding drugs and protest, the Establishment and the Generation Gap, there weren't really many *idea* novels born out of the time. Most young writers, without that many print outlets in the first place, suddenly wanted to write for film. "Their" stories were being written by older hacks for youth-pursuing movies.

The young writers, like their generation, were groping through a dynamic and chaotic time, most not yet reflecting upon or articulating that moment. At the same time they were rejecting history and the standard forms of authorship, without yet grasping their own. It was a time in which the continuity in all things was broken, the Tin Pan Alley tradition and its evergreens giving way to the new Top Forty and the Golden Oldies of only a decade before, a romantic movie tradition scrapped in favor of a flirtation with ultra-cool, often cruel and unfeeling exercises in kicks and despair. Margaret Mead described the country at that time as two separate and different tribes superimposed on the same island, the prewar and the post-, the old and the new, the latter appearing like some atomic mutation to the former. Maybe history will record that it came together better than anyone predicted at the time. Yet for all of the mass participation and talk about the arts, it did not prove to be a particularly productive or informative period for literature.

Worse, during that period I saw too many young raw talents informed by accelerated sophistication and disillusion, not fired by reason and imagination but thrown on the pyre of life-burning drugs, creative waste and frivolous indulgence, burned out without even a solid ash left behind.

So I went to London. I believe Abe Lastfogel sensed my growing ennui, or else he would never have contrived that assignment to the London office. I welcomed it not only because it brought me to London and closer to Bill, but because it promised a new perspective and perhaps a recharging of enthusiasm for my work. Had I not been ready to consider leaving the business, I probably would not have been so susceptible to the idea of wedding bells. Perhaps marriage only symbolized escape from the business. At any rate, I made the move and believed myself ready at last to sign that contract "till death do us part." I sailed in the spring of 1966.

Nominally, I was still in charge of literary operations in the American offices and I reported in when I felt like it. I made frequent trips on client business, becoming increasingly disturbed by what struck me as the shambles into which the department I had built was falling. My achievements in London were hardly spectacular. I was a good caretaker, at least.

I put together a Jerry Lewis film, *Don't Raise the Bridge, Lower the River*. Robert Joseph, a writer-producer client who had done a number of Broadway shows, including Giraudoux's *Tiger at the Gates*, which I had unsuccessfully attempted to package as a film with Fred Zinnemann directing and Gore Vidal screenwriting, happened to be in London, and we had good times laughing about the past, without putting together any monuments in the present.

Bill and I faced the weekdays, and the glow of those romantic weekend retreats began to grow dim. On those weekends it was simply so good to see each other that everything was beautiful. We looked different in the Monday-morning light.

His daughter, very devoted and protective of him, took an immediate dislike to me and satisfied herself that I was an American fortune hunter, lusting after her father's money.

I suddenly gave serious consideration to the reality involved in this dream of marriage. I did not want to live in the English countryside, in a place which was too far from London. I did not want to retire. Forgive me, I did not want to be married.

I kidded him—I warned him, really—that if I married him, I'd get up and drink pink gin at eight-thirty in the morning just so I could make it through the day with those dreary English provincials in Warwickshire. It would have been a catastrophe to marry him. There was a unison sigh of relief when we finally admitted that to each other. It had been beautiful, a romance to cherish, not to spoil. We had no regrets.

Irving Hoffman was still watching over me. When I left for England, Irving dispatched a number of his decorated king-size typed letters asking his various industry friends in London to extend their welcome to me. One letter went to Robert Goldstein, who was the production chief of Twentieth in London and was also the host with the most to the film colony at that time. His home was a famous traffic stop for film people passing through, and invitations to his Sunday brunches were prized. Upon receipt of Irving's letter, Bob promptly called me to extend an invitation. I couldn't make it. Another invitation. I didn't make it. More invitations, and I always had something else to do, something that kept me out of town on Sunday.

Finally, just to dispel any notion that I was the terribly unsocial Manhattanite, I showed up. I had been there for just a few minutes when a charming and very attractive young man crossed the room toward me.

"I've always wanted to meet you," he said.

I turned to Nunnally Johnson and whispered, "Who is he?"

It was Kenneth Hyman, who had just produced *The Dirty Dozen*. He was also vice-president of Seven Arts Productions, the company run by his father, Eliot Hyman, who had realized the tremendous profits to be had from distributing feature films to television, had snatched up vast libraries of films and made a fortune before turning to the financing of new features. Kenny asked me to have lunch with him the following week.

At that luncheon he confided to me that his father was about to buy out Warner Brothers. He said that he was anxious for me to be with them in the new venture. Somehow, I didn't take him seriously. Kenny will always look like a young man, with that healthy glow that certain Thomas Mann consumptives carry. We had lunch several more times after that. Of course I was flattered by his continued offer, but blithely informed him that I wasn't looking for a job.

Meanwhile, Abe Lastfogel had been counting the months. Finally he called to say that if I wasn't going to go through with my marriage, it was about time I came back to New York. I agreed in an instant and started packing. I really wanted to go home.

When I returned to the New York office, somehow it wasn't the same. Whatever feelings of affection I had for the place and the job were gone. Although I was uncertain of my next step, I knew I had to leave.

But for the moment, there was still plenty of activity in the literary department. Chaim Potok, who had come to me before I left for London, had the number-two novel on the best-seller lists, *The Chosen*. Arlene Friedman, who had done most of the legwork for the book, had submitted it to more than a dozen publishers before she placed it. It was a fine vindication of her confidence, but she, like most of my girls, had been long gone by that time.

I was infuriated with the deal that the agency had made for another of the new clients, Mario Puzo. They had foolishly given Paramount Pictures a two-year option on *The Godfather* for $3,500 against a purchase price of $85,000!

I had read the partial manuscript and knew its potential for print and film. The contracts had not yet been signed, so I implored Mario to walk away from the commitment and give us a chance to get the deal the book deserved. But Mario had been struggling so long and had never had any picture interest in anything he had done. He had debts and a large family. He needed the money. I told him that I could get the agency to advance him the cash he needed now, but not to throw away such a valuable property. It was too late. The money was already earmarked and he took it.

The film was a gold mine, but Mario got just that $85,000, unheard of for a best seller in our time. Sure, he got $500 a week in expense money in addition to his salary while he was on the Coast working on the screenplay, but that went for the rent on his Beverly Hills Hotel suite, with little change left over.

The joy had certainly gone out of the business for me, and I now decided what I would do. I applied to the New York State University at Stony Brook. Since moving to the Three Village area on Long Island, I had taken an interest in the university, establishing an annual scholarship for writers and helping to arrange for distinguished speakers on campus.

It was about this time that the trade papers and the daily newspapers broke the story that Eliot Hyman was buying out Warner Brothers and that Kenny Hyman would be the head of production at the studio. I called Kenny at the Seven Arts offices in New York with congratulations.

"I'm glad you called," he responded. "It's very funny, but I was just about to get in touch with you." He suggested that we have lunch, and again he said that he wanted me to join them in the new management at Warner. I didn't even ask what the job was. The idea of going to a motion picture company didn't appeal to me at all, particularly a Hollywood studio. It had taken me long enough to get out of the movie business. The New York end of it had been sorry enough, and on my trips to Hollywood, I had always appreciated the second half of a round-trip ticket better than the first.

Despite my refusal of that unspecified job, I agreed to meet Kenny's father. As we entered Eliot Hyman's office Kenny said, "Dad, the lady said no."

"I would have done a better job on her," said Eliot.

As Kenny walked me to the elevator, he spoke one of those lines so typical of and dear to the hearts of the eternal Hollywood optimists: "Let's not close the door on this."

With that, the elevator doors snapped shut.

The offer was revived at regular intervals for weeks, like a running gag, all the lines and responses remaining the same.

Then one day I was talking to a neighbor of mine on the Island, sharing my green-pastures fantasy of the ideal academic life to which I was planning to retire. "It will be so perfect," I sighed, "really marvelous, no more interoffice politics, no bickering, no pressures."

I raved on at some length, picturing some sort of pastoral literary salon, with me as the tiptoeing book fairy, gently pollinating great novels amidst the blossoms of upturned minds.

My friend burst out laughing, recounting from her own passing knowledge some of the special political games that worm their way into the groves of academe, suggesting the possible reception of entrenched and possibly unpublished departmental heads to this interloper from the world of commerce. She even offered the opinion that some of those budding young geniuses I pictured might not be all that receptive to practical counsel that might be contrary to some of their more romantic attitudes. Hadn't I met enough postgraduate authors to know that? It was a quick, hard-eyed look at education as another kind of business, subject to the same follies and frauds as any other. Suddenly it wasn't that easy to imagine myself as the benevolent Miss Chips of the English department, shuffling down the auditorium aisle on my eightieth birthday to a standing ovation from a quarter century of tearful graduate faces grown famous and graying at the temples. Darn that dream!

"Well now, what is this movie job they keep offering you?" she asked, as the houselights came up and the caroling of appreciative students at my cottage door faded away forever.

"Hmm? Oh, I don't know. I never asked."

"Don't you think maybe you need an agent to find out for you? You're terrible about yourself. How can you turn down a job before you know what it is?"

The next morning I arrived early at the airport for a flight to Washington, D.C., and stopped at the closest phone booth, dialing the number of Seven Arts.

"Kenny, exactly what is the job?"

"Helen, you really don't expect me to tell you over the telephone, do you? Where are you?"

"I'm at the airport. I have to go to Washington to take care of some business for Justice Douglas. I'll be back on Wednesday."

"Call me and come in when you get back." Click.

"You are going to be vice-president in charge of world-wide story operations," said Kenny Hyman when I returned.

The job would give me the authority to try to carry out ideas which promised aggressive new life to an industry which needed it desperately. Maybe, just maybe . . . I was hooked.

"How much do you want?"

"How much do you want to give me?" He quoted a highly amusing figure, with lots of fringe benefits.

"My contract is three years," said Kenny. "Do you want to conform to mine or would you feel safer with a five-year contract?"

"Three years. I'll never last it out anyhow."

Later I brazened. "You know, the Morris Agency always paid for my car, and when I have to go anywhere at night, they permit me to hire a limousine."

"Don't be silly," Kenny countered. "You will have a Lincoln or its equivalent and a full-time chauffeur. Do you have a lawyer? I'll have a rough draft of the contract drawn up and you can show it to him."

When my lawyer looked up from the contract, he said, "You must have negotiated this for yourself. This is a *great* contract."

"I didn't negotiate it. Kenny Hyman gave it to me."

I quit my job at the Morris Agency, after twenty-three years, on June 5, the day the Israeli Six-Day War broke out. I tried to reach Abe Lastfogel on the telephone at his office in Beverly Hills, but he was out, very likely involved in some effort in support of Israel. I was really relieved that I had been unable to reach him. I knew he would be hurt, that he had to be hurt. Even if he had expected my resignation for some time, it would still come as a shock. I would do anything not to hurt him, anything short of staying on.

Frances Lastfogel was in New York. I called her, explained my decision and told her that I had tried to reach Abe to let him know of my resignation before he heard of it from someone else. She was furious with me, striking out angrily, arguing that I could not do this to them, that she was very upset and irate. Her words and her tone made it clear enough.

She called me back a short time later and said, "Helen, you have a perfect right to live your life the way that you feel best, but you know that Abe will never get over it."

I then sent a telegram to Abe. He called me when he received it to say that he was coming to New York. When he arrived, I met him at the agency. He told his secretary to hold all his calls, and we went into his office. He looked out the window for a long time. There were tears in his eyes, and in mine.

"You could at least have given me the courtesy of discussing it with me before you accepted this job," he said.

"If I had, you would only have tried to talk me out of it, wouldn't you? This was the only way."

"Yes," he said, and he understood, though the hurt remained.

It is common practice in large companies for defectors to be swiftly packed up and smuggled out through the service door, lest they infect the troops or steal next season's game plan. That was particularly true in the agency business. Empty your desk and hit the streets! Instead, the William Morris Agency persuaded me to stay on until mid-August.

I had planned to take a month's vacation. I had booked passage on the *Michelangelo*. I also had to have conferences with Eliot Hyman, but he was so involved with corporate problems that he had to keep postponing dates. Finally I had to cancel the *Michelangelo* booking. It was almost time to report to Kenny in Hollywood.

The Morris Agency did one more unusual thing. Nat Lefkowitz gave a luncheon in my honor the day I left. As we were saying our goodbyes, he leaned over and said very quietly, "You can change your mind, you know. Abe can get you out of your Warner contract."

I answered, "Nobody really understands. I just don't want to be in the agency business any more. I've had it!"

EPILOGUE

So I took the job at Warner Brothers–Seven Arts as vice-president in charge of world-wide story operations. It seemed, at first, to present a great challenge—and it was indeed remunerative. I was excited about what I thought I could accomplish, and thrilled and eager to get started.

I even moved to California. I bought a house in Beverly Hills, small according to Hollywood standards, but pretty, with a lovely garden and view and swimming pool—but no screening room and tennis court, which greatly disappointed some of my associates. I did not participate in the great American sport of the status race, knowing full well that executive jobs at studios, for the most part, have no track records.

Unfortunately, the job turned out to be neither fun nor rewarding, and long before my contract expired, I asked out, knowing Universal wanted me; after a holiday of four days, I started there. I was a vice-president again. At Warner there had been six vice-presidents; at Universal, I think there were about two dozen. Titles at Universal were awarded as gold stars were given at elementary schools in my day.

I rather enjoyed Universal. I never seemed to be an integral part of it, but as a spectator, I found it had some very amusing moments. At both studios it was a revelation and an education to witness power politics at work.

Again I quit. And simultaneous with my exit from Universal, I was offered what seemed like a prestigious assignment at *Reader's Digest*. I was put in charge of motion picture productions. Lila and DeWitt Wallace, the illustrious founders of that unique organization, were very cordial to me, as were some of their staff. But why they thought the entertainment business was one of their métiers, I'll never know. Their Midas touch did not extend to their entry into show business. I had warned them from the beginning that they could take their money to Las Vegas and have the same chance at winning. They would never have produced *Star Wars* or *Saturday Night Fever* or even *Jaws*, but neither would I, even had I been given the opportunity.

Being associated with three enormous companies, I cannot calculate how many people I met, possibly thousands. Those I really respected were the craftsmen—or craftspersons: the film editors, the cinematographers, the set designers, the costume designers and, of course, a number of directors. Last, but by no means least, the writers. I'm so old-fashioned that I still believe a good film cannot be produced from a poor script. Even in the land of the lotus eaters, writers remained my first and true love.

But now, as Virginia Woolf said, "Things have dropped from me. I have outlived certain desires." In retrospect, I have nothing to complain about. More important, I have no regrets. And even more important—I had and I have a talent for luck.

INDEX